Yu-Gi-Oh! THE DUELISTS OF THE ROSES ™

Associate Product Manager: Jill Hinckley
Project Editor: Teli Hernandez
Editorial Assistant: Carrie Ponseti

ISBN: 0-7615-4250-7
Library of Congress Catalog Card Number: 2003101373
Printed in the United States of America

03 04 05 06 GG 10 9 8 7 6 5 4 3 2 1

Prima's Official Strategy Guide

Elliott Chin

Prima Games
A Division of Random House, Inc.

3000 Lava Ridge Court
Roseville, CA 95661
(800) 733-3000
www.primagames.com

Contents

Acknowledgements

Prima Games would like to thank Dennis Lee at Konami. The author would like to thank his wife, Amy Ng.

Introduction

You've watched Yugi duel his archrival Kaiba on Saturday mornings, fought your own card battles against your friends, and taken on the card kings of Egypt in *Yu-Gi-Oh! Forbidden Memories*. Now, you can experience *Yu-Gi-Oh!* on the Playstation®2. The newest *Yu-Gi-Oh!* video game offers awesome monsters in full 3D, more than 850 cards, and new rules that will test your knowledge of Duel Monsters.

In *Yu-Gi-Oh! The Duelists of the Roses*, you'll face off against familiar friends and foes, such as Tea, Tristan, Mai, Ishtar, Seto, and Pegasus. You'll also encounter some interesting new twists.

The battle between good and evil is more pronounced than ever before. Now, you're forced to choose sides. You are the Rose Duelist, and you have been Summoned through time to settle the War of the Roses. There can be only one king of England, and you will help choose him. Will you fight for Yugi or will you serve Seto? The fate of England is in your hands.

The War of the Roses

In 1485, a bloody civil war between the Yorkists and the Lancastrians threatens to tear apart the British Empire. The war was called the War of the Roses because both factions chose the rose to represent their cause, with the Yorkists choosing the white rose and the Lancastrians the red rose. Led by the usurper Richard III, the Yorkists are dangerously close to victory.

The Duelists of the Roses takes place in England in 1485 during the War of the Roses. You battle across England, Ireland, and France. At first only a little of the territory is open to you, but as you defeat duelists, you earn the right to move to new areas and wage new duels. And once you've beaten a duelist, you can return to duel him or her again. Eventually, you can travel freely between areas, dueling as much as you like.

Seto and his White Rose Duelists are helping the Yorkists seize power in England.

Hoping to put an end to the war and restore his legitimate claim to the crown, the Lancastrian heir Henry Tudor, known as Yugi to his close friends, asks his druid advisor Simon McMooran to Summon from the future the legendary Rose Duelist. Only the Rose Duelist has the power to fight the Yorkist's most powerful weapon, the mysterious card-wielding duelist named Seto and his seven White Rose Crusaders. These eight have used their powerful magical cards to conquer all of England, and Yugi's own duelists are too weak to battle them. Only you, the Rose Duelist of legend, has any hope of defeating the eight duelists of the White Rose.

You have been Summoned to duel Seto and help Yugi reclaim the throne.

Now, on a dark night in Stonehenge, the magic ritual Summoning you to 1480s has finished. Simon has given you a deck of cards and a purpose. The fate of the English isles rests on your shoulders, Rose Duelist. Only you can defeat Seto and restore order to England. Only you have the power to wield the Magic Cards!

What's New?

There are many differences between *Yu-Gi-Oh! The Duelists of the Roses* and previous *Yu-Gi-Oh!* video games, as well as a few differences from the trading card game. While most of the basics are the same, you should note a few changes.

Deck Leaders

The Deck Leader is a new element that represents you on the playing Field.

You are now represented on the Field by your Deck Leader, a creature card promoted from the ranks of your deck to serve as your avatar in the game. Your Deck Leader has no ATK or DEF rating but Summons your cards and suffers when damage gets through during monster battles. In *Yu-Gi-Oh! The Duelists of the Roses*, the Deck Leader is you! That also means creatures can attack you directly if they move next to you. If your Deck Leader is under fire from enemy creatures, move him out of harm's way.

Playing Field

Move around the Field with your cards, corner the opposing Deck Leader, and attack his cards.

Introduction

Duels are played on a dueling Field, a 7x7 grid made up of different terrain squares. You Summon cards onto this Field, and move your cards around it. Battles between monsters are also resolved on the Field. However, if you want your creature to fight your opponent's monster, you must move it toward the enemy on the playing Field. To directly attack the opposing Deck Leader, simply maneuver your creatures into position around him. This ability to move around the Field is one of the most important changes to the game, along with the new Deck Leaders.

New Summoning Field

Your Summoning Field is now the squares adjacent to your Deck Leader.

The Summoning Field is the eight squares surrounding your Deck Leader. In some cases, you would have fewer squares to Summon onto. If, for example, you are at the corner of the Field, you would have only three squares. You are still limited to five creature cards and five spells on the Field at a time.

Summon Points

Unlike previous *Yu-Gi-Oh!* video games, there are no star chips. You start off with four Summoning Points on the first turn and gain three more points every turn thereafter. Each creature card has a Summoning Point Cost, which you must pay before you can Summon the creature onto the Field. You can have a maximum of 12 Summoning Points.

No Tribute

You no longer have to tribute weaker monsters to Summon higher-cost monsters. If you have enough Summoning Points to pay for a monster, you can play it.

Easier Fusions

You no longer have to use the Polymerization card to start a monster Fusion. In fact, there is no Polymerization card, nor is there a Fusion side deck. Instead, you simply designate two monsters from your hand to fuse into a single creature. If the two creatures are compatible, they merge into a Fusion creation and appear on the playing Field.

New Victory Conditions

New features have led to new victory conditions. If you occupy all of the opposing Deck Leader's Summoning Field, you win.

Some new victory conditions have been introduced and an old one taken out. Unlike in the card game, you do not automatically lose the duel if you run out of cards to draw. There are also two new methods for winning a duel. Each duel runs for 100 turns. If you have more Life Points (LP) than your opponent when turn 0 rolls around, then you win. With the introduction of board movement on the Field, you can also win if you occupy all your opponent's Summoning squares, thereby preventing him or her from Summoning any cards into the game.

Leaving Egypt for England

Now that we've covered some of the new features in brief, let's take a closer look at the game basics. If you're already familiar with *Yu-Gi-Oh!*, consider the next section a refresher course. But carefully read the information on the new features. You'll need every advantage if you want to unite England and be forever known as the King of Games.

3

Dueling Basics and Deck Strategies

Yu-Gi-Oh! The Duelists of the Roses faithfully recreates nearly all of the rules of the *Yu-Gi-Oh!* card game. With a few exceptions, what you expect from the card game is what you'll see on the screen. However, be sure to read over the descriptions of the cards in the Cards section, as some cards have been altered to better fit the gameplay of *The Duelists of the Roses*.

When you first load the game, you have four options. You can start a New Game, Continue a previous game, play a Custom Game, or Trade cards with another player.

Beginning Game Options

Your options at the beginning of the game.

New Game

This is where you play the story-based Campaign mode. When you start this game, you are told about the history of the War of the Roses and asked to choose sides. You can play for Yugi or Seto. This mode is the meat of the game, and it's where you play the most challenging duels, gain the most cards, and unlock passwords for valuable new cards. For information on the campaign duelists, the best decks to use, and strategies for beating the story-based game, read the "Campaign Walkthrough."

Continue

This option lets you continue your progress in the campaign from your saved game. Unfortunately, you can only have one game file on a memory card at a time.

Custom Game

You can play other human opponents in a Custom Game, or duel against the computer while it uses your own decks. Custom Games are a vital part of your strategy, and a perfect means to gain multiple copies of cards you have, to learn from the computer how to best use your cards, and as a way of testing out new Fusions and strategies. Read "Custom Games and Trading" for more information.

Trade

If you have two PS2 memory cards in your memory bays, you can trade cards between saved game files. You can trade with your friends, or use multiple memory cards and the Trade feature to give yourself more cards for your campaign saved game. Read "Custom Games and Trading" for more information.

Dueling Basics

In this game, defeat your competition in a game of dueling monsters and spells. You face off against the opposing duelist, with each of you taking turns drawing cards and playing them onto the Field. Once your cards are on the Field, you maneuver them into position to attack your enemy's cards or your enemy's Deck Leader.

Deck Size

You are limited to a maximum deck size of 40 cards, not counting your Deck Leader. You never can have more than three copies of the same card in your deck.

Life Points

You and your opponent each start out with 4,000 Life Points (LP). In the campaign, this amount is fixed. However, in Custom Games, you can adjust the number of starting LP.

 **TIP**

Sometimes you are stuck with an early hand full of weak creatures. To open up several slots in your hand for the next round of hopefully better cards, designate multiple creatures to Summon onto the Field. Although only one of them makes it to the playing Field, all are ejected from

your hand. Every card except the last gets bounced into your Graveyard, so make sure you won't need those cards. And if you're lucky, you might even stumble onto a Fusion this way.

Turn Structure

- In Campaign mode, you always go first. In Two-Player mode, player one always goes first.
- The round begins with the Standby Phase. During this phase, any magic effects from spells or creatures are activated. These include increases or decreases to creature ATK and DEF that are supposed to occur every turn, or Life Point gains that occur each turn as a result of a creature's special effect.
- During your Standby Phase, you draw as many cards as needed to replenish your hand up to your maximum of five cards.
- After this phase is the Main Phase. During this phase, you can Summon one card onto the playing Field by paying the appropriate Summoning Point Cost.
- Cards are played face-down when first Summoned onto the Field.
- During the Main Phase, each of your monster and spell cards on the Field can move. Moving a card onto an enemy card initiates an attack or triggers a trap. A card does not have to move; it can remain in its current square.
- Flipping a card face-up counts as movement and is often done with cards that have special effects when flipped.
- Your Deck Leader can also take a move action during the same turn it Summons a card.
- When you finish taking all your actions and movements for your Deck Leader, monsters, and spells, you declare the end of your turn.
- Your opponent then goes through the same round phases as you.
- You and your opponent continue until one of you achieves one of the four victory conditions.

TIP

Keep drawing cards and never leave your hand stagnant. But save up Summoning Points so you can play the really big creatures. Rather than waste Summoning Points by playing low-level creatures, play a Magic Card. Power-up cards don't need to stay in your hand. Play them in your Summoning Field to free up a slot in your hand; and when you get a creature that benefits from the Power-up, Summon it onto the same square as the Power-up to equip the creature.

Five Card Limit

You are limited to five cards in your hand at a time, and you can have no more than five monsters and five spells on the Field at a time. If you have no room to place more cards, move your Deck Leader over a card you don't want. This forces the card into the Graveyard. If you want to replace a monster with a better one, move one of your creatures into another friendly creature's square. The moving creature bumps the stationary creature off the Field. However, if the two are a Fusion match, then they perform a Fusion. Either way, you just made room for another monster.

One Card Per Turn

You can only Summon one card onto the Field per turn. You can combine multiple cards from your hand into one card, however, such as merging two cards to create a Fusion creature or adding a Power-up card to a creature before you play it.

NOTE

The powerful Magic Card, Solomon's Lawbook, is the only way to play two cards in one turn. After you play your first card, flip Solomon's Lawbook face-up, which activates the card. Your hand is restored to five cards, and you can play another card.

Summoning Points

You start each duel with four Summoning Points. Each round thereafter, you gain three more Summoning Points during your Standby Phase. You can never have more than 12 Summoning Points at a time.

Summoning Field

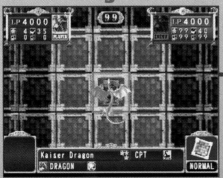

The blue squares are your Summon Squares.

Because of the move to a 7x7 playing Field and the ability to move your cards around, the Summoning Field now exists around your Deck Leader. You can Summon your cards into any square adjacent to your Deck Leader. If there are no available squares at the end of your turn, you lose the game.

Victory Conditions

You win the game when one of four conditions is met:

- **You reduce your opponent's Deck Leader's Life Points to zero.**
- **The turn counter runs down to zero and you have more Life Points than your opponent.**
- **You occupy all your opponent's Summoning Area with your own cards so he or she is unable to Summon any of his or her own cards at the beginning of his turn.**
- **You equip Exodia the Forbidden One as your Deck Leader and begin your round with the Right Arm of the Forbidden One, Left Arm of the Forbidden One, Right Leg of the Forbidden One, and the Left Leg of the Forbidden One in your Summoning Area and in the face-up position. These are very rare cards, but at least one character in the campaign can win this way.**

Card Battles

A battle ensues when a creature of yours moves into a square occupied by an enemy creature card.

To ensure that you win, make sure all the factors are in your favor. When battling the computer in Campaign mode, the opposing duelists use every advantage against you; in fact, the maps are designed to favor your computer opponent.

Many factors boost your creature's ATK/DEF ratings. If possible, boost your creature's innate strength, rather than using it plain.

Ways to Improve ATK/DEF Strength

- **Terrain: +500 points to ATK/DEF**
- **Power-up Cards: +300 to +700 points to ATK/DEF**
- **Friendly Effect Creatures: +100 to +1,000 points to ATK/DEF**
- **Magic Cards: +600 points to all creatures of a type**

The easiest way to boost a creature's ATK is by equipping it with a Power-up card. Power-up cards affect only one creature. Be sure that the Power-up card applies to the creature, or else when merging the two (whether in your hand or on the Field), the Power-up will bounce the other card off the Field if they are not compatible. For example, the Power-up card Dragon Treasure does not affect Thunder Dragon, despite the name. If you try to equip Thunder Dragon with Dragon Treasure, Thunder Dragon will be destroyed.

The second easiest way to increase a creature's strength is by making it fight on favorable terrain, which gives it a bonus 500 points. Sometimes, standing your ground on favorable terrain is all that keeps you from losing. And if your favorable terrain turns out to be the unfavorable terrain for your enemy's creatures, that is a net difference in 1,000 points in your creatures' favor.

Certain Magic Cards boost all creatures of a type. In essence, it gives a power up to all the creatures of that type on the Field. Cards such as Winged Trumpeter, for instance, give a +600 boost to all Fairies on the Field. Rain of Mercy boosts the strength of all Plants on the Field by 600. If you have even one of these cards, you have a huge advantage over your opponent. While your opponent might be able to power up one creature to high levels, with these Magic Cards you can pump up all your creatures, quickly outpacing your foe.

Finally, some creature cards have special Flip effects that boost the strength of friendly creatures. When flipped face-up, they give anywhere from +100 to +1,000 bonus points. Some creatures, such as Gyakutenno Megami, give a one-time bonus, while others, such as Pumpking the King of Ghosts, give a bonus at the beginning of every round. Also, some cards must be in defense position to give their strength boost, while others simply bestow their bonus when flipped. Refer to the "Cards" section to see the cards that give this benefit.

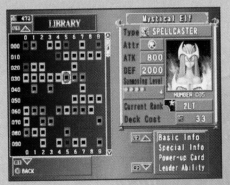

Sample Creatures with Power-Up Effects

- **Fairy King Truesdale (#670):** While this card is face-up in the defense position, the power of all your Plant monsters increases by 500 points.
- **Gyakutenno Megami (#368):** When this card is flipped face-up, all your monsters with ATK of 1,000 or below are increased by 1,000 points.
- **Hoshiningen (#383):** Your Light monsters are strengthened by 300 points when this card is flipped face-up.
- **Hourglass of Courage (#390):** If LP is over 1,000 when this card is destroyed in battle, your monsters' strengths are increased by 1,000 points, and your LP is reduced by 1,000!
- **Mystical Elf (#035):** When this card is flipped face-up, it powers up all of your own Light monsters by 800 points.
- **Pumpking the King of Ghosts (#108):** While this card is face-up in the defense position, all Zombie monsters are increased by 100 points at the start of each turn.

Ways to Reduce Opposing ATK/DEF

Learning how to reduce the strength of enemy monsters is important. An easy way to deal damage to your opponent is to weaken his monsters and then rip through them to deliver damage to the enemy Deck Leader.

Trap Cards are a very effective way to reduce monster ATK and DEF. Cards such as Spellbinding Circle, Mesmeric Control, and Tears of the Mermaid spellbind opposing creatures and reduce their strength. These Trap Cards give yourself time to set up good maneuvers and weaken the enemy.

Another good way to decrease enemy monster strength is with Effects Monsters, such as the Sectarian of Secrets or Koragashi. Both reduce an enemy monster 300 points when killed in battle. Koragashi

does it to all creatures in horizontal and vertical spaces relative to its position when it is destroyed. Set these creatures up in defense position and then let the enemy creatures attack you for a nasty surprise.

You can also weaken a monster's ATK and DEF rating by making it battle your monsters on unfavorable terrain. Lure a

fiend to fight in the Forests, or better yet, use a Magic Card to change the terrain around it into Forests, thus chopping off 500 points from its strength.

 TIP

One insidious Trap Card to use is Reverse Trap. This permanent trap takes all power ups and reduces the equipped monster by the same number, reversing the effects of all Power-up Cards. It is the perfect way to punish the enemy's monsters—you deprive him of his expected 500-point increase and also reduce his strength by 500 points. However, this card reverses all Power-up Cards played, including yours.

New Concepts
Deck Leader

Your Deck Leader is the most important part of your deck. You start with a Deck Leader that comes prepackaged for the deck you choose at the game's beginning. However, you can eventually choose new leaders from your existing creatures. All of your creature cards have a beginning rank of NCO (non-commissioned officer). As your creatures are used in duels, however, they gain experience and eventually rise in rank. There are 13 ranks, and certain ranks confer special abilities to your Deck Leader.

Deck Leader Ranks

- NCO, Non-commissioned Officer
- 2LT, Second Lieutenant
- 1LT, First Lieutenant
- CPT, Captain
- MAJ, Major
- LTC, Lieutenant Colonel
- COL, Colonel
- BG, Brigadier
- RAD, Rear Admiral
- VAD, Vice Admiral
- ADM, Admiral
- SA, Senior Admiral
- SD, Secretary of Defense

 NOTE

When a creature of a name rises in rank, all creatures of that name you own also rise in rank. Thus, it is not just individual monsters that improve. So when your Kaiser Dragon is promoted, all your Kaiser Dragons get promoted.

Your monsters achieve new rank only after successfully performing in duels. That means they must be on the playing Field and win several battles before they gain enough experience points to be promoted. Each successive rank requires more and more successfully won battles, making it harder to achieve higher rank. At their highest rank, certain creature types can have from three to five special abilities. Be warned though: You must win dozens of battles before you can crack even the lower ranks. And getting to a high-enough rank to gain your first Deck Leader Ability will take even longer. But once you get there, the abilities can be a tremendous help.

 NOTE

Creatures gain very little experience while acting as Deck Leaders. A creature won't advance as quickly as if he were fighting normally. They must fight on the Field against other cards to get promoted.

When you designate a Deck Leader, it loses any Effects it has. So Fairy King Truesdale cannot give friendly Plant creatures a +500 bonus to strength while it is Deck Leader. Deck Leaders are simply your means to Summon cards and are your physical representation on the Field. They have no attack and confer no creature effects beyond their Leader Abilities.

Sample Leader Abilities

There are several more abilities than these in the game. Half the fun is finding them out for yourself.

- **Extended Support Range:** Extends the range at which the Deck Leader's other abilities operate. Range increases from the 3x3 space around the Leader to a 5x5 space.
- **Increased Movement:** The Deck Leader can move two squares instead of one.
- **Increased Strength for Same-Type Friendlies:** All monsters of the same type as the Leader gain 500 bonus points to ATK/DEF when in the Leader's support range.
- **Movement Bonus for Same Type Friendlies:** Creatures of the same type as the Leader can move an additional square per turn when within the support range. This movement bonus is not in addition to the movement bonus for favorable terrain.
- **Weaken Specific Enemy Type:** Enemy creatures of one specific type have their ATK/DEF reduced by 500 points when within the Deck Leader's support range.

Movement

During each round, you can move your Deck Leader and your cards. Each card, whether it is a monster or a spell, can normally only move one square per turn, horizontally or vertically. Moving diagonally counts as a two-square move.

Monsters can sometimes move more than one square per turn if they begin their turn face-up and on favorable terrain. If those two conditions are met, then creature cards can move two squares or diagonally. Spell cards can never move more than one square per turn. To see a list of which monsters favor which terrain, refer to the "Terrain" section.

This insect monster can move two spaces because it began its round face-up on Forest terrain.

A Deck Leader can avoid one monster forever.

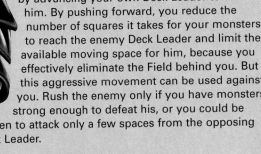

But multiple monsters can eventually corner it.

NOTE

Once a Trap Card is face-up, it can no longer move. When moving a Trap Card into position, always keep it face-down. If you accidentally flip it, it will remain immobile. The same happens if your enemy has creatures or Magic Cards that flip up your face-down cards.

TIP

If your Trap Cards and Flip Effect Cards have been neutralized or immobilized by being flipped face-up against your will, use the Magic Card, Darkness Approaches, to flip them face-down.

NOTE

You can move your Deck Leader one square per turn. Deck Leaders do not gain any benefit for being in their type's favorable terrain. Just as they lose their ATK/DEF rating when made into Deck Leaders, they also no longer benefit or suffer from terrain conditions. Only if you gain the Leader Ability, Increased Movement, can you move two squares per round.

TIP

To get a quick sneak attack on a Deck Leader, hold a favorable terrain card in reserve behind your monster. When there are two spaces between your monster and the Deck Leader, the enemy will assume that it will take two turns for you to reach it and might not move right away. But if you flip a terrain card behind the monster, you suddenly give it favorable terrain, and the monster can now move two squares and attack the Leader directly.

Moving your Deck Leader is a very strategic part of your duel. If you can corner the opposing Deck Leader, you can attack him directly. To do so, chase the enemy Leader with more than one creature.

If you are simply moving one space per turn, it becomes difficult to attack a Leader with a single monster. Have two creatures move toward the Deck Leader from opposite directions, intercepting the Leader. In avoiding one of your monsters, the enemy Leader ends up running into the other.

You also can corner the enemy Deck Leader by advancing your own Deck Leader toward him. By pushing forward, you reduce the number of squares it takes for your monsters to reach the enemy Deck Leader and limit the available moving space for him, because you effectively eliminate the Field behind you. But this aggressive movement can be used against you. Rush the enemy only if you have monsters strong enough to defeat his, or you could be open to attack only a few spaces from the opposing Deck Leader.

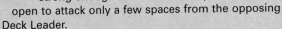

The Deck Leader is being chased into the corner. From here, it is easy to occupy Summoning Squares and surround him.

- **Magic Cards:** Spell cards that do not fall into the previous categories. These include cards that deal direct damage to enemy Deck Leaders, that heal, that give bonus points to all creatures on the Field, that transport you across the Field, that alter the Field terrain, or produce other miscellaneous magic effects.

Card Types and Attributes

There are two kinds of cards: Spells and Monsters. Spell cards are further divided into various types.

Categories of Spell Cards

- **Power-up Cards:** Spell cards that directly boost the power of a single creature type. Must be equipped on a single monster during Summoning or moved onto a monster on the playing Field. Can affect enemy monsters if run into on the Field.

- **Trap Cards:** Spell cards that usually create an undesirable effect when triggered by the enemy's actions.

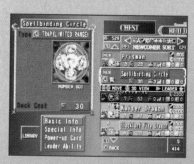

- **Ritual Cards:** Spell cards that sacrifice three specific monsters to create a new, better monster. Monsters created by your Ritual Card appear only for the duel and do not go into your Chest afterward.

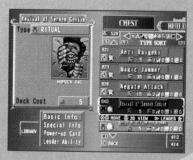

Monster Cards

You use Monster Cards to duel your opponent. It is mostly through your monster battles that you hurt and ultimately defeat your competition's Deck Leader. Monsters all have different statistics that tell you a little something about them. They are known by their Type, Attribute, Attack, Defense, Deck Cost, and any Special Effects.

There are three kinds of Monster Cards: Normal, Effects, and Ritual Monsters. The majority of monsters are Normal—nothing but their ATK/DEF rating. Effects Monsters have special abilities that come into play during specific circumstances, such as being flipped face-up, being destroyed, or when attacking. Refer to the "Cards" section for a detailed list of all Effects Monsters and their individual abilities. Ritual Monsters are created from Ritual Cards, and require the sacrifice of creatures. Ritual Monsters never exist in your Chest on their own. They only appear when the right creatures and Ritual Card are on the Field.

Fusions

Unlike in the *Yu-Gi-Oh!* card game, Fusion monsters are not a separate category of creatures. While you can create them by fusing other creatures, the Fusion result is also a monster that exists as a Normal monster card. However, if you create a monster through Fusion, it exists for the duel only, and does not appear in your Chest afterward.

To create a Fusion, designate two or more creatures and then try Summoning them onto the playing Field together. If the creatures are a match for Fusion, they will merge into a new creature. If they are not a match, then all creatures except for the last in the chain are removed from the game. Refer to the "Fusion" section for more information.

Type

There are 21 types in the game and every monster is divided into these 21 types. (Type is simply what kind of creature the card is.) This is important for knowing what Power-ups affect them. Also very important is the fact that each type of monster has different favorable and unfavorable terrain.

On favorable terrain, monsters gain strength and movement bonuses. On unfavorable terrain, they suffer ATK/DEF penalties. Machine and Dinosaur types for instance, have Wastelands as a favorable terrain, while Fish and Plants have it as unfavorable terrain. Refer to the Terrain Effects Chart to see each type's favorable and unfavorable terrain. In some cases, a type might have multiple favorable or unfavorable terrains.

This terrain has just been turned into Mountains to give these Dragons an advantage.

Type also sometimes determines how creatures interact with each other. Some monsters, for example, have bonuses against other creature types. Also, some creatures are more likely to fuse with some types than others. Warriors, for example, fuse well with Beasts, Zombies, and Winged Beasts, but not so well with Dragons.

Attribute

A creature's attribute is important for determining how monsters react to each other after a battle. There are six attributes in the game, and some are weak against others. If a creature of a certain attribute is attacked by a creature of a weaker attribute, even if that creature dies in battle, it might still impede the winner by virtue of its superior attribute.

For example, Water trumps Fire, so if a Fire creature defeats a Water creature in battle, the Fire creature will be spellbound for one turn, even though it won the battle. However, if the roles were reversed, and the Water creature won, the Fire creature would not spellbind the Water creature, because Fire is inferior to Water.

NOTE

When a creature is spellbound, it is frozen in its current position, whether attack or defense, and cannot move for one round.

It does not matter who initiates the attack and whether the defender is in attack or defense position. Anytime a creature of a superior attribute loses in battle to a creature of an inferior attribute, the winning creature is spellbound. This occurs even when the losing monster does not die, as when it is repelled by a monster with higher defense.

ATTRIBUTE RELATIONSHIPS

- Water spellbinds Fire
- Fire spellbinds Earth
- Earth spellbinds Wind
- Wind spellbinds Dark
- Dark spellbinds Light
- Light spellbinds Water

NOTE

Only directly related attributes have any affect on each other. A Water monster battling a Wind monster produces no effect. Water only has a spellbinding relationship to Light and Fire. Likewise, Fire only has a spellbinding relationship with Water and Earth.

Use spellbinding to your advantage. Sometimes it's worth sacrificing a small amount of LP just to paralyze an opponent's tough monster. This is especially useful when you need to buy time to draw a game-winning card. Spellbinding is best used when your creature is in defense position and you can lure a monster with the weaker attribute to attack you.

Terrain

The game's 10 terrain types are: Crush, Dark, Forest, Labyrinth, Meadow, Mountain, Normal, Sea, Toon, and Wasteland. Creatures in favorable terrain gain a +500 bonus to ATK and DEF. When face-up, they also can move two squares instead of one. Unfavorable terrain imposes no movement penalty, but reduces ATK and DEF by 500 points. Two of these terrain types, Crush and Labyrinth, also have special features.

Special Terrain Types

Crush terrain destroys any monsters of ATK 1,500 or greater that steps onto it, regardless of whether they are face-up or face-down. Only monsters with ATK below 1,500, spell cards, and your Deck Leader can traverse Crush terrain.

Labyrinth terrain is impassable. Only a select few Effects Monsters can successfully move over Labyrinth terrain. All monsters can attack an enemy creature that is on Labyrinth terrain, but after winning, the victorious creature cannot move into the Labyrinth square unless it also has the ability to move through Labyrinths. Labyrinth is also special because it does not get changed by terrain-altering Magic Cards, such as Forest, Mountain, and Yami.

Terrain-Altering Cards

Turn terrain to your advantage by using terrain-altering cards. All terrain types except for Labyrinth can be altered by the Magic Cards listed below, which affect all terrain within a two-space area of the activating card. There are also a few more cards, including creature cards, that can alter terrain but that aren't listed here. However, creatures that alter terrain affect only a one-space area.

- **Burning Land:** Changes terrain to Normal.
- **Forest:** Changes terrain to Forest.
- **Earthshaker:** Randomly shifts position of all terrain and changes Labyrinth squares to Normal.
- **Mountain:** Changes terrain to Mountain.
- **Sogen:** Changes terrain to Meadow.
- **Toon World:** Changes terrain to Toon.
- **Yami:** Changes terrain to Dark.

TERRAIN EFFECTS

	CRUSH	DARK	FOREST	LABYRINTH	MEADOW	MOUNTAIN	NORMAL	SEA	TOON	WASTELAND
Aqua	—	—	—	—	—	—	—	Fav	Unf	Unf
Beast	—	—	Fav	—	—	—	—	—	Unf	—
Beast-warrior	—	—	Fav	—	Fav	—	—	—	Unf	—
Dinosaur	—	—	—	—	—	—	—	—	Unf	Fav
Dragon	—	—	—	—	—	Fav	—	—	Unf	—
Fairy	—	Unf	—	—	—	Fav	—	—	Unf	—
Fiend	—	Fav	Unf	—	—	—	—	—	Unf	—
Fish	—	—	—	—	—	—	—	Fav	Unf	Unf
Immortal	Fav	—	—	—	—	—	—	—	Unf	—
Insect	—	—	Fav	—	—	—	—	—	Unf	—
Machine	—	—	—	—	—	—	—	Unf	Unf	Fav
Plant	—	—	Fav	—	—	—	—	—	Unf	Unf
Pyro	—	—	Fav	—	—	—	—	Unf	Unf	—
Reptile	—	—	—	—	—	—	—	—	Unf	—
Rock	—	—	—	—	—	—	—	—	Unf	Fav
Sea Serpent	—	—	—	—	—	—	—	Fav	Unf	Unf
Spellcaster	—	Fav	—	—	Unf	—	—	—	Unf	—
Thunder	—	—	—	—	—	Fav	—	Fav	Unf	—
Warrior	—	—	—	—	Fav	—	—	—	Unf	—
Winged Beast	—	—	—	—	—	Fav	—	—	Unf	—
Zombie	—	Fav	—	—	—	Unf	—	—	Unf	Fav

Dueling Basics and Deck Strategies

Deck Management

Half of a successful winning strategy lies not on the playing Field but in your deck management. Knowing what cards to bring to battle can guarantee victory. Having a poorly designed deck can spell certain defeat.

Deck Cost

This game uses a card's Deck Cost to balance strong decks. In the Campaign mode, you cannot engage in a duel if your Total Deck Cost is higher than your opponent's. You can only duel someone in the campaign if you have a numerically inferior deck.

Every card in the game has a Deck Cost. The more powerful the monster or spell, the higher the cost. Cards such as Blue-Eyes White Dragon (DC 55) or Mirror Force (DC 99), are much more expensive than ineffectual cards such as Dancing Elf (DC 5) and Fake Trap (DC 5).

Because of this limit in the campaign, you are forced to balance your high-powered cards with their cost, ensuring that you do not overload your deck with unbeatable high-level cards. In Custom Games, however, there is no such limitation. In games against other players, you can build a deck with as high a Deck Cost as you want.

Constructing the Perfect Deck

There is no such thing as the perfect deck. However, as you play through the campaign, you will discover deck strategies that work best for you. Try to have a focus or a theme. If you want to build a Dragon deck, then add sufficient power ups such as Dragon Treasure and terrain cards such as Mountain. If you want to go with Plants, Zombies, or Fairies, include the best-supporting creatures and cards possible.

Finally, tailor your deck to your opponent. If you know you are facing Seto, who is famous for his Dragons, then add several Dragon-killing monsters to your deck, such as Dragon Seeker or Javelin Beetle. If you are dueling Necromancer, than add cards such as Eternal Rest to destroy his Zombies, or Rogue Doll, which kills any Zombie it faces.

MUST-HAVE DECK COMBOS

Here are must-have cards for those who want to adhere to the following sample deck themes. It doesn't hurt to have three of each card, because in some cases, such as Pumpking's strength boost for Zombies, multiple cards stack their effects. Some decks, such as the Fairy deck, showcase a creature type that is weak on its own but immensely powerful if stacked with the proper Power-up Cards. Other decks, such as Dragon, stand on the strength of their creatures alone, and have few supporting cards.

Dragon
Dragon Treasure
Gust Fan
Mountain

Fairy Deck
Bright Castle
Cyber Shield
Gust Fan
Gyakutenno Megami
Hoshiningen
Mountain
Mystical Elf
Silver Bow and Arrow
Winged Trumpeter

Plant Deck
Fairy King Truesdale
Forest
Rain of Mercy
Vile Germs

Zombie
Dark Energy
Dokurorider
Pumpking the King of Ghosts
Violet Crystal
Witch of the Black Forest

Machine Deck
Limiter Removal
Machine King
Machine Conversion Factory
Mechanical Spider
Robotic Knight

Creatures: Big Versus Little

As you're constructing your deck, you could either pack your deck with high-powered creatures with steep Summon Costs or lots of little creatures with cheap Summon Costs. The advantage to the first strategy is that you have the stronger creatures, but you have to wait longer to play them, so you lose the numerical advantage.

With low-level monsters, you can play them frequently, but your creatures are too weak to stand up to stronger foes. If you build a deck with low-level creatures, make sure each one can fuse with another. That way, you offset the disadvantage of not being able to play stronger monsters.

Have a good range of creatures, but concentrate on higher-level creatures. You are limited to five monsters anyway, so in the long run you don't lose much of a competitive advantage by not having more creatures out early. Besides, your opponent's five Fairy Dragons won't stand a chance against your one Blue-Eyes White Dragon. The only drawback to a high-level creature deck is that there aren't enough Summoning Points to go around. For these decks, add several Gate Deegs and Berfomets, creature cards that have a special Flip Effect that gives you maximum points as soon as they are flipped face-up on the Field.

The other disadvantage of having a deck emphasis on strong, high-level monsters is that you are very vulnerable to traps and spells. If you go this route, add an Ancient Tree of Enlightenment to your deck to neutralize all traps. And add a few Monster Reborn cards so you can revive your heavy monsters if they get lost.

Ratio of Monsters to Spells

In the beginning of the game, your deck is almost 80 percent creatures and 20 percent spells. But as your game progresses, even out that ratio until it hovers at around 50 percent. The most powerful opponents you face have spell-heavy decks. When facing Darkness-ruler, Pegasus, and Manawyddan fab Llyr, it usually isn't their creatures that do you in, but their well-placed and numerous spell cards.

Start by slowly replacing your weaker monsters with Trap and Power-up Cards. You get them more frequently than other Magic Cards from the Graveyard Slot Machine. Next on your list should be a few healing Magic Cards and direct damage Magic Cards. Eventually, you have a deck composed of high-cost creatures and many useful spells.

Ratio of Spells to Traps

A little more difficult to ascertain is the ratio of different spell cards. You always should have two or three Trap Cards that spellbind and weaken your opponent. When starting out, get your hands on an instant death Trap Card (if possible), such as Bear Trap, and add it to your deck. But later on, these cards aren't as good, because you have enough strong creatures to protect yourself. Also, leaving a weakened creature around is sometimes more beneficial to you than completely destroying it, because you can attack the weakened and spellbound monster to get at the enemy Deck Leader.

Make sure to add a terrain card for your most dominant type. If you are using mostly Dragons and Fairies, add a Mountain card to your deck. If your deck consists of Plants and Insects, add a Forest card. About a third of your spell cards should be various Trap Cards. The other third can be Power-up Cards, and the final third should be miscellaneous Magic Cards.

TIP

Because you go from duelist to duelist in the campaign, it's a good idea to create a low-cost deck and a high-cost deck. That way, you don't have to keep adjusting your deck before every single duel.

Cost should be no limit in your high-cost deck. But in your low-cost deck, add cheap Fusions to get stronger monsters for less Deck Cost. Find the cheapest component creatures to achieve the desired Fusion, rather than just throwing in two creatures because they match. Refer to the "Fusion" section for more details.

In your low-cost deck, leave room to throw in one or two powerful spell cards as befits your upcoming duel, but keep the rest of the deck modest.

MUST-HAVE CARDS

Here are a few cards that can instantly make any deck better. As you find them, make room for them in your deck.

Creature Cards

Berfomet
Blast Sphere
Gate Deeg
Hourglass of Courage
Hourglass of Life
Tenderness

Healing Cards

Dian Keto the Cure Master
Gift of the Mystical Elf
Goblin's Secret Remedy
Soul of the Pure

Direct Damage Cards

Just Desserts
Ookazi
Riryoku
Tremendous Fire

Miscellaneous

Burning Land
Dark Hole
Earthshaker
Graverobber
Harpie's Feather Duster
Magic Drain
Monster Reborn
Raigeki
Solomon's Lawbook
Yellow Luster Shield

When to Give Up Fusions for Better Cards

At some point, ditch the cards that can make a Fusion for a better Normal monster. By the time you have several Kaiser Dragons, Red-Eyes B. Dragon, and a Blue-Eyes White Dragon, it's no longer necessary to keep a Baby Dragon and a Kaminarikozou in your deck.

In the campaign, a large part of that decision-making depends on who you are fighting. Because you must have a lower Total Deck Cost than the opponent you face, it makes sense to eschew some higher-cost cards in favor of two lower-cost cards that can make a Fusion. But if cost is not a limit, or if you are facing high Deck Cost opponents such as Yugi, Pegasus, and Manawyddan fab Llyr, throw out all your weak cards and load up with high-cost cards.

Once you have higher-cost cards, those two Fusion components are taking up valuable spots in your deck that could go to a great Magic Card, such as Solomon's Lawbook or Earthshaker.

And relying on Fusions in your deck means you are much more likely to run into a situation where you are desperately waiting to draw that second monster, while the opponent is killing you with his high-ATK Normal Monster. You're much more constrained by the luck of the draw.

So, as soon as you can dump a Fusion in favor of two other cards, even a spell card or an equal or slightly weaker monster, do so. Retain only those Fusions that are far and away more powerful than any Normal Monster, such as Meteor Black Dragon, or that have a Special Effect you cannot duplicate with any of your other cards.

How to Get Better Cards

As you play through the campaign, you will quickly realize you need better cards. Here is how you can upgrade your deck by acquiring new cards.

Graveyard Slot Machine

Every time you defeat an opponent in the campaign, you are taken to the Graveyard Slot Machine. As you stop the Slot Machine, you gain the cards you see. This is the best way to gain new cards. If you see a particular duelist using a card you especially like, then keep playing him or her until you get that card. It could take you several tries, but this is the easiest way to get cards you want.

When playing the Graveyard Slot Machine, if you hit the same image three times in a row, you are rewarded with a rare card not normally available from the Slot Machine.

Reincarnation

Do not neglect to use the Reincarnation feature in the game. After every five duels, you can go into your Chest and Reincarnate a card. The card must be in your Chest, and not your deck. Then press L3. That card is removed from your Chest, and you gain three new cards instead.

The three cards each have a Deck Cost slightly lower than the cost of the original card, so if you want stronger cards, you must sacrifice some of your best cards. This is where Custom Games come in very handy. If you have a Sanga of the Thunder, a card with a Deck Cost of 56, you can keep battling against yourself in Custom Game to get multiple copies of it to Reincarnate later.

 TIP

The best way to gain many new cards quickly, short of entering passwords, is to use two memory cards to continually Reincarnate a card and trade it back to yourself. Have an original save game file on your first memory card. After each Reincarnation attempt, save your new game onto the second memory card. Then trade the new cards on memory card two to memory card one. Since you won't be saving over your game on memory card one, you can keep reloading it and Reincarnating cards, and then save the new cards onto memory card two. Repeat until you're satisfied with the cards you've gained.

Custom Games

Sometimes you already have the cards you want, but you'd like more of them. In this case, you can use the Custom Game option to help yourself out.

If you play against the CPU in Custom Game, it uses your own deck against you. When you win, you get to access the Graveyard Slot Machine just as you would in a campaign duel, except in this instance, the cards available in the Slot Machine are drawn from your deck. So if you have a Magic Jammer and you want more, play against your own deck in Custom Game several times and win. It's the quickest way to gain multiple copies of cards you already have.

Campaign Introduction

Once you select a New Game, you are whisked through time to 1485 and Stonehenge. Waiting for you is Simon McMooran, High Druid and Henry Tudor's advisor. Henry Tudor, as you soon find out, is otherwise known as Yugi.

Simon describes the desperate situation to you: England is in the midst of civil war between the Yorkists and Lancastrians. The Lancastrian heir to the throne, Yugi, has been exiled to France, while the Yorkist usurper, Richard III, is poised to take all of England. It seems Richard III is unbeatable in battle as long as his White Rose Duelists hold the eight White Rose Cards. None of Yugi's friends have been able to defeat their leader Seto, and so you have been Summoned to duel his White Rose Duelists and claim all eight of their White Rose Cards. Without them, Seto and his followers will be unable to stop Yugi.

But just as you are about to pledge allegiance to the Lancastrians, Seto appears and offers you a deal. He tells you that the Yorkists have all but won, and all they need to cement victory are Yugi's eight Red Rose Cards. If you are willing to retrieve those eight cards, then he will send you home promptly.

Now you must choose: join Yugi or follow Seto. Go with Yugi first and then serve Seto. The Yugi side of the story is more fleshed out, with a few cutscenes, while the Seto side is just a dueling marathon. And after you beat the game, you automatically replay from the Seto side anyway.

Yugi Campaign Overview

After you join Yugi's side and help him defeat the White Rose Duelists in anticipation of his upcoming invasion of England, you have two options.

You start the game at Wilford Haven, with two paths leading to Chester and Tewkesbury. You can duel Weevil Underwood in Chester or Rex Raptor in Tewkesbury.

Weevil is the easier of the two, so duel him first.

When you win, two more paths open up. You can duel Pegasus in Lancashire or Keith in Towton. Both are too hard at this point, so go back to Tewkesbury and duel Rex Raptor. When you beat him, he also opens up two paths to you: Necromancer in Exeter and Darkness-ruler in St. Albans.

Duel Necromancer first, even though he is a dead-end in the campaign trail. Once you defeat Darkness-ruler, your trail leads back to Keith—duel him. Pegasus is by far the toughest challenge of the eight White Rose Duelists, so hold off on dueling him until the last possible moment.

If you beat Keith, the trail continues to Labyrinth-ruler in Newcastle. He is also a dead-end, so after you defeat him, return to Pegasus. After you beat him, the trail goes to Ishtar in the Isle of Man. When you defeat her, you meet with Yugi in a cutscene. He tells you the invasion is on schedule and to meet him in Bosworth.

At Bosworth, Richard III is waiting for you. After you defeat him, a White Rose Duelist switches sides. Then, it's off to Stonehenge to duel Seto. But after you defeat him, the final duelist awaits: the Card Guardian Manawyddan fab Llyr. When he finally crumbles in defeat, the game ends. Thanks to your help, Yugi regains his crown and you can go home knowing that you fulfilled your destiny as the Rose Duelist.

NOTE

Save your game before the final duel with Manawyddan fab Llyr. After you defeat him, you'll be prompted to save your game. Save your game only if you have a second memory card, otherwise, all your progress in the Yugi game is erased and you can't duel any of the White Rose Duelists to gain more cards.

Seto Campaign Trail

You can play Seto's campaign by choosing him first or by winning the Yugi campaign. After you do that, you can replay the game from Seto's viewpoint. There are no forks in Seto's campaign. It's a straight line to Yugi and then back to Stonehenge.

Your first duel is with Tea at Windsor. After you beat her, move on to London and T. Tristan Grey. Beyond him in Canterbury lies Lady Margaret Mai Beaufort, the woman who told Yugi to Summon you to England.

After you defeat her, hop to Dover to catch a ship bound for France. The captain, Mako, agrees to take you but then drops anchor in the middle of the straits. It turns out he has been paid to make sure you never reach France!

You fight him in the Straits of Dover. Defeat him and he drops you off at the port of Boulogne, where the campaign trail leads you to the duelist Joey in Amiens. After beating him, you continue to Paris, where J. Shadi Morton is eager to duel you. From this point, the Seto campaign ramps up in difficulty. The next stop is Le Mans, and the duelist Jasper Dice Tudor. Defeat him and you move on to Bakura in Rennes. Finally, Yugi waits for you in Brest.

But it's not over until the Card Guardian sings. Seto has Summoned Card Guardian Manawyddan fab Llyr to Stonehenge. He has his reasons for doing so, but soon learns that the Guardian cannot be controlled. Your moment of destiny is at hand, as Seto urges you to banish the Guardian. If you do that, then you are forever in Seto's debt, and he gladly sends you home with his thanks.

At this point, you can replay the game from Yugi's side. Or if you have already done so, all your progress in both campaigns opens up and you can duel all the duelists as often as you like, dueling for fun or for the cards! You've earned it.

Your Starting Deck

Before setting out on your dueling conquests, choose a starting deck. In fact, you choose your deck before you pick sides. Each has its own strengths and weaknesses. Look at each deck's card list and Fusions before you decide which one is best. Then you are ready to take on the White and Red Rose Duelists!

NOTE

There are many decks to choose from, but they are presented three at a time. Because decks are determined by your name, you'll need to enter a new name if you want a new set of decks to choose from. We found 16! How many can you find?

- Airknight Parshath
- Birdface
- Fairy King Truesdale
- King Tiger Wanghu
- Kyruel
- Luminous Soldier
- Maiden of Aqua
- Molten Behemoth
- Patrician of Darkness
- Robotic Knight
- Serpentine Princess
- Tactical Warrior
- The Illusory Gentleman
- Thunder Nyan-Nyan
- Twin-Headed Behemoth
- Wolf Axwielder

Airknight Parshath

Vital Stats

- Main Monster Types: Fairy, Warrior, Dragon, Winged Beast
- Main Attributes: Light, Wind, Earth, Water
- Deck Cost: 822
- Average Monster Summon Level: 3.47
- Average Monster ATK/DEF: 1,011/1,054

This Fairy deck doesn't have strong monsters. However, it has some good Effect Monsters that pump your troops. Hoshingen adds +300 to all your Light Monsters. Since most of your monsters are Light, this is an immense help. Playing your Winged Trumpeter Magic Card adds another +600 strength to those Fairies. As soon as you can, acquire a Dancing Elf so that you can create the Mystical Elf Fusion, which gives your Light Monsters another +800 points. That's +1,700 bonus to all your Fairy monsters!

This deck also has an excellent Trap Card, Tears of the Mermaid, making it one of the best decks at crippling a strong enemy monster. The Airknight of Parshath deck is also good against Machines, since it has LaLa Li-oon that hurts all Machine Monsters.

Good Fusions

- **Dark Witch:** Doma The Angel of Silence + Maiden of the Moonlight
- **Punished Eagle:** Masaki the Legendary Swordsman + Mavelus
- **Garvas:** Master & Expert + Faith Bird
- **Nekogal #2:** Maiden of the Moonlight + Silver Fang
- **Kairyu-Shin:** White Dolphin + Fairy Dragon

Complete Card Listing

NAME	ATK/DEF	TYPE
Arma Knight	1,000/1,200	Aqua
Arma Knight	1,000/1,200	Aqua
Bright Castle	—	Power-up
Doma the Angel of Silence	1,600/1,400	Fairy
Fairy Dragon	1,100/1,200	Dragon
Faith Bird	1,500/1,100	Winged Beast
Flame Manipulator	900/1,000	Pyro
Griggle	350/300	Plant
Hoshingen	500/700	Fairy
Kaminarikozou	700/600	Thunder
Key Mace	400/300	Fairy/Effect
Kurama	800/800	Winged Beast
LaLa Li-oon	600/600	Thunder
Lunar Queen Elzaim	750/1,100	Fairy
Maiden of the Moonlight	1,500/1,300	Spellcaster
Masaki the Legendary Swordsman	1,100/1,100	Warrior
Masaki the Legendary Swordsman	1,100/1,100	Warrior
Master & Expert	1,200/1,000	Beast
Master & Expert	1,200/1,000	Beast
Mavelus	1,300/900	Winged Beast
Moon Envoy	1,100/1,100	Warrior
Moon Envoy	1,100/1,100	Warrior
Mountain	—	Magic
Orion the Battle King	1,800/1,500	Fairy
Orion the Battle King	1,800/1,500	Fairy
Peacock	1,700/1,500	Winged Beast
Petit Dragon	600/700	Dragon
Petit Dragon	600/700	Dragon
Protector of the Throne	800/1,500	Warrior
Rainbow Flower	400/500	Plant
Silver Bow and Arrow	—	Power-up
Silver Fang	1,200/800	Beast
Spirit of the Harp	800/2,000	Fairy
Spirit of the Harp	800/2,000	Fairy
Tears of the Mermaid	—	Trap (Limited Range)
The Judgement Hand	1,400/700	Warrior
The Little Swordsman of Aile	800/1,300	Warrior
White Dolphin	500/400	Fish
Winged Egg of New Life	1,400/1,700	Fairy
Winged Trumpeter	—	Magic

Birdface

Vital Stats

- Main Monster Types: Winged Beast, Spellcaster, Dragon, Beast
- Main Attributes: Wind, Dark, Light, Earth
- Deck Cost: 814
- Average Monster Summon Level: 3.41
- Average Monster ATK/DEF: 1,084/944

The Birdface deck has mostly Winged Beasts. Many of them are strong, although no individual monster tops 2,000 ATK. However, you can make very strong Fusions with this deck, including at least two Crimson Sunbirds (2,300 ATK). Most of your monsters can be made stronger with this deck's good Power-up cards, including the Magic Card Windstorm of Etaqua, which boosts all Winged Beasts on the Field. As soon as you get this deck, battle yourself in Custom Game to acquire a Birdface card to add to your deck, which will further strengthen your Winged Beast monster cards.

   This deck is good at altering terrain, not because of its Mountain spell card, but because of Yamatano Dragon Scroll. If you can flip it face-up in the defense position for three rounds, it transforms into Yamadron, a Dragon that transforms all adjacent squares into Normal terrain *every time it attacks!* This deck lacks good Traps, Effects Monsters, and spells.

Good Fusions

- Crimson Sunbird: Fireyarou + Blue-Winged Crown
- Punished Eagle: Harpie Lady + Princess of Tsurugi
- Garvas: Dark Rabbit + Kurama
- Dark Witch: Shining Frienship + Princess of Tsurugi
- Nekogal #2: LaMoon + Hane-Hane

Complete Card Listing

Name	ATK/DEF	Type
Baby Dragon	1,200/700	Dragon
Bat	300/350	Machine/Effect
Blue-Winged Crown	1,600/1,200	Winged Beast
Claw Reacher	1,000/800	Fiend
Corroding Shark	1,100/700	Zombie
Dancing Elf	300/200	Fairy
Dark Gray	800/900	Beast
Dark Rabbit	1,100/1,500	Beast
Dark Shade	1,000/1,000	Fiend
Djinn the Watcher of the Wind	700/900	Spellcaster
Fireyarou	1,300/1,000	Pyro
Follow Wind	—	Power-up
Gust Fan	—	Power-up
Hane-Hane	450/500	Beast/Effect
Harpie Lady	1,300/1,400	Winged Beast
Hitotsu-Me Giant	1,200/1,000	Beast-warrior
House of Adhesive Tape	—	Trap (Limited Range)
Hurricail	900/200	Spellcaster/Effect
Insect Soldiers of the Sky	1,000/800	Insect
Killer Needle	1,200/1,000	Insect
Kurama	800/800	Winged Beast
LaMoon	1,200/1,700	Spellcaster
Larvas	800/1,000	Beast/Effect
Lucky Trinket	600/800	Spellcaster/Effect
Meda Bat	800/400	Fiend
Monstrous Bird	2,000/1,900	Winged Beast
Moon Envoy	1,100/1,000	Warrior
Mountain	—	Magic
Parrot Dragon	2,000/1,300	Dragon
Princess of Tsurugi	900/700	Warrior
Shining Friendship	1,300/1,100	Fairy/Effect
Skull Red Bird	1,550/1,200	Winged Beast
Spirit of the Books	1,400/1,200	Winged Beast/Effect
Spirit of the Winds	1,700/1,400	Spellcaster
Windstorm of Etaqua	—	Magic
Wing Eagle	1,800/1,500	Winged Beast
Winged Dragon, Guardian of the Fortress #1	1,400/1,200	Dragon
Wings of Wicked Flame	700/900	Pyro
Witch's Apprentice	550/500	Spellcaster
Yamatano Dragon Scroll	900/300	Dragon/Effect

Fairy King Truesdale

Vital Stats

- Main Monster Types: Insect, Plant, Beast
- Main Attributes: Dark, Earth, Water, Wind
- Deck Cost: 822
- Average Monster Summon Level: 3.29
- Average Monster ATK/DEF: 991/1,034

Fairy King Truesdale offers a good beginning deck because of its Rain of Mercy Power-up, Acid Trap Hole, and several monsters with ATK or DEF above 1,500. When you acquire the deck, go into a Custom Game and play against yourself until you win a Fairy King Truesdale to add to your deck. This gives all your Plants a +500 bonus if the Fairy King is face-up in play. The deck consists mostly of Insects and Plants, meaning you will fare well against Weevil and Tea, but your deck's strength will taper off later in the game. Insects are not the strongest of creatures either, but you do have some excellent Fusions, including Nekogal #2 and Mystical Sand.

Good Fusions

- Bean Soldier: Mushrooom Man + Mushroom Man #2
- Flower Wolf: Dark Gray + Abyss Flower
- Mystical Sand: Queen of Autumn Leaves + Stone Armadiller
- Nekogal #2: Queen of Autumn Leaves + Dark Gray
- Queen of Autumn Leaves: Arlownay + Tentacle Plant

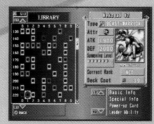

Complete Card Listing

Name	ATK/DEF	Type
Abyss Flower	750/400	Plant
Acid Trap Hole	—	Trap (Limited Range)
Alinsection	950/700	Insect
Ancient One of the Deep Forest	1,800/1,900	Beast
Arlownay	800/1,000	Plant
Basic Insect	500/700	Insect
Beaked Snake	800/900	Reptile
Big Insect	1,200/1,500	Insect
Dark Gray	800/900	Beast
Dig Beak	500/800	Beast
Forest	—	Magic
Great Bill	1,250/1,300	Beast
Hercules Beetle	1,500/200	Insect
Hunter Spider	1,600/1,400	Insect
Insect Armor with Laser Cannon	—	Power-up
Insect Soldiers of the Sky	1,000/800	Insect
Kattapillar	250/300	Insect
Killer Needle	1,200/1,400	Insect
Korogashi	550/400	Insect
Kwagar Hercules	1,900/1,700	Insect
Liquid Beast	950/800	Aqua
Man-Eating Plant	800/600	Plant
Mon Larvas	1,300/1,400	Beast
Mushroom Man	800/600	Plant
Mushroom Man #2	1,250/800	Warrior
Petit Angel	600/900	Fairy
Petit Dragon	600/700	Dragon
Petit Moth	300/200	Insect
Rain of Mercy	—	Magic
Rose Spectre of Dunn	2,000/1,800	Plant
Stone Armadiller	800/1,200	Rock
Tentacle Plant	500/600	Plant
Trent	1,500/1,800	Plant
Twin Long Rods #2	850/700	Aqua
Vile Germs	—	Power-up
Witch of the Black Forest	1,100/1,200	Spellcaster

King Tiger Wanghu

Vital Stats

- Main Monster Types: Beast
- Main Attributes: Earth, Dark, Water
- Deck Cost: 832
- Average Monster Summon Level: 3.27
- Average Monster ATK/DEF: 1,027/978

This deck's monster count is made of Beasts, with a few Fiends and Machines for Fusions. Aside from the powerful Firewing Pegasus (2,250 ATK), this deck has mediocre monsters. However, it can play some good Fusions, like Stone D., Chimera, and Rose Spectre of Dunn. Most of the strong monsters and Fusions in this deck favor Forest terrain, which this deck can create with its Forest spell card.

In fact, this deck's main strength is its strong magic. You can heal yourself with Goblin's Secret Remedy for 1,000 LP, negate any attack move with the Block Attack Trap, and destroy the creature with the lowest ATK anywhere on the Field with Fissure.

Good Fusions

- Chimera the Flying Mythical Beast: Flower Wolf + Fungi of the Musk
- Stone D.: Darkfire Dragon + Rock Ogre Grotto #2
- Nekogal #2: Gazelle the King of Mythical Beasts + Enchanting Mermaid
- Flower Wolf: Armored Rat + Rainbow Flower
- Flame Swordsman: Flame Snake + Kojikocy

Complete Card Listing

Name	ATK/DEF	Type
Ancient One of the Deep Forest	1,800/1,900	Beast
Armored Rat	950/1,100	Beast
Beast Fangs	—	Power-up
Block Attack	—	Trap (Full Range)
Dark Assailant	1,200/1,200	Zombie
Darkfire Dragon	1,500/1,250	Dragon
Djinn the Watcher of the Wind	700/900	Spellcaster
Enchanting Mermaid	1,200/900	Fish
Feral Imp	1,300/1,400	Fiend
Firewing Pegasus	2,250/1,800	Beast
Fissure	—	Magic
Flame Snake	400/450	Pyro
Forest	—	Magic
Frenzied Panda	1,200/1,000	Beast
Fungi of Musk	400/300	Fiend/Effect
Ganigumo	600/800	Insect/Effect
Gazelle the King of Mythical Beasts	1,500/1,200	Beast
Giant Flea	1,500/1,200	Insect
Goblin's Secret Remedy	—	Magic
Hane-Hane	450/500	Beast/Effect
Haniwa	500/500	Rock
Hitodenchak	600/700	Aqua/Effect
Hitotsu-Me Giant	1,200/1,000	Beast-warrior
Hunter Spider	1,600/1,400	Insect
Kojikocy	1,500/1,200	Warrior
Larvas	800/1,000	Beast/Effect
Leo Wizard	1,350/1,200	Spellcaster
Mechanical Spider	400/500	Machine
Megirus Light	900/600	Fiend
Meotoko	700/600	Beast
Monsturtle	800/1,000	Aqua
Mystical Moon	—	Power-up
Mystical Sheep #2	800/1,000	Beast/Effect
Rainbow Flower	400/500	Plant
Rock Ogre Grotto #2	700/1,400	Rock
Sparks	—	Magic
Spike Clubber	1,700/1,800	Machine
Tomozaurus	500/400	Dinosaur
Trakadon	1,300/800	Dinosaur
Wolf	1,200/800	Beast

Kyruel

Vital Stats

- Main Monster Types: Fiend, Zombie, Spellcaster, Dragon
- Main Attributes: Dark, Wind
- Deck Cost: 780
- Average Monster Summon Level: 3.42
- Average Monster ATK/DEF: 1,098/990

The Kyruel deck is composed of Fiends, Zombies, and Dragons. Despite its low Deck Cost, it is a powerful deck, with three monsters at 2,000 ATK or higher. To balance out these strong monsters, the deck also has a number of weak creatures. Luckily, most of them can be formed into Fusions, such as Metal Dragon or Dragon Zombie.

This deck also lacks good traps. However, it does have the Paralyzing Potion Power-up Card that paralyzes any monster it touches. It gives this deck an excellent way to deal with monsters that are too strong for your creatures. The Kyruel deck also has good Effect Monsters, like Phantom Dewan and Fiend's Hand. This deck has strong monsters and decent spells. It has a few weak monsters and is missing a terrain-altering card. If you get a bad draw, this deck can let you down.

Good Fusions

- Metal Dragon: Wicked Dragon with the Ersatz Heads + Mechanical Snail
- Dragon Zombie: Blackland Fire Dragon + Shadow Spectre
- Skelgon: Dragon Zombie + Fiend's Hand
- Armored Zombie: Unknown Warrior of Fiend + Shadow Spectre
- Magical Ghost: Masked Sorcerer + Shadow Spectre

Complete Card Listing

Name	ATK/DEF	Type
Air Eater	2,100/1,600	Fiend
Air Eater	2,100/1,600	Fiend
Barox	1,380/1,530	Fiend
Barox	1,380/1,530	Fiend
Blackland Fire Dragon	1,500/1,200	Dragon
Call of the Haunted	—	Magic
Cyber Commander	750/750	Machine/Effect
Dark Titan of Terror	1,300/1,100	Fiend
Eatgaboon	—	Trap (Limited Range)
Fiend Castle	—	Power-up
Fiend's Hand	600/600	Zombie/Effect
Hinotama	—	Magic
King of Yamimikai	2,000/1,530	Fiend
Kuriboh	300/200	Fiend/Effect
Madjinn Gunn	600/800	Fiend
Magical Labyrinth	—	Magic
Man-Eating Treasure Chest	1,600/1,000	Fiend
Masked Clown	500/700	Warrior
Masked Sorcerer	900/1,400	Spellcaster
Mechanical Snail	800/1,000	Machine
Mechanical Snail	800/1,000	Machine
Neck Hunter	1,750/1,900	Fiend
Neck Hunter	1,750/1,900	Fiend
Necrolancer the Timelord	800/900	Spellcaster
Paralyzing Potion	—	Power-up
Phantom Dewan	700/600	Spellcaster/Effect
Shadow Specter	500/200	Zombie/Effect
Shadow Specter	500/200	Zombie/Effect
Solitude	1,050/1,000	Beast-warrior/Effect
Sparks	—	Magic
The Bistro Butcher	1,800/1,000	Fiend
Three-Headed Geedo	1,200/1,400	Fiend
Unknown Warrior of Fiend	1,000/500	Warrior
Unknown Warrior of Fiend	1,000/500	Warrior
Ushi Oni	2,150/1,950	Fiend
Wicked Dragon with the Ersatz Heads	900/900	Dragon
Wicked Dragon with the Ersatz Heads	900/900	Dragon
Witch's Apprentice	550/500	Spellcaster
Wretched Ghost of the Attic	550/400	Fiend
Wretched Ghost of the Attic	550/400	Fiend

Luminous Soldier

Vital Stats

- Main Monster Types: Warrior, Fairy, Spellcaster, Fish
- Main Attributes: Light, Earth, Water
- Deck Cost: 826
- Average Monster Summon Level: 3.44
- Average Monster ATK/DEF: 1,076/1,027

The Luminous Soldier deck is one of the best in terms of monsters and Fusions. It is one of only two decks with the Kaiser Dragon card, the strongest individual monster in any of the starters. This also means it has the best Fusion of any starting deck: Twin-Headed Thunder Dragon, a 2,800 ATK monster! And it has several other Fusions with ATK over 2,000. Play a Custom Game against this deck to see its great Fusions. Unfortunately, Luminous Soldier has virtually no Effects Monsters, Traps, or spell cards. This deck is all about the monsters. Which means if you run into a deck with stronger monsters, you have no means of dealing with them. Luckily, with Burning Land (the lone Magic Card), you can at least wipe out any terrain advantage the enemy might have.

Good Fusions

- Twin-Headed Thunder Dragon: Kaiser Dragon + Thunder Dragon
- Bracchio-raidus: Trakadon + Hard Armor + Kanikabuto
- Punished Eagle: Hinotama Soul + Winged Dragon, Guardian of the Fortress #2 + Swordsman from a Foreign Land
- Mystical Sand: Amazon of the Seas + Haniwa
- Flame Cerebrus: Silver Fang + Charubin the Fire Knight

Complete Card Listing

NAME	ATK/DEF	TYPE
Airknight Parshath	1,900/1,400	Fairy
Amazon of the Seas	1,300/1,400	Fish
Arma Knight	1,000/1,200	Aqua
Armail	700/1,300	Warrior
Armail	700/1,300	Warrior
Beaver Warrior	1,200/1,500	Beast-Warrior
Bright Castle	—	Power-up
Burning Land	—	Magic
Charubin the Fire Knight	1,100/800	Pyro
Eldeen	950/1,000	Spellcaster
Eldeen	950/1,000	Spellcaster
Fake Trap	—	Trap (Full Range)
Goddess with the Third Eye	1,200/1,000	Fairy
Goddess with the Third Eye	1,200/1,000	Fairy
Haniwa	500/500	Rock
Hard Armor	300/1,200	Warrior
Hero of the East	1,100/1,000	Warrior
Hinotama Soul	600/500	Pyro/Effect
Kaiser Dragon	2,300/2,000	Dragon
Kaminarikozou	700/600	Thunder
Karan the Swordmistress	1,400/1,400	Warrior
Kanikabuto	650/900	Aqua
Karbonala Warrior	1,500/1,200	Warrior
Lady of Faith	1,100/800	Spellcaster
Legendary Sword	—	Power-up
Leo Wizard	1,350/1,200	Spellcaster
Moon Envoy	1,100/,1,000	Warrior
Moon Envoy	1,100/1,000	Warrior
Neo the Magic Swordsman	1,700/1,000	Spellcaster
Ocubeam	1,550/1,650	Fairy
Oscillo Hero	1,250/700	Warrior
Silver Fang	1,200/800	Beast
Swordsman from a Foreign Land	250/250	Warrior
Thunder Dragon	1,600/1,500	Thunder
Tiger Axe	1,300/1,000	Beast-warrior
Trakadon	1,300/800	Dinosaur
White Dolphin	500/400	Fish
White Dolphin	500/400	Fish
Wing Egg Elf	500/1,300	Fairy
Winged Dragon, Guardian of the Fortress #2	1,200/1,000	Winged Beast

Maiden of Aqua

Vital Stats
- Main Monster Types: Aqua, Sea Serpent, Fish
- Main Attributes: Water, Dark
- Deck Cost: 823
- Average Monster Summon Level: 3.29
- Average Monster ATK/DEF: 991/1,012

This is another deck whose Leader you want to add to your library by playing yourself in the Custom Game. Maiden of The Aqua boosts all your Aqua monsters 500 points. Play Star Boy and you get another +300 points, for +800 points total. This pumping up is necessary because with a few exceptions, the monsters in this deck are average. It's Fusions are also mediocre, except for the amazing Aqua Dragon. It always has ATK 2,750 because it transforms every square in which it battles into Sea terrain.

The strength of this deck is that it can alter terrain fairly well, with three Effects Monsters that can turn surrounding spaces into Sea squares, which is favorable terrain for your creatures.

This deck has one good Trap, one good spell card, and only a few Power-ups.

Good Fusions
- Aqua Dragon: Kairyu-Shin + Akihiron
- Kairyu-Shin: Koumori Dragon + White Dolphin
- Metal Dragon: Koumori Dragon + Mechanical Snail
- Bolt Escargot: Bolt Penguin + Night Lizard

Complete Card Listing

Name	ATK/DEF	Type
Akihiron	1,700/1,400	Aqua
Ameba	300/350	Aqua/Effect
Aqua Chorus	—	Magic
Aqua Madoor	1,200/2,000	Spellcaster
Bio Plant	600/1,300	Fiend
Bolt Penguin	1,100/800	Thunder
Fiend Kraken	1,200/1,400	Aqua
Flying Penguin	1,200/1,000	Aqua
Giant Red Seasnake	1,800/800	Aqua
Hitodenchak	600/700	Aqua
Kairyu-Shin	1,800/1,500	Sea Serpent/Effect
Kanikabuto	650/900	Aqua
Koumori Dragon	1,500/1,200	Dragon
Krokodilus	1,100/1,200	Reptile
Liquid Beast	950/800	Aqua
Man-eating Black Shark	2,100/1,300	Fish
Mechanical Snail	800/1,000	Machine
Megirus Light	900/600	Fiend
Night Lizard	1,150/1,300	Aqua
Night Lizard	1,150/1,300	Aqua
Penguin Soldier	750/500	Aqua/Effect
Power of Kaishin	—	Power-up
Psychic Kappa	400/1,000	Aqua/Effect
Sea Kamen	1,100/1,300	Aqua
Sea Kamen	1,100/1,300	Aqua
Star Boy	550/500	Aqua/Effect
Takriminos	1,500/1,200	Sea Serpent
Takriminos	1,500/1,200	Sea Serpent
Tears of the Mermaid	—	Trap (Limited Range)
Tentacle Plant	500/600	Plant
The Eye of Truth	—	Magic
The Furious Sea King	800/700	Aqua/Effect
The Melting Shadow	500/700	Aqua
Turtle Raccoon	700/900	Aqua/Effect
Turtle Tiger	1,000/1,500	Aqua
Twin Long Rods #1	900/700	Aqua
White Dolphin	500/400	Fish
Yado Karu	900/1,700	Aqua
Zarigun	600/700	Aqua
Zarigun	600/700	Aqua

Molten Behemoth

Vital Stats

- Main Monster Types: Pyro, Rock, Beast-warrior, Warrior
- Main Attributes: Earth, Dark, Fire, Wind
- Deck Cost: 841
- Average Monster Summon Level: 3.59
- Average Monster ATK/DEF: 1,127/1,077

This deck has a good selection of strong Rock and Pyro monsters, including some with high ATK and others with high DEF. However, the terrain card in this deck, Wasteland, only helps Rocks. Thus, this deck doesn't benefit from terrain as much as more unified decks, since the two monster types don't share favorable a terrain.

The key to maximizing this deck is playing in a Custom Game and winning a Molten Behemoth. It will give your Pyro monsters +500 strength. With your Power-up cards, you can thus get your Flame Cerebrus to an incredible ATK/DEF of 4,100/3,800.

This deck has no Traps, mediocre Effects Monsters, and few spells, although it does have two direct damage Magic Cards (Hinotama).

Good Fusions

- Crimson Sunbird: Mavelus + Fire Eye
- Stone D.: Blackland Fire Dragon + Destroyer Golem
- Flame Cerebrus: Wolf + Dragon Piper
- Punished Eagle: Mavelus + Rhaimundos of the Red Sword
- Megazowler: Morphing Jar + Krokodilus

Complete Card Listing

NAME	ATK/DEF	TYPE
Acid Crawler	900/700	Insect
Battle Ox	1,700/1,000	Beast-warrior
Blackland Fire Dragon	1,500/800	Dragon
Burning Spear	—	Power-up
Cyber Soldier of Darkworld	1,400/1,200	Machine
Dark Rabbit	1,100/1,500	Beast
Destroyer Golem	1,500/1,000	Rock
Dragon Piper	200/1,800	Pyro/Effect
Electric Lizard	850/800	Thunder/Effect
Fire Eye	800/600	Pyro/Effect
Fireyarou	1,300/1,000	Pyro
Flame Cerebrus	2,100/1,800	Pyro
Flame Ghost	1,000/800	Zombie/Effect
Flame Manipulator	900/1,000	Pyro
Flame Snake	400/450	Pyro
Giant Flea	1,500/1,200	Insect
Hinotama	—	Magic
Hinotama	—	Magic
Hitotsu-Me Giant	1,200/1,000	Beast-warrior
Hitotsu-Me Giant	1,200/1,000	Beast-warrior
Kagemusha of the Blue Flame	800/400	Warrior
Krokodilus	1,100/1,200	Reptile
Mavelus	1,300/900	Winged Beast
Mavelus	1,300/900	Winged Beast
Millenium Golem	2,000/2,200	Rock
Morphing Jar	700/600	Rock
Rhaimundos of the Red Sword	1,200/1,300	Warrior
Rhaimundos of the Red Sword	1,200/1,300	Warrior
Salamandra	—	Power-up
Sectarian of Secrets	700/500	Spellcaster/Effect
Shovel Crusher	900/1200	Machine
Spring of Rebirth	—	Power-up
Stone Statue of the Aztecs	300/2,000	Rock
That Which Feeds on Life	1,200/1,000	Fiend
Three-Headed Geedo	1,200/1,400	Fiend
Three-Legged Zombie	1,100/800	Zombie
Tripwire Beast	1,200/1,300	Thunder
Wasteland	—	Magic
Winged Dragon, Guardian of the Fortress #1	1,400/1,200	Dragon
Wolf	1,200/800	Beast

Patrician of Darkness

Vital Stats

- Main Monster Types: Zombie, Warrior, Fiend, Insect
- Main Attributes: Dark, Earth
- Deck Cost: 815
- Average Monster Summon Level: 3.29
- Average Monster ATK/DEF: 1,068/959

This deck is very powerful for a starting deck, mostly because of the great Fusions that you can make. Remember how to create Pumpking the King of Ghosts and play him every match. In long games, it makes you incredibly strong. Play yourself a few times in Custom Game to get enough of the right creatures to play two Pumpkings. Getting multiple Ookazi is also nice. Another great Fusion is Great Mammoth of Goldfine. You already have one in the deck, but you can play two with the Fusion, giving this deck great power in the early game.

Good Fusions

- Cyber Soldier: Cyber-Stein + Skull Stalker
- Garvas: Skullbird + Skull Stalker
- Great Mammoth of Goldfine: Mammoth Graveyard + Phantom Ghost
- Pumpking the King of Ghosts: Snakeyashi + Zombie Warrior
- Stone D.: Stone Ghost + Lesser Dragon

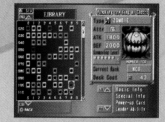

Complete Card Listing

NAME	ATK/DEF	TYPE
Akakieisu	1,000/800	Spellcaster
Basic Insect	500/700	Insect
Blue-Eyed Silver Zombie	900/700	Zombie
Crass Clown	1,350/1,400	Fiend
Cursebreaker	—	Power-up
Cyber-Stein	700/500	Machine
Dark Assailant	1,200/1,200	Zombie
Dimensionhole	—	Magic
Disk Magician	1,350/1,000	Machine
Dokuroizo the Grim Reaper	900/1,200	Zombie
Dragon Zombie	1,600/0	Zombie
Fiend's Hand	600/600	Zombie
Gokibore	1,200/1,400	Insect
Great Mammoth of Goldfine	2,200/1,800	Zombie
Gruesome Goo	1,300/700	Aqua
Kagemusha of the Blue Flame	800/400	Warrior
Kattapillar	250/300	Insect
Lesser Dragon	1,200/1,000	Dragon
Lisark	1,300/1,300	Beast
Living Vase	900/1,100	Plant
Mammoth Graveyard	1,200/800	Dinosaur
Obese Marmot of Nefariousness	750/800	Beast
Ookazi	—	Magic
Phantom Ghost	600/800	Zombie
Saggi the Dark Clown	600/500	Spellcaster
Shadow Ghoul	1,600/1,300	Zombie
Shadow Specter	500/200	Zombie
Skull Servant	300/200	Zombie
Skull Stalker	900/800	Warrior
Skullbird	1,900/1,700	Winged Beast
Snakeyashi	1,000/1,200	Plant
Stone Ghost	1,200/1,000	Rock
Sword of Dark Destruction	—	Power-up
The Statue of Easter Island	1,100/1,400	Rock
Trial of Nightmare	1,300/900	Fiend
Violet Crystal	—	Power-up
Witty Phantom	1,400/1,300	Fiend
Yami	—	Magic
Zanki	1,500/1,700	Warrior
Zombie Warrior	1,200/900	Zombie

Robotic Knight

Vital Stats

- Main Monster Types: Machine, Warrior
- Main Attributes: Dark, Earth
- Deck Cost: 830
- Average Monster Summon Level: 3.40
- Average Monster ATK/DEF: 1,075/1,062

This is a well-constructed deck with powerful monsters. Most of the monsters are Machines, and there is an Effects Monster and two Magic Cards that pump them up. Cyber Commander adds +300 to all Machines, Limiter Removal boosts their strength another 600, and the Wasteland card changes surrounding spaces to the Machine's favorable terrain. Play yourself to add Robotic Knight to your deck so you gain a further +300 points to your Machines. This deck's Fusions are good, but not better than its best monsters.

Robotic Knight has a Bear Trap that kills any monster with 2,000 ATK or less. If you support your monsters with the right Magic Cards and Effects Monsters, this becomes one very formidable deck.

Good Fusions

- Stone D.: Darkfire Dragon + Destroyer Golem
- Mystical Sand: Ogre of the Black Shadow + Invader of the Throne + Rock Ogre Grotto #2
- Metal Dragon: Lesser Dragon + Steel Scorpion
- Cyber Saurus: Little D + Jinzo #7
- Sword Arm of Dragon: Uraby + Unknown Warrior of Fiend

Complete Card Listing

Name	ATK/DEF	Type
Bat	300/350	Machine/Effect
Bear Trap	—	Trap (Limited Range)
Brave Scizzar	1,300/1,000	Machine
Brave Scizzar	1,300/1,000	Machine
Burglar	850/800	Beast
Cyber Commander	750/700	Machine/Effect
Cyber-Stein	700/500	Machine/Effect
Darkfire Dragon	1,500/1,250	Dragon
Destroyer Golem	1,500/1,000	Rock
Fireyarou	1,300/1,000	Pyro
Holograh	1,100/700	Machine
Invader From Another Dimension	950/1,400	Fiend
Invader of the Throne	1,350/1,700	Warrior
Jinzo #7	500/400	Machine
Kamionwizard	1,300/1,100	Spellcaster
Lesser Dragon	1,200/1,000	Dragon
Limiter Removal	—	Magic
Little D.	1,100/700	Dinosaur
Machine Conversion Factory	—	Power-up
Madjinn Gunn	600/800	Fiend
Masaki the Legendary Swordsman	1,100/1,100	Warrior
Mechanical Spider	400/500	Machine
Ogre of the Black Shadow	1,200/1,400	Beast-warrior
Pendulum Machine	1,750/2,000	Machine
Rock Ogre Grotto #2	700/1,400	Rock
Royal Guard	1,900/2,200	Machine
Space Megatron	1,400/2,000	Machine
Space Megatron	1,400/2,000	Machine
Sparks	—	Magic
Steel Ogre Grotto #2	1,900/2,200	Machine
Steel Scorpion	250/300	Machine
Steel Scorpion	250/300	Machine
Tyhone	1,200/1,400	Winged Beast
Unknown Warrior of Fiend	1,000/500	Warrior
Uraby	1,500/800	Dinosaur
Wasteland	—	Magic
Wilmee	1,000/1,200	Beast
Winged Cleaver	700/700	Insect
Zombie Warrior	1,200/900	Zombie
Zombie Warrior	1,200/900	Zombie

Serpentine Princess

Vital Stats

- Main Monster Types: Reptile, Dinosaur, Spellcaster, Aqua
- Main Attributes: Earth, Water, Dark
- Deck Cost: 840
- Average Monster Summon Level: 3.26
- Average Monster ATK/DEF: 1,075/1,004

The monsters of the Serpentine Princess deck aren't very strong, but the deck has good Fusions. With the right draw, you can play up to four Bracchio-raidus monsters (ATK 2,200): Get four Megazowlers (through drawing or Fusion) and fuse them with your four Aqua monsters. Play Wasteland to make them (and your Machine and other Dinosaur monsters) even stronger.

Play against yourself immediately to win a Serpentine Princess for your deck. It adds +900 points to your Reptiles, and when combined with the Sebek's Blessing Magic Card, bumps your Reptile cards to between 2,300 and 3,300 strength!

The best thing about this deck is its Effects Monsters. For instance, Yashinoki gives you 500 LP when flipped face-up, Ancient Jar renders all spellbinding permanent, and Sinister Serpent reduces your opponent's Summoning Points to 0 when destroyed. Another plus of this deck is Paralyzing Potion, which neutralizes any enemy monster.

Good Fusions

- Bracchio-raidus: Megazowler + Flying Penguin
- Megazowler: Ancient Jar + Yormungarde
- Sword Arm of Dragon: Uraby + Dragon Statue
- Cyber Saurus: Steel Scorpion + Crawling Dragon #2
- Metal Dragon: Wicked Dragon with the Ersatz Head + Machine Attacker

Complete Card Listing

Name	ATK/DEF	Type
Abyss Flower	750/400	Plant
Ancient Jar	400/200	Rock/Effect
Ancient Sorcerer	1,000/1,300	Spellcaster
Aqua Madoor	1,200/2,000	Spellcaster
Behegon	1,350/1,000	Aqua
Crawling Dragon #2	1,600/1,200	Dinosaur
Dragon Statue	1,100/900	Warrior
Drooling Lizard	900/800	Reptile
Emperor of the Land and Sea	1,800/1,500	Reptile
Flame Ghost	1,000/800	Zombie/Effect
Flying Penguin	1,200/1,000	Aqua
Giga-tech Wolf	1,200/1,400	Machine
Grappler	1,300/1,200	Reptile
Grappler	1,300/1,200	Reptile
Hitodenchak	600/700	Aqua/Effect
Machine Attacker	1,600/1,300	Machine
Masked Sorcerer	900/1,400	Spellcaster
Megazowler	1,800/2,000	Dinosaur
Mysterious Puppeteer	1,000/1,500	Warrior
Mystic Lamp	400/300	Spellcaster/Effect
Paralyzing Potion	—	Power-up
Phantom Dewan	700/600	Spellcaster
Power of Kaishin	—	Power-up
Pragtical	1,900/1,500	Dinosaur
Raise Body Heat	—	Power-up
Sebek's Blessing	—	Magic
Sinister Serpent	300/250	Reptile/Effect
Steel Scorpion	250/300	Machine
Stone Armadiller	800/1,200	Rock
The Wandering Doomed	800/600	Zombie
Toon Alligator	800/1,600	Reptile
Two-Headed King Rex	1,600/1,200	Dinosaur
Uraby	1,500/800	Dinosaur
Uraby	1,500/800	Dinosaur
Wasteland	—	Magic
Wetha	1,000/900	Aqua
Wicked Dragon with the Ersatz Head	900/900	Dragon
Yashinoki	800/600	Plant/Effect
Yormungarde	1,200/900	Reptile
Yormungarde	1,200/900	Reptile

Tactical Warrior

Vital Stats

- Main Monster Types: Warrior
- Main Attributes: Earth, Dark, Light
- Deck Cost: 830
- Average Monster Summon Level: 3.42
- Average Monster ATK/DEF: 1125/959

This deck possesses many strong individual monsters, and some very good Fusions. Since most of the monsters in the deck are Warriors, they benefit greatly from the terrain-altering card Sogen. You can also add the Deck Leader, Tactical Warrior, to your deck via the Custom Game for a boost, as it gives +300 points to all your Warriors. This deck has few Effects monsters, but one that it does have, Swordsman from a Foreign Land, can be used once per duel to eliminate a strong enemy monster.

There is one trap, but it has limited utility since it only works on monsters with 1,500 ATK or below. On the plus side, this deck does have a direct damage Spell Card.

Good Fusions

- Bracchio-raidus: Two-mouth Darkruler + M-Warrior #2 + Guardian of the Sea
- Chimera the Flying Mythical Beast: Master & Expert + Baron of the Fiend Sword
- Stone D. Stone Ghost + Blackland Fire Dragon
- Nekogal #2: Nekogal #1 + Moon Envoy
- Flame Swordsman: Charubin the Fire Knight + The Judgement Hand

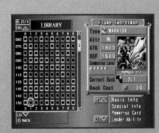

Complete Card Listing

NAME	ATK/DEF	TYPE
Amazon of the Seas	1,300/1,400	Fish
Ancient Lizard Warrior	1,400/1,100	Reptile
Axe Raider	1,700/1,150	Warrior
Baron of the Fiend Sword	1,550/800	Fiend
Battle Steer	1,800/1,300	Beast-warrior
Blackland Fire Dragon	1,500/800	Dragon
Charubin the Fire Knight	1,100/800	Pyro
Cyber Soldier of Darkworld	1,400/1,200	Machine
Eatgaboon	—	Trap (Limited Range)
Empress Judge	2,100/1,700	Warrior
Final Flame	—	Magic
Giltia the D. Knight	1,850/1,500	Warrior
Grappler	1,300/1,200	Reptile
Griggle	350/300	Plant
Guardian of the Sea	1,300/1,000	Aqua
Hard Armor	300/,1200	Warrior
Hitotsu-Me Giant	1,200/1,000	Beast-warrior
Jinzo #7	500/400	Machine
Kumootoko	700/1,400	Insect
Kuwagata	1,250/1,000	Insect
Legendary Sword	—	Power-up
M-Warrior #1	1,000/500	Warrior/Effect
M-Warrior #2	500/1,000	Warrior/Effect
Masked Clown	500/700	Warrior
Master & Expert	1,200/1,000	Beast
Moon Envoy	1,100/1,000	Warrior
Mystic Clown	1,500/1,000	Fiend
Nekogal #1	1,100/900	Beast
Neo the Magic Swordsman	1,700/1,000	Spellcaster
Queen's Double	350/300	Warrior/Effect
Rock Ogre Grotto +1	800/1,200	Rock
Sogen	—	Magic
Swordsman from a Foreign Land	250/200	Warrior/Effect
The Judgement Hand	1,400/700	Warrior
The Wandering Doomed	800/600	Zombie
Two-Mouth Darkruler	900/700	Dinosaur
Wicked Dragon with the Ersatz Head	900/900	Dragon
Winged Dragon, Guardian of the Fortress #1	1,200/1,000	Winged Beast
Zanki	1,500/1,700	Warrior
Zombie Warrior	1,200/900	Zombie

The Illusory Gentleman

Vital Stats

- Main Monster Types: Spellcaster, Zombie, Fiend, Aqua
- Main Attributes: Dark, Light, Water, Wind
- Deck Cost: 847
- Average Monster Summon Level: 3.28
- Average Monster ATK/DEF: 1,064/990

The monsters in The Illusory Gentleman deck have a good strength, but no single monster tops 1,900 ATK. To hold your own against stronger decks, use Fusions, Power-ups, and your terrain card, Yami. You can get some good Fusions with this deck, although they aren't numerous.

This deck has good spells, including Magic Jammer, which neutralizes an enemy's spell card, and Magical Neutralizing Force Field, which erases all Power-ups on monsters and ends all spellbinding. The deck also has a healing card and a very good trap that damages and spellbinds an opposing monster. Thanks to the Rogue Doll, this deck is also good against Zombies.

Good Fusions

- Soul Hunter: Beaked Snake + Mech Mole Zombie
- Punished Eagle: Takuhee + Fiend Sword
- Dark Elf: Ancient Elf + Fairywitch
- Rose Spectre of Dunn: Green Phantom King + Ancient Brain
- La Jinn the Mystical Genie of the Lamp: Dark Artist + Lord of the Lamp

Complete Card Listing

Name	ATK/DEF	Type
Ameba	300/350	Aqua/Effect
Ancient Brain	1,000/700	Fiend
Ancient Elf	1,450/1,200	Spellcaster
Beaked Snake	800/900	Reptile
Black Pendant	—	Power-up
Book of Secret Arts	—	Power-up
Crow Goblin	1,850/1,600	Winged Beast
Dark Artist	600/1,400	Fiend
Doma the Angel of Silence	1,600/1,400	Fairy
Fairy of the Fountain	1,600/1,100	Aqua
Fairywitch	800/1,000	Spellcaster
Fiend Sword	1,400/800	Warrior
Green Phantom King	500/1,600	Plant/Effect
Hinotama	—	Magic
Illusionist Faceless Mage	1,200/2,200	Spellcaster/Effect
Key Mace	400/300	Fairy/Effect
Koumori Dragon	1,500/1,200	Dragon
Kuriboh	300/200	Fiend/Effect
Lord of the Lamp	1,400/1,200	Fiend
Magic Jammer	—	Trap (Full Range)
Magical Ghost	1,300/1,400	Zombie
Magical Neutralizing Force Field	—	Magic
Mech Mole Zombie	500/400	Machine/Effect
Mesmeric Control	—	Trap (Limited Range)
Monster Eye	250/350	Fiend/Effect
Musician King	1,750/1,500	Spellcaster
Rare Fish	1,500/1,200	Fish
Red Medicine	—	Magic
Rogue Doll	1,600/1,000	Spellcaster/Effect
Shadow Specter	500/200	Zombie/Effect
Spirit of the Mountain	1,300/1,800	Spellcaster
Spirit of the Winds	1,700/1,400	Spellcaster
Star Boy	550/500	Aqua/Effect
Takuhee	1,450/1,000	Winged-Beast
The 13th Grave	1,200/900	Zombie
The Unhappy Maiden	0/100	Spellcaster/Effect
Three-Legged Zombie	1,100/800	Zombie
Water Girl	1,250/1,000	Aqua
Water Magician	1,400/1,000	Aqua
Yami	—	Magic

Thunder Nyan-Nyan

Vital Stats

- Main Monster Types: Thunder, Plant, Spellcaster
- Main Attributes: Earth, Water, Dark, Wind
- Deck Cost: 830
- Average Monster Summon Level: 3.36
- Average Monster ATK/DEF: 1,098/944

Thunder Nyan-Nyan is a deck composed mostly of Thunder monsters. They favor Mountain terrain, and this deck has a Mountain spell card. Unfortunately, this deck does not have very strong monsters, with the highest ATK being Kaminari Attack's 1,900. However, as with most decks of this nature, Thunder Nyan-Nyan has strong Fusions, like Crimson Sunbird.

If you get Thunder Nyan-Nyan from playing yourself in Custom Game, this card gives all your other Thunder cards a movement boost, giving you a big tactical advantage in duels.

This deck has no good Traps or spell cards, but it does have some good Effects Monsters, especially against a Machine deck.

Good Fusions

- Crimson Sunbird: Crow Goblin + Wings of Wicked Flame
- Mystical Sand: Stone Ghost + Red Archery Girl
- Chimera the Flying Mythical Beast: King Fog + Lisark
- Punished Eagle: Red Skull Bird + Oscillo Hero
- Kaminari Attack: Electric Lizard + Curtain of the Dark Ones + Djinn the Watcher of the Wind

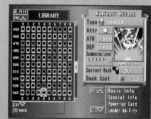

Complete Card Listing

Name	ATK/DEF	Type
Baby Dragon	1,200/700	Dragon
Barrel Lily	1,100/600	Plant
Beautiful Headhuntress	1,600/800	Warrior
Bolt Escargot	1,400/1,500	Thunder
Bright Castle	—	Power-up
Crow Goblin	1,850/1,600	Winged Beast
Curtain of the Dark Ones	600/500	Spellcaster/ Effect
Dark Assailant	1,200/1,200	Zombie
Djinn the Watcher of the Wind	700/900	Spellcaster
Electric Lizard	850/800	Thunder/Effect
Electric Snake	800/900	Thunder/Effect
Firegrass	700/600	Plant
Fusionist	900/700	Beast
Goddess of Whim	950/700	Fairy
Horn of Light	—	Power-up
House of Adhesive Tape	—	Trap (Limited Range)
Hyosube	1,500/900	Aqua
Kaminari Attack	1,900/1,400	Thunder
Kaminarikozou	700/600	Thunder
Killer Needle	1,200/1,000	Insect
King Fog	1,000/900	Fiend
Lisark	1,300/1,300	Beast
Meda Bat	800/400	Fiend
Mega Thunderball	750/600	Thunder/Effect
Minar	850/750	Insect
Monster Eye	250/300	Fiend/Effect
Mountain	—	Magic
Necrolancer the Timelord	800/900	Spellcaster
Ocubeam	1,550/1,650	Fairy
Oscillo Hero	1,250/700	Warrior
Oscillo Hero #2	1,000/500	Thunder/Effect
Rainbow Flower	400/500	Plant
Red Archery Girl	1,400/1,500	Aqua
Skull Red Bird	1,550/1,200	Winged-Beast
Spirit of the Winds	1,700/1,400	Spellcaster
Stone Ghost	1,200/1,000	Rock
The Thing That Hides in the Mud	1,200/1,300	Rock
Trent	1,500/1,800	Plant
Tripwire Beast	1,200/1,300	Thunder
Wings of Wicked Flame	700/600	Pyro

Twin-Headed Behemoth

Vital Stats

- Main Monster Types: Dragon, Spellcaster, Winged Beast
- Main Attributes: Dark, Earth, Light, Wind
- Deck Cost: 825
- Average Monster Summon Level: 3.31
- Average Monster ATK/DEF: 1,029/983

This is the game's Dragon deck. It has the strongest card in any starting deck, the Kaiser Dragon, and also has some very strong Fusions, such as B. Dragon Jungle King and Chimera the Flying Mythical Beast.

Of all the decks, this one stands on its own the most. It has no weaknesses, unlike the Zombie deck's vulnerability in Wasteland. But it has the fewest power ups; nothing like Fairy King Truesdale's Rain of Mercy or Patrician of Darkness's Pumpking the King of Ghosts. And it doesn't have a good Magic Card, like the Zombie deck's Ookazi or the Insect/Plant deck's Acid Trap Hole. So potentially, the other two decks could be more powerful, but when played straight out of your hand, the Twin-Headed Behemoth has the strongest cards.

Good Fusions

- B. Dragon Jungle King: Crawling Dragon + Arlownay
- Chimera the Flying Mythical Beast: Kurama + Wretched Ghost of the Attic
- Dark Witch: Goddess with the Third Eye + Lunar Queen Elzaim
- Punished Eagle: Fiend Reflection #1 + Unknown Warrior of Fiend
- Skelgon: Baby Dragon + Flame Ghost + Ghoul with an Appetite
- Thunder Dragon: Baby Dragon + Kaminarikozou

Complete Card Listing

Name	ATK/DEF	Type
Anthrosaurus	1,000/850	Dinosaur
Arlownay	800/1,000	Plant
Armored Lizard	1,500/1,200	Reptile
Baby Dragon	1,200/700	Dragon
Crawling Dragon	1,600/1,400	Dragon
Curtain of the Dark Ones	600/500	Spellcaster/Effect
Dark-Piercing Light	—	Magic
Dragon Treasure	—	Power-up
Eldeen	950/1,000	Spellcaster
Fairy Dragon	1,100/1,200	Dragon
Fiend Reflection #1	1,300/1,400	Winged Beast
Firegrass	700/600	Plant
Flame Ghost	1,000/800	Zombie/Effect
Ghoul with an Appetite	1,600/1,200	Zombie
Goddess with the Third Eye	1,200/1,000	Fairy
Great Bill	1,250/1,300	Beast
Guardian of the Labyrinth	1,000/1,200	Warrior
House of Adhesive Tape	—	Trap (Limited Range)
Kaiser Dragon	2,300/2,000	Dragon
Kaminarikozou	700/600	Thunder
Kurama	800/800	Winged Beast
Lesser Dragon	1,200/1,000	Dragon
Little Chimera	600/550	Beast
Lunar Queen Elzaim	750/1,100	Fairy
Mechanical Snail	800/1,000	Machine
Minar	850/750	Insect
Mountain	—	Magic
Mystic Lamp	400/300	Spellcaster/Effect
Ogre of the Black Shadow	1,200/1,400	Beast-warrior
Petit Dragon	600/700	Dragon
Psychic Kappa	400/1,000	Aqua/Effect
Sectarian of Secrets	700/500	Spellcaster/Effect
Sky Dragon	1,900/1,800	Dragon
Sorcerer of the Doomed	1,450/1,200	Spellcaster
Unknown Warrior of Fiend	1,000/500	Warrior
Wall of Illusion	1,000/1,850	Fiend/Effect
Winged Dragon Guardian of the Fortress #2	1,200/1,000	Winged Beast
Wow Warrior	1,250/900	Fish
Wretched Ghost of the Attic	550/400	Fiend
Zarigun	600/700	Aqua

Wolf Axwielder

Vital Stats

- Main Monster Types: Beast-warrior, Beast, Warrior, Aqua
- Main Attributes: Earth, Water, Dark
- Deck Cost: 814
- Average Monster Summon Level: 3.26
- Average Monster ATK/DEF: 1,064/977

The Wolf Axwielder deck has an average assortment of monsters, with nothing approaching the strongest monsters of decks like Kyruel or Twin-Headed Behemoth. It also only possesses one Power-up Card. Use the deck's Sogen spell card to boost your monsters. This card changes terrain to Meadow, which is favorable for this deck's majority of Beast-warriors.

With the mediocre monsters create good Fusions. You can create over half a dozen monsters with 2,000 ATK or more, as well as an equal number of monsters between 1500 and 2,000.

This deck has few spells, although it can heal your LP by 200 points and has a Trap Card that spellbinds opponents.

Good Fusions

- Crimson Sunbird: Faith Bird + Wicked Wings of Flame
- Bracchio-raidus: Lava Battleguard + Uraby + Turu-Purun
- Punished Eagle: Faith Bird + Armail
- Rabid Horseman: Battle Ox + Mystic Horseman
- Rose Spectre of Dunn: Abyss Flower + Lord of Zemia

Complete Card Listing

NAME	ATK/DEF	TYPE
Abyss Flower	750/400	Plant
Armail	700/1,300	Warrior
Axe of Despair	—	Power-up
Battle Ox	1,700/1,000	Beast-Warrior
Bolt Penguin	1,100/800	Thunder
Burglar	850/800	Beast
Darkworld Thorns	1,200/900	Plant
Drooling Lizard	900/800	Reptile
Faith Bird	1,500/1,100	Winged Beast
Garoozis	1,800/1,500	Beast-warrior
Great White	1,600/800	Fish
Haniwa	500/500	Rock
Hero of the East	1,100/1,000	Warrior
Hinotama	—	Magic
Hyo	800/1,200	Warrior/Effect
Ice Water	1,150/900	Aqua
Infinite Dismissal	—	Trap (Limited Range)
Kamakiriman	1,150/1,400	Insect
Kamionwizard	1,300/1,100	Spellcaster
Lava Battleguard	1,550/1,800	Warrior/Effect
Lord of Zemia	1,300/1,000	Fiend
Milus Radiant	300/250	Beast/Effect
Mooyan Curry	—	Magic
Morphing Jar	700/600	Rock
Mystic Horseman	1,300/1,550	Beast
Nekogal #1	1,100/900	Beast
Ogre of the Black Shadow	1,200/1,400	Beast-warrior
One Who Hunts Souls	1,100/1,000	Beast-warrior
Rhaimundos of the Red Sword	1,200/1,300	Warrior
Rude Kaiser	1,800/1,600	Beast-warrior
Shovel Crusher	900/1,200	Machine
Sogen	—	Magic
The Melting Red Shadow	500/700	Aqua
Tiger Axe	1,300/1,100	Beast-warrior
Torike	1,200/600	Beast
Turu-Purun	450/500	Aqua/Effect
Uraby	1,500/800	Dinosaur
Wing Egg Elf	500/1,300	Fairy
Wings of Wicked Flame	700/600	Pyro
Witch's Apprentice	550/500	Spellcaster

Campaign Walkthrough

After meeting with Yugi, you leave France and sail back to the English port of Wilford Haven to pave the way for his advancing army. You must defeat the Lancastrians's Rose Duelists to give Yugi any hope of success in the upcoming War of the Roses.

For your first duel, you can choose to fight Weevil or Rex.

There are two paths before you disembark at Wilford Haven. Two of Seto's Red Rose Duelists block your path. Weevil Underwood holds the castle of Chester in the north and Rex Raptor controls Tewkesbury in the south. Choose to duel Weevil first—he's the easier foe.

Weevil Underwood
Vital Stats

- **Name:** Weevil Underwood
- **Location:** Chester
- **Deck Cost:** 854
- **Deck Leader:** Basic Insect
- **Deck Leader Rank:** First Lieutenant
- **Leader Abilities:** None
- **Primary Terrain:** Forest

Chester

LEGEND
- **F**   Forest
- **W**   Wasteland

Weevil's creatures are among the weakest you face throughout the game, but as your first duel, he poses quite a challenge.

His greatest advantage is the map's terrain. Because his deck is composed almost exclusively of Insects and Plants, both of which have an affinity for Forests, his creatures gain a +500 bonus to ATK and DEF when fighting on most of the map. Thanks to this bonus, most creatures Weevil throws at you are in the mid 1,000s to low 2,000s in ATK and DEF. Unless you also have a Forest-friendly deck, that is too strong for most of your starting creatures, especially when Weevil adds a few Power-up cards to make his Insects even stronger. Battle these creatures with your Fusions.

NOTE

Weevil uses Magic and Trap Cards sparingly. Watch out for Bear Trap, which destroys one creature with 2,000 ATK or less.

Combat Weevil's terrain advantage with terrain-altering cards, such as Mountain, which can change Forest squares into Mountains. This brings his creatures down to a more manageable level. And, if you have creatures favorable to the new terrain, you get the advantage.

The only *really* scary cards in his deck are Perfectly Ultimate Great Moth and Javelin Beetle. Luckily, it takes Weevil six rounds to Summon the Perfectly Ultimate Great Moth once he plays a Larva of Moth card. If you see this card, take down Weevil quickly before the Summoning is complete. Javelin Beetle, meanwhile, is a rare Ritual Card, meaning Weevil has to sacrifice three specific creatures to Summon it. Aside from these two rare dangers, though, you should have little trouble defeating Weevil and claiming your first Rose Card.

NOTE

Goblin's Secret Remedy is a card to claim off Weevil in the Graveyard Slot Machine. This is a Magic Card that heals 1,000 LP. Keep playing Weevil so you can snag this card, which comes in handy in later duels.

Cards to Watch Out For
Perfectly Ultimate Great Moth

Type: Insect
Attribute: Earth
Attack: 3,500
Defense: 3,000
Effect: While this card is face-up in the defense position, all enemy monsters are reduced by 100 points each turn.

Javelin Beetle

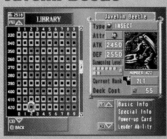

Type: Insect
Attribute: Earth
Attack: 2,450
Defense: 2,550
Effect: 600 bonus points added in battle against Dragon monsters.

Rose Spectre of Dunn

Type: Plant
Attribute: Dark
Attack: 2,000
Defense: 1,800
Effect: None

Creature Stats: Weevil Underwood

- Main Race: Insect
- Average Creature Attack: 1,214
- Average Creature Defense: 1,364

Sample Card List: Weevil Underwood

NAME	ATK/DEF	TYPE
Bear Trap	—	Trap
Block Attack	—	Trap
Big Insect	1,200/1,500	Insect
Cocoon of Evolution	—	Magic
Dungeon Worm	1,800/1,500	Insect/Effect
Giant Flea	1,500/1,200	Insect
Giant Scorpion of the Tundra	1,100/1,200	Insect
Goblin's Secret Remedy	—	Magic
Gokibore	1,200/1,400	Insect
Hercules Beetle	1,500/2,000	Insect
Hunter Spider	1,600/1,400	Insect
Infinite Dismissal	—	Trap
Insect Armor with Laser Cannon	—	Power-up
Javelin Beetle Pact	—	Ritual
Kamakiriman	1,150/1,400	Insect
Killer Needle	1,200/1,000	Insect
Kumootoko	700/1,400	Insect
Kuwagata	1,250/1,000	Insect
Kwagar Hercules	1,900/1,700	Insect
Larva of Moth	0/2,000	Insect/Effect
Larvae Moth	500/400	Insect/Effect

NAME	ATK/DEF	TYPE
Laser Cannon Armor	—	Power-up
Man-Eater Bug	450/600	Insect/Effect
Needle Worm	750/600	Insect
Negate Attack	—	Trap
Nightmare Scorpion	900/800	Insect/Effect
Petit Moth	300/200	Insect
Pupa of Moth	0/2,000	Insect/Effect

Rex Raptor
Vital Stats

- **Name:** Rex Raptor
- **Location:** Tewkesbury
- **Deck Cost:** 960
- **Deck Leader:** Two-Headed King Rex
- **Deck Leader Rank:** Major
- **Leader Abilities:** Movement Bonus for Same Type Friendlies
- **Primary Terrain:** Wasteland and Labyrinth

Tewkesbury

LEGEND
L   Labyrinth
W   Wasteland

After your first duel with Rex Raptor, you'll quickly realize that he isn't the pushover that Weevil was. His deck consists primarily of high-attack Dinosaurs, and his terrain consists of alternating lines of Wasteland and Labyrinth. Wasteland is favorable land for Dinosaurs, granting them +500 strength, while Labyrinth is impassable terrain.

The alternating lines of Labyrinth terrain make it impossible to attack enemy creatures from multiple angles. On Rex's map, you must confront his creatures head-on if you want to cross to his Deck Leader's side of the field.

Because of the terrain and Rex's ample Power-up cards, nearly all the dinosaurs he plays have ATK in the low 2,000s, and some, such as the two Bracchio-raiduses, can have ATK of 3,200! Altering the terrain is your best strategy for neutralizing this duelist's terrain advantage. Keep in mind, though, that most terrain-altering cards have no effect on Labyrinth squares, so they'll remain as impassable obstacles.

To help you fight Rex's Dinosaurs, use Traps such as Mesmeric Control and Tears of the Mermaid to weaken his creatures, then follow up by attacking with your own Fusion creatures. Use your own Power-up cards to make them even stronger. Having Dinosaur, Machine, Rock, and Zombie creatures helps you, because they get a bonus on Wasteland terrain. Conversely, you're in trouble if your deck consists of Aqua, Fish, Plants, and Sea Serpents.

NOTE

Use the tight terrain to your advantage. If you have traps following directly behind your strongest creatures, Rex's Dinosaurs can't avoid them. When they attack your lead card, your trap triggers, spellbinding and weakening the opposing creature.

NOTE

In Rex's Graveyard Slot Machine, you can gain Bracchio-raidus, one of the most powerful creatures available to you this early in the game. Repeat your duels with Rex until you land this card, which will be your strongest for a long time.

Cards to Watch Out For
Bracchio-raidus

Type: Dinosaur
Attribute: Aqua
Attack: 2,200
Defense: 2,000
Effect: None

Megazowler

Type: Dinosaur
Attribute: Earth
Attack: 1,800
Defense: 2,000
Effect: None

Breath of Light

Type: Magic
Usage: One-time
Effect: Destroys all Rock creatures on the field.

Creature Stats: Rex Raptor
- **Main Race:** Dinosaur
- **Average Creature Attack:** 1,432
- **Average Creature Defense:** 1,170

Sample Card List: Rex Raptor

Name	ATK/DEF	Type
Anthrosaurus	1,000/850	Dinosaur
Armored Lizard	1,500/1,200	Reptile
Crawling Dragon #2	1,600/1,200	Dinosaur
Invigoration	—	Power-up
Little D	1,100/700	Dinosaur
Mammoth Graveyard	1,200/800	Dinosaur
Pragtical	1,900/1,500	Dinosaur
Raise Body Heat	—	Power-up
Red Medicine	—	Magic
Sparks	—	Magic
Stain Storm	—	Magic
Sword Arm of Dragon	1,750/2,030	Dinosaur
Tomozaurus	500/400	Dinosaur
Trakadon	1,300/800	Dinosaur
Two-Headed King Rex	1,600/1,200	Dinosaur
Two-Mouth Darkruler	900/700	Dinosaur
Uraby	1,500/800	Dinosaur

Necromancer
Vital Stats

- **Name:** Necromancer
- **Location:** Exeter
- **Deck Cost:** 795
- **Deck Leader:** Pumpking the King of Ghosts
- **Deck Leader Rank:** Colonel
- **Leader Abilities:** Extended Support Range, Increased Strength for Same Type Friendlies
- **Primary Terrain:** Wasteland and Meadow

Exeter

LEGEND
- **M** Meadow
- **S** Sea
- **W** Wasteland

Do some deck shuffling before you duel Necromancer. His total Deck Cost is far below that of any other White Rose Duelist you face, so you must shave some high-cost cards from your deck. Refer to the "Dueling Strategies and Deck Basics" section for help.

Get rid of some high-level creatures, but make sure you can still field a good Fusion or two. Put Warriors and Beast-warriors in your deck, and go into the duel with Trap Cards to weaken Necromancer's own creatures.

Necromancer is aggressive and will send his creatures to you rather than waiting defensively on his turf. His Deck Leader will move into the top left corner and sit there, because that entire area of the map is Zombie-friendly Wasteland terrain. Fight your battles on the Meadow where you start.

Hurry if you see Necromancer's Deck Leader play Pumpking the King of Ghosts in the face-up and defense position. This monster card gives all his Zombies +100 strength every turn. If you let the duel drag on, you could be facing Zombies with strengths of 2,000, then 3,000, and even 4,000. If you rush Necromancer, though, his Leader Ability and terrain combine to give his nearby Zombies +1,000 ATK/DEF points. Terrain-altering cards are useful.

But if you don't have to go after Necromancer, let him come to you. You can destroy his Zombies on the Meadows, letting your excess damage pass through to his Deck Leader. Use Trap Cards and spellbinding relationships to freeze Necromancer's creatures in attack position to make this possible. Because most of Necromancer's creatures have the Dark attribute, attack him with Wind attribute monsters.

Although Zombies are by themselves weak, with Necromancer's suite of cards and Leader abilities, they can be deadly. Watch out.

NOTE

Necromancer's ace in the hole is Dark Hole, which sends all creatures on the Field into the Graveyard. Don't be surprised if you see this card played just when you have all your creatures surrounding his Deck Leader. Be prepared to play yet another host of monster cards to beat him.

NOTE

If you play the Graveyard Slot Machine right, you can snag the great Dark Hole card. Because your monsters will still be much weaker than your opposing duelist's for at least the next few opponents, having this card to destroy enemy creatures is a life-saver.

Cards to Watch Out For
Pumpking the King of Ghosts

Type: Zombie
Attribute: Dark
Attack: 1,800
Defense: 2,000
Effect: While this card is face-up in the defense position, all Zombie monsters are increased 100 points at the start of each turn!

Dokurorider

Type: Zombie/Ritual
Attribute: Dark
Attack: 1,900
Defense: 1,850
Effect: During movement, transforms terrain of entered space into Wasteland terrain!

Dark Hole

Type: Magic

Usage: One-time

Effect: Destroys all monster and spell cards on the Field!

Creature Stats: Necromancer

- **Main Race:** Zombie
- **Average Creature Attack:** 1,158
- **Average Creature Defense:** 876

Sample Card List: Necromancer

NAME	ATK/DEF	TYPE
Alinsection	950/700	Insect
Armored Zombie	1,500/0	Zombie
Blocker	850/1,800	Machine/Effect
Blue-Eyed Silver Zombie	900/700	Zombie/Effect
Call of the Haunted	—	Magic
Clown Zombie	1,350/0	Zombie
Cyber-Stein	700/500	Machine/Effect
Dark Energy	—	Power-up
Dark Hole	—	Magic
Dokuroizo the Grim Reaper	900/1,200	Zombie/Effect
Dragon Zombie	1,600/0	Zombie
Fiend's Hand	600/600	Zombie/Effect
Ganigumo	600/800	Insect/Effect
Graveyard and the Hand of Invitation	700/900	Zombie/Effect
Minar	850/750	Insect
Nightmare Scorpion	900/800	Machine/Effect
Revival of Dokurorider	—	Ritual
Shadow Ghoul	1,600/1,300	Zombie/Effect
Shadow Specter	500/200	Zombie/Effect
Skelgon	1,700/1,900	Zombie/Fusion
Skull Servant	300/200	Zombie/Effect
The Snake Hair	1,500/1,200	Zombie/Effect
Violet Crystal	—	Power-up
Wood Remains	1,000/900	Zombie/Effect
Yaiba Robo	1,000/1,300	Machine/Effect
Yaranzo	1,300/1,500	Zombie
Zombie Warrior	1,200/900	Zombie

Darkness-ruler
Vital Stats

- **Name:** Darkness-ruler
- **Location:** St. Albans
- **Deck Cost:** 982
- **Deck Leader:** King of Yamimakai
- **Deck Leader Rank:** Colonel
- **Leader Abilities:** Increased Strength for Same Type Friendlies
- **Primary Terrain:** Dark

St. Albans

LEGEND
- **D** Dark
- **F** Forest

Now that the easier challenge of Necromancer has been dealt with, it's time to turn to Darkness-ruler.

Darkness-ruler is stronger than Necromancer. It's not just his creatures that make him tough, though. He also has lots of devious trap and power ups. Darkness-ruler will be your most frustrating duel yet, because he fights dirty.

This is too good to be true. Darkness-ruler's Deck Leader looks defenseless, but you can bet those are all traps surrounding him.

Watch out for his Gorgon's Eye. You cannot move your creatures into defense position if this card is in play. If you do, they will be permanently spellbound in the attack position. Darkness-ruler then follows up with a creature attack, and more damage gets dealt to you because your monster is weakened. Because you can't enter defense position, avoid battle unless you know your creature is stronger than your opponent's.

Use cards such as Dark-Piercing Light to reveal Darkness-ruler's face-down cards, and use lots of spell-binding creatures and traps to freeze his creatures before they can attack you.

Darkness-ruler uses mostly Fiends in his deck. He has several creatures, such as King of Yamimakai and Summoned Skull, with starting attacks in the 2,000s. But Darkness-ruler can easily raise those numbers by 1,500 to 2,000 points! The Dark terrain gives all his creatures a +500-point bonus, and his Leader Ability also gives Fiends in a 3x3 area around him another +500 points to ATK and DEF. Finally, Darkness-ruler can also play Castle of Dark Illusions, which further boosts Fiend strength.

TIP

If you don't have terrain-altering cards, withdraw your Deck Leader and creatures into one of the two Forest corners in the map. Darkness-ruler's creatures are aggressive and will follow you in, but Forest is unfavorable terrain for Fiends.

To beat Darkness-ruler you must erase his Dark terrain and place terrain favorable to your own creatures. Use Trap Cards to weaken his creatures, and draw them away from Darkness-ruler's Leader so you negate the Leader Ability. If Gorgon's Eye and Castle of Dark Illusions are in play, destroy those cards immediately.

NOTE

Darkness-ruler uses many traps to lure your creatures in close and then kills them when they are weak. But he also has the negative Power-up Card, Paralyzing Potion, which permanently spellbinds any enemy creature that moves into its occupied square. Use cards to reveal Darkness-ruler's face-down cards.

Cards to Watch Out For
Gorgon's Eye

Type: Trap (Full Range)
Usage: Permanent and continuous
Effect: Permanent trap that triggers when an enemy card completes its move in the defense position! Automatically cancels the enemy card's move and eternally spellbinds it.

Castle of Dark Illusions

Type: Fiend
Attribute: Dark
Attack: 920
Defense: 1,930
Effect: While this card is face-up in the DEF position, all FIEND monsters are awarded the power-up bonus of 500 points.

Time Seal

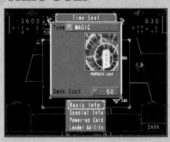

Type: Magic
Usage: One-time
Effect: Permanently spell-binds the monster with the highest ATK on the Field!

Creature Stats: Darkness-ruler
- **Main Race:** Fiend
- **Average Creature Attack:** 1,430
- **Average Creature Defense:** 1,344

Sample Card List: Darkness-ruler

NAME	ATK/DEF	TYPE
Acid Trap Hole	—	Trap
Barox	1,380/1,530	Fiend
Big Eye	1,200/1,000	Fiend/Effect
Crass Clown	1,250/1,400	Fiend
Dark Chimera	1,610/1,460	Fiend
Dark Prisoner	600/100	Fiend/Effect
Fiend Castle	—	Power-up
Infinite Dismissal	—	Trap
Invisible Wire	—	Trap
Job-Change Mirror	800/1,300	Fiend
King of Yamimakai	2,000/1,530	Fiend
Lord of Zemia	1,300/1,000	Fiend
Malevolent Nuzzler	—	Power-up
Mask of Darkness	900/400	Fiend/Effect
Mesmeric Control	—	Trap
Midnight Fiend	800/600	Fiend
Neck Hunter	1,750/1,900	Fiend
Paralyzing Potion	—	Power-up
Reaper of the Cards	1,380/1,930	Fiend/Effect
Ryu-Kishin Powered	1,600/1,200	Fiend
Shadow Spell	—	Trap
Summoned Skull	2,500/1,200	Fiend/Fusion
Tears of the Mermaid	—	Trap
Terra the Terrible	1,200/1,300	Fiend
Time Seal	—	Magic

Keith
Vital Stats

- **Name:** Keith
- **Location:** Towton
- **Deck Cost:** 1,027
- **Deck Leader:** Slot Machine
- **Deck Leader Rank:** Lieutenant Colonel
- **Leader Abilities:** Movement Boost for Same Type Friendlies
- **Primary Terrain:** Wasteland and Labyrinth

Towton

LEGEND

L	Labyrinth
W	Wasteland

After the devious traps and deceptive strategies of Darkness-ruler, Keith is a refreshing return to straightforward dueling... until you look at his deck lineup. His Machines are a relentless force of metal and muscle.

Keith's terrain is somewhat like Rex's, in that Labyrinth squares make it difficult to maneuver. As in that previous level, you're forced to tackle the enemy head-on, without the ability to skirt around or surround his monsters. So always lead with your best creatures. Here it is imperative to have traps following your monsters. Keith's Machines are too strong for any of your creatures, and he uses numerous power ups to make them even tougher. You need to cut them down to size, and traps accomplish that perfectly. Terrain-altering magic comes in very handy, as usual.

TIP

Most of your creatures cannot beat even Keith's average Machines. When you play those creatures, place them in the defense position so that no LP damage gets through to you when they get destroyed.

If you are using a strong creature deck, such as a Dragon deck, be prepared for some painful losses. You simply cannot beat Keith in a head-on slugfest. Many of Keith's monsters start out in the 2,000 range, and that's without power ups or special help from other monsters. Add in creatures such as Robotic Knight and several Limiter Removal Power-up Cards, and you can expect to see monsters in the mid to high 3,000s. Take a page from Darkness-ruler's rulebook and be sneaky. In addition to traps, use lots of Effects Monsters that destroy the enemy creature when they die, such as Fiend's Hand, or that damage them when killed, such as Sectarian of Secrets and Skull Stalker.

TIP

The Zombie deck is the best starting deck to use against Keith. It has four advantages. First, Zombies favor Wasteland terrain. Second, it has Pumpking, who beefs up Zombies every turn. Third, it has good Effects Monsters that can destroy or damage Keith's Machines. Fourth, it has a monster (Shadow Ghoul) that can move through Labyrinth squares. If you didn't choose Zombies as your first deck, play Necromancer several times to get some key Zombies to make your deck stronger against Keith's.

Whatever deck you use, include healing spell cards to prolong your lifespan. A mere 4,000 LP will not cut it against Keith. Also, stack your deck with direct damage spells such as Ookazi. Play the previous duelists to get these spell cards. You'll need them here. But be warned: Keith uses Magic Jammer to neutralize spell cards.

Cards to Watch Out For
Barrel Dragon

Type: Machine
Attribute: Dark
Attack: 2,600
Defense: 2,200
Effect: When this card is flipped face-up, 1 card other than own is randomly selected for destruction!

Metalzoa

Type: Machine/Fusion
Attribute: Dark
Attack: 3,000
Defense: 2,300
Effect: None

Machine King

Type: Machine
Attribute: Dark
Attack: 2,200
Defense: 2,000
Effect: While this card is flipped face-up, this card is strengthened by 100 points for every Machine monster on the Field (including itself).

Creature Stats: Keith

- Main Race: Machine
- Average Creature Attack: 1,615
- Average Creature Defense: 1,600

Sample Card List: Keith

Name	ATK/DEF	Type
7 Completed	—	Power-up
Brave Scizzar	1,300/1,000	Machine
Dice Armadillo	1,650/1,800	Machine
Giant Mech-Soldier	1,750/1,900	Machine
Giga-Tech Wolf	1,200/1,400	Machine
Golgoil	900/1,600	Machine/Effect
Ground Attacker Bugroth	1,500/1,000	Machine
Holograh	1,100/700	Machine
Invisible Wire	—	Magic
Launcher Spider	2,200/2,500	Machine
Limiter Removal	—	Magic
Machine Conversion Factory	—	Magic
Magic Jammer	—	Trap
Mechanical Spider	400/500	Machine
Metalmorph	—	Power-up
Patrol Robo	1,100/900	Machine/Effect
Robotic Knight	1,600/1,800	Machine/Effect
Saber Slasher	1,450/1,500	Machine
Shovel Crusher	900/1200	Machine
Slot Machine	2,000/2,300	Machine
Space Megatron	1,400/2,000	Machine
Zoa	2,600/1,900	Fiend

Labyrinth-ruler
Vital Stats

- **Name:** Labyrinth-ruler
- **Location:** Newcastle
- **Deck Cost:** 1,016
- **Deck Leader:** Monster Tamer
- **Deck Leader Rank:** Brigadier
- **Leader Abilities:** None
- **Primary Terrain:** Labyrinth

Newcastle

LEGEND	
C	Crush
D	Dark
F	Forest
L	Labyrinth
M	Meadow
N	Normal
S	Sea
W	Wasteland

As his name suggests, Labyrinth-ruler's map is an annoying maze. Labyrinth walls block any up and down movement on the map except on the left and right column. Unfortunately, Crush squares occupy both of these columns, so you have to walk an "S" path to get to the top of the map.

Worse yet, Labyrinth-ruler has plenty of monsters that can walk right through Labyrinth terrain, such as Labyrinth Tank and Dungeon Worm. While your creatures are attempting a circuitous route to the enemy Deck Leader, his monsters are coming straight toward you.

The first monsters Labyrinth-ruler sends at you aren't too tough, but that's only because they have to pass through the Crush terrain. Don't be fooled. Once you pass over to his side, he has some very tough monsters waiting for you. But by this point, you have some pretty strong monsters of your own. Of course, the Crush squares limit their effectiveness, preventing you from taking your high-level monsters up the map.

Detour around Crush and Labyrinth terrain.

Use terrain-altering cards to change the Crush squares on both paths into traversable terrain—anything that won't kill your high-level monsters when passing through. Then move in with your strong monsters. Take advantage of any weak creatures Labyrinth-ruler sends through the Crush squares. You can easily kill those, so battle them just when they leave a Crush square so you can damage the enemy Deck Leader. But despite your best efforts, Labyrinth-ruler might play his Labyrinth Wall Spell Card, which changes a square back into Labyrinth terrain, sealing off entryways toward him.

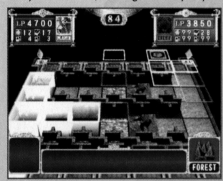

If you can't alter the Crush terrain, use creatures with ATK ranges close to 1,500. Any monsters Labyrinth-ruler sends through the Crush squares can't be over 1,500 ATK either. So if you send a 1,450 ATK monster, followed by a trap, you can do some decent damage. You won't win the game quickly this way, but you can whittle away at Labyrinth-ruler's LP.

Labyrinth-ruler often keeps very powerful monsters, such as Sanga of the Thunder, on his side of the map, in order to destroy any of your creatures that get through. Most fearsome of all is his Ritual Monster, Gate Guardian. Be wary of any creatures in defense position near Labyrinth-ruler.

NOTE

In a map where it is difficult to reach the opponent, use direct damage spells. Labyrinth-ruler uses Final Flame and Ookazi, Magic Cards that do 200 and 500 damage, respectively.

Cards to Watch Out For
Sanga of the Thunder

Type: Thunder
Attribute: Light
Attack: 2,600
Defense: 2,200
Effect: When damage is inflicted to LP in battle, the damage amount is reduced to 0!

Labyrinth Tank

Type: Machine
Attribute: Dark
Attack: 2,400
Defense: 2,400
Effect: Can enter Labyrinth squares!

Shift

Type: Magic
Usage: One-time
Deck Cost: 50
Effect: Your monster with the highest ATK on the Field is transported to the space where this card is activated!

Creature Stats: Labyrinth-ruler

- **Main Race:** Warrior and Insect
- **Average Creature Attack:** 1,457
- **Average Creature Defense:** 1,311

Sample Card List: Labyrinth-ruler

NAME	ATK/DEF	TYPE
Acid Crawler	900/700	Insect
Beautiful Headhuntress	1,600/800	Warrior
Cockroach Knight	800/900	Insect
Dream Clown	1,200/900	Warrior/Effect
Dungeon Worm	1,800/1,500	Insect/Effect
Eatgaboon	—	Trap
Final Flame	—	Magic
Gate Guardian Ritual	—	Ritual
Goblin's Secret Remedy	—	Magic
Hero of the East	1,100/1,000	Warrior
Jirai Gumo	2,200/100	Insect/Effect
Kattapillar	250/300	Insect
Kazejin	2,400/2,200	Spellcaster/Effect
Labyrinth Wall	—	Magic
Laser Cannon Armor	—	Power-up
Magical Labyrinth	—	Magic
Monster Tamer	1,800/1,600	Warrior/Effect
Needle Worm	750/600	Insect
Ookazi	—	Magic
Sanga of the Thunder	2,600/2,000	Thunder/Effect
Shadow Ghoul	1,600/1,300	Zombie/Effect
Suijin	2,500/2,400	Aqua/Effect
Wall Shadow	1,600/3,000	Warrior/Effect

Pegasus
Vital Stats

- **Name:** Pegasus
- **Location:** Lancashire
- **Deck Cost:** 1,254
- **Deck Leader:** Illusionist Faceless Mage
- **Deck Leader Rank:** Vice Admiral
- **Leader Abilities:** Extended Support Range, Increased Strength for Same Type Friendlies
- **Primary Terrain:** Toon

Lancashire

LEGEND

L	Labyrinth
M	Meadow
N	Normal
O	Toon
S	Sea

Pegasus has the most powerful deck of the White Rose Duelists. He gives you one of the toughest challenges in the entire Yugi campaign.

NOTE

Pegasus's Leader Ability gives all friendly Spellcasters in a 5x5 area surrounding him 500 bonus strength points.

The focus of Pegasus's deck is strong Magic Cards, Trap Cards, and Toon monsters. Of these three, his spells are the most dangerous. Watch out for Tremendous Fire, Brain Control, and Change of Heart. Tremendous Fire does 1,000 damage directly to your LP. Brain Control and Change of Heart are less direct, but potentially more dangerous, as they let Pegasus control your creatures for one turn. He is smart enough to play them only when one of your creatures is in a square next to you. Then he makes it attack you.

To counter Pegasus's spells, put three Magic Jammers in your deck. Unfortunately, Pegasus has two Brain Controls, two Tremendous Fires, one Change of Heart, and one Mimicat. And bad news for Dragon-deck users: he also has two Dragon Capture Jars, so you will run out of Magic Jammers. To make things easier, move your monsters away from you after Summoning them so they can't attack you in one round. To counter Tremendous Fire, add healing cards to your deck.

You can't afford to sit back. Rush Pegasus before his spells defeat you. But Pegasus is very defensive, never sending his monsters beyond the Toon terrain.

Toon terrain is unfavorable to all monsters except for special Toon monsters. All your creatures will suffer a 500-point reduction to ATK/DEF on Toon terrain! But Pegasus' monsters are Toons, meaning they get a +500 bonus in Toon spaces. So the net difference between your monsters and his is 1,000! And that's before Pegasus uses power ups. You must change the Toon terrain to stand a chance. But Pegasus has two Toon World cards to change the terrain back.

When advancing on Pegasus, be wary of any face-down cards on the Field. Pegasus has several traps that spellbind and damage your creatures, such as Spellbinding Circle, and traps that destroy them, such as Invisible Wire. The spell-binding traps are worse because a weak monster on the Field often leads to damage to your Deck Leader when the monster dies in battle. Don't use weak monsters as decoys first, because if they get spellbound, Pegasus's monsters can overwhelm them and severely damage you in the process. Use Dark-Piercing Light to reveal them for what they are. Or enter the password to add Ancient Tree of Enlightenment to your deck to completely neutralize all traps. Unfortunately, that also renders Magic Jammer useless.

Pegasus's Deck Leader is surrounded by cards. These are most likely Trap Cards and Magic Cards.

Cards to Watch Out For
Brain Control

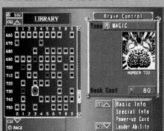

Type: Magic
Usage: One-time
Deck Cost: 80
Effect: Take control of opponent's highest ATK monster for one turn!

Change of Heart

Type: Magic
Usage: One-time
Deck Cost: 80
Effect: Select one of the opponent's cards on the Field and control it for 1 turn!

Mimicat

Type: Magic
Usage: One-time
Deck Cost: 80
Effect: Select, revive, and control 1 card from either Graveyard.

Creature Stats: Pegasus

- Main Race: Dragon, Fiend, Spellcaster
- Average Creature Attack: 1,422
- Average Creature Defense: 1,455

Sample Card List: Pegasus

Name	ATK/DEF	Type
Bickuribox	2,300/2,000	Fiend/Toon
Bright Castle	—	Power-up
Curse of Millennium Shield	—	Ritual
Dark Rabbit	1,100/1,500	Beast/Toon
Dragon Capture Jar	—	Magic
Dragon Piper	200/1,800	Pyro
Fiend Castle	—	Power-up
Flame Swordsman	1,800/1,600	Warrior/Fusion
Garma Sword Oath	—	Ritual
Genin	600/900	Spellcaster/Effect
Illusionist Faceless Mage	1,200/2,200	Spellcaster/Effect
Invisible Wire	—	Magic
Magical Neutralization Force Field	—	Magic
Manga Ryu-Ran	2,200/2,600	Dragon/Toon
Megamorph	—	Power-up
Mesmeric Control	—	Trap
Niwatori	900/800	Winged Beast/Effect
Parrot Dragon	2,000/1,300	Dragon/Toon
Rogue Doll	1,600/1,000	Spellcaster/Effect

Name	ATK/DEF	Type
Saggi the Dark Clown	600/1,500	Fiend/Toon
Spellbinding Circle	—	Trap
Stuffed Animal	1,200/900	Beast/Toon
Swordstalker	2,000/1,600	Warrior/Effect
Toon Alligator	800/1,600	Reptile/Toon
Toon Summoned Fiend	2,500/1,200	Fiend/Toon
Toon World	—	Magic
Tremendous Fire	—	Magic

Ishtar
Vital Stats

- Name: Ishtar
- Location: Isle of Man
- Deck Cost: 861
- Deck Leader: Witch of the Black Forest
- Deck Leader Rank: Colonel
- Leader Abilities: Increased Strength for Same Type Friendlies
- Primary Terrain: Crush and Sea

Isle of Man

LEGEND

C	Crush
S	Sea
W	Wasteland

After the punishing Machines of Keith and the overwhelming magic of Pegasus, Ishtar is a breeze. Her Deck Cost is much lower than the recent duelists you have faced, so you must pare down your deck. But this time, you should have about 10 to 20 battles' worth of new cards, so you can make much more intelligent choices about how to build. Now, you can assemble a lean but powerful deck.

Ishtar's map is a central island of Crush squares bordered by Sea. She moves quickly to occupy the middle of this island, where she stays and throws monsters at you. She is quite aggressive. Get to the middle of the island first so you can control the duel's tempo. By being closer to her, you can more easily move monsters around her, provided you change the Crush terrain. Bring one or two terrain-reforming cards to the duel for that.

Ishtar doesn't have many strong cards, because she is designed to play on Crush. But she still sends them aggressively against you anyway. Hold your ground with strong face-down monsters, and you can batter Ishtar by defending against her monsters' low attacks.

If Ishtar plays her best card, Mirror Wall, you might be in trouble. This full-range trap cuts the ATK of all your monsters in half, which suddenly gives Ishtar the advantage again. Get rid of this card when it appears.

If you do change the terrain to something besides Crush, then Ishtar brings out her better monsters. However, your best monsters should still be stronger. Some of her monsters, such as Kairyu-Shin, can change the terrain around them to Sea squares when flipped face-up, turning the terrain to Ishtar's advantage.

For the most part, though, if you concentrate on playing good monsters and spells, you can win. Don't bring in Machine or Pyro monsters in case Ishtar does convert the entire level to Sea. It's also a good idea to have some Aqua, Fish, Sea Serpents, or Thunder creatures in your deck. Ishtar has many of those monsters in her own deck.

Traps aren't key here, because your monsters should be stronger than Ishtar's, but they can make you unbeatable, especially if you add power ups to your monsters. Replay Labyrinth-ruler and Pegasus to get a few Tremendous Fire and Ookazi cards and use them against Ishtar to make this duel a rout.

With Ishtar beaten, it's time to travel to Bosworth to await Yugi's arrival.

Cards to Watch Out For
Mirror Wall

Type: Trap
Usage: One-time
Deck Cost: 80
Effect: Permanent trap that triggers when an enemy initiates an attack against your Leader or other cards on the Field and reduces the ATK of the enemy by half!

Invitation to a Dark Sleep

Type: Spellcaster
Attribute: Dark
Attack: 1,500
Defense: 1,800
Effect: When this card is flipped face-up, all enemy cards are spellbound for 1 turn!

Shadow of Eyes

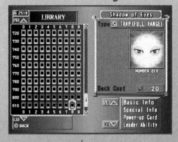

Type: Trap
Usage: One-time
Deck Cost: 20
Effect: Permanent trap that triggers when an enemy card completes its move in the defense position! Automatically changes the card to offense position!

Creature Stats: Ishtar
- **Main Race:** Aqua
- **Average Creature Attack:** 1,166
- **Average Creature Defense:** 1,143

Sample Card List: Ishtar

Name	ATK/DEF	Type
30,000-Year White Turtle	1,250/2,100	Aqua
Aqua Chorus	—	Power-up
Aqua Madoor	1,200/2,000	Spellcaster
Baby Dragon	1,200/700	Dragon
Bolt Escargot	1,400/1,500	Thunder
Bolt Penguin	1,100/800	Aqua
Boulder Tortoise	1,450/2,200	Aqua
Cursebreaker	—	Power-up
Destroyer Golem	1,500/1,000	Rock
Fake Trap	—	Trap
Gemini Elf	1,900/900	Spellcaster
Great White	1,600/800	Fish
High Tide	—	Power-up
Immortal Thunder	1,500/1,300	Thunder/Effect
Kairyu-Shin	1,800/1,500	Sea Serpent/Effect
Kaminarikozuo	700/600	Thunder
Koumori Dragon	1,500/1,200	Dragon/Fusion
Monsturtle	800/100	Aqua
Penguin Knight	900/800	Aqua/Effect
Penguin Soldier	750/500	Aqua/Effect
Power of Kaishin	—	Power-up
Spring of Rebirth	—	Power-up
Star Boy	550/500	Aqua/Effect
Takriminos	1,500/1,200	Sea Serpent
Turtle Oath	—	Ritual
Water Elemental	900/700	Aqua
Waterdragon Fairy	1,100/700	Aqua/Effect
Winged Dragon Guardian of the Fortress #1	1,400/1,200	Dragon
Yado Karu	900/1,700	Aqua
Zarigun	600/700	Aqua

Richard Slysheen of York
Vital Stats

- Name: Richard Slysheen of York
- Location: Bosworth
- Deck Cost: 1,039
- Deck Leader: Battle Steer
- Deck Leader Rank: Secretary of Defense
- Leader Abilities: Level Cost Reduction for Summoning Same Type, Extended Support Range, Movement Bonus for Same Type Friendlies
- Primary Terrain: Meadow

Bosworth

LEGEND
M Meadow
T Mountain

The campaign's story finally picks up after you beat Ishtar and your path leads back to the heart of England. Waiting for you at Bosworth is the usurper himself, Richard Slysheen of York. Remember what Yugi said in the beginning of the game? He lands at Bosworth, and Richard is waiting for him. Mistaking you for a loyal supporter, he challenges you to a friendly duel.

Put your strong deck back together, because Richard has some fairly strong monsters. Most of his deck monsters are Beast-warriors and Warriors, which favor the Meadows that make up most of this level. Their ATK/DEF ratings hover around 2,000 and can be in the mid to high 2,000s with power ups and the terrain. Your best strategy is to take away the terrain advantage.

Because of the map's openness, Richard rushes you with his Warriors and Beast-warriors. You need high DEF monsters to absorb the brunt of this onslaught. Add Trap Cards behind these defenders to weaken Richard's monsters, then follow up with attacks from your own high ATK monsters.

Richard's Deck Leader, meanwhile, stays at his end of the map, protected by Acid Trap Hole, a trap that instantly kills any creature with 4,000 ATK or less. Even worse, he has the powerful Magic Card, Raigeki. Once played and flipped face-up, it destroys all monsters in vertical and horizontal lines extending from its original square. Do not move

your monsters in straight lines. Stagger them or move them diagonally against each other. Or add a few Magic Jammers to your deck.

Although Richard's monsters are strong, he shouldn't be too tough if you've updated your deck with stronger creatures of your own.

After you defeat Richard, Pegasus arrives to inform him that you are the Rose Duelist. Incensed at being deceived, he is about to vent his wrath on you when suddenly, Pegasus declares that he is switching sides. Impressed with your strength, he decides to join Yugi.

Yugi's troops arrive and take back the English island, but your work is still not done. Seto escapes, and so it falls to you to defeat the final—and most dangerous—of all White Rose Duelists.

NOTE

Richard's Graveyard Slot Machine has quite a few good high ATK/DEF creatures such as Panther Warrior and Rude Kaiser. Come back to add some muscle to your deck.

Cards to Watch Out For
Acid Trap Hole

Type: Trap
Usage: One-time
Deck Cost: 30
Effect: Disposable trap that triggers against armor with ATK of 4,000 or below and destroys it.

Judge Man

Type: Warrior
Attribute: Earth
Attack: 2,200
Defense: 1,500
Effect: None

Raigeki

Type: Magic
Usage: One-time
Deck Cost: 80
Effect: Destroys all monsters located in vertical and horizontal lines from the activated space!

Creature Stats:
Richard Slysheen of York

- **Main Race:** Beast-warrior, Warrior
- **Average Creature Attack:** 1,366
- **Average Creature Defense:** 1,152

Sample Card List:
Richard Slysheen of York

NAME	ATK/DEF	TYPE
Acid Trap Hole	—	Trap
Armed Ninja	300/300	Warrior/Effect
Axe of Despair	—	Power-up
Battle Ox	1,700/1,000	Beast-warrior
Battle Steer	1,800/1,300	Beast-warrior
Beautiful Headhuntress	1,600/800	Warrior
Cursebreaker	—	Power-up
Empress Judge	2,100/1,700	Warrior
Guardian of the Labyrinth	1,000/1,200	Warrior
Hard Armor	300/1,200	Warrior
Judge Man	2,200/1,500	Warrior
Kagemusha of the Blue Flame	800/400	Warrior
Legendary Sword	—	Power-up
Masaki the Legendary Swordsman	1,100/110	Warrior
Millennium Golem	2,000/2,200	Rock
M-Warrior #1	1,000/500	Warrior
M-Warrior #2	500/1,000	Warrior
Panther Warrior	2,000/1,600	Beast-warrior
Raigeki	—	Magic
Revival of Senmen Genjin	—	Ritual
Rude Kaiser	1,800/1,600	Beast-warrior
Swamp Battleguard	1,800/1,500	Warrior/Effect
Sword of Dragon's Soul	—	Power-up
The Judgement Hand	1,400/700	Warrior

Seto
Vital Stats

- **Name: Seto**
- **Location: Stonehenge**
- **Deck Cost: 1,184**
- **Deck Leader: Blue-Eyes White Dragon**
- **Deck Leader Rank: Secretary of Defense**
- **Leader Abilities: Level Cost Reduction for Summoning Same Type and Increased Movement**
- **Primary Terrain: Normal and Meadow**

Stonehenge

LEGEND

F	Forest
L	Labyrinth
M	Meadow
N	Normal

Seto has escaped to Stonehenge and is eager to battle you. He insulted you when you first arrived into the past, so now it's payback time.

But you must be on top of your game to make Seto eat his words. The map is straightforward, with an arena of Normal spaces in the middle surrounded by Meadows. Most of the arena is walled in by Labyrinth squares.

Seto is quick to unleash his Blue-Eyes White Dragon, an immensely powerful monster. He has several Dragon Treasure power ups and Mountain Cards as well, so he can let loose a monster in the mid 4,000s!

Many of Seto's other monsters are also Dragons, although he also has some good support Spellcasters and Warriors. His Lord of D. makes all his Dragons immune to spell effects, while his Swordstalker provides strength on the Meadow squares. Watch out for the Hourglass of Courage, which when killed, gives all of Seto's surviving monsters +1,000 bonus strength points, and the Hourglass of Life, which revives up to four of the strongest monsters from both Graveyards when it dies! Spellbinding

these two monsters is your best bet, because you prevent those effects from occurring and tie up one more monster slot that would otherwise be used for Seto's heavier monsters.

It will take a good combination of power ups, Effects Monsters, and traps to bring down Seto's Dragons, but don't celebrate too quickly. Seto has three Blue-Eyes White Dragons, and multiple other monsters. Don't let Seto play his Ritual Card, Ultimate Dragon, which Summons a Blue-Eyes Ultimate Dragon, the most powerful monster in the entire game. So kill his Blue-Eyes White Dragon as soon as possible.

One very annoying Trap Card Seto plays is Royal Decree, which nullifies all your traps. Traps are important here, but you can't use them until you can destroy this card.

When you go on the offensive to catch Seto's Deck Leader, notice that he can move two squares per turn! This is faster than any of your monsters, so go at him from multiple angles. Use the layout of the map to your advantage and sandwich the Deck Leader between your two strongest monsters.

If you are winning, Seto attempts a Destiny Draw, and could draw a very powerful card such as Mirror Force. This is immensely powerful and destroys all monsters in the attack position.

When you defeat Seto, this is not the end! Seto tricked you into dueling him so that he could Summon the ultimate Card Guardian, Manawyddan fab Llyr! Now your final duel awaits!

NOTE

Seto gives great Graveyard Slot Machine cards. You can snag Meteor Dragon and Red-Eyes B. Dragon, the two components for the Meteor B. Dragon, an ATK 3,500/DEF 2,000 monster!

Cards to Watch Out For
Blue-Eyes White Dragon

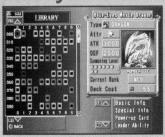

Type: Dragon
Attribute: Light
Attack: 3,000
Defense: 2,500
Effect: None

Royal Decree

Type: Trap
Range: Full Range
Usage: Permanent and continuous
Effect: Permanent trap that triggers against any activated Trap Card and nullifies the card!

Raigeki

Type: Magic
Usage: One-time
Deck Cost: 80
Effect: Destroys all monsters located in vertical and horizontal lines from the activated space!

Creature Stats: Seto

- Main Race: Dragon
- Average Creature Attack: 1,721
- Average Creature Defense: 1,626

Sample Card List: Seto

NAME	ATK/DEF	TYPE
Axe of Despair	—	Power-up
Battle Ox	1,700/1,000	Beast-warrior
Blue-Eyes White Dragon	3,000/2,500	Dragon
Dragon Treasure	—	Power-up
Gear Golem the Moving Fortress	800/2,200	Machine
Gift of the Mystical Elf	—	Magic
Hannibal Necromancer	1,400/1,800	Spellcaster/Effect
Hourglass of Courage	1,100/1,200	Fairy/Effect
Invitation to a Dark Sleep	1,500/1,800	Spellcaster/Effect
Judge Man	2,200/1,500	Warrior
Kageningen	800/600	Warrior/Effect
Kaiser Dragon	2,300/2,000	Dragon
La Jinn the Mystical Genie of the Lamp	1,800/1,000	Fiend
Legendary Sword	—	Power-up
Lord of D.	1,200/1,100	Spellcaster/Effect
Magic Jammer	—	Trap
Mikazukinoyaiba	2,200/2,350	Dragon
Monster Reborn	—	Magic

NAME	ATK/DEF	TYPE
Mystic Horse	1,300/1,550	Beast
Raigeki	—	Magic
Shadow Spell	—	Trap
Sky Dragon	1,900/1,800	Dragon
Steel Ogre Grotto #2	1,900/2,200	Machine
Sword of Dark Destruction	—	Power-up
Swordsman from a Foreign Land	250/250	Warrior/Effect
Swordstalker	2,000/1,600	Warrior/Effect
Ultimate Dragon	—	Ritual

Manawyddan fab Llyr (version one)
Vital Stats

- Name: Manawyddan fab Llyr (version one)
- Location: Stonehenge
- Deck Cost: 1,985
- Deck Leader: Skull Knight
- Deck Leader Rank: SD
- Leader Abilities: Extended Support Range, Increased Strength for Same Type Friendlies, Weaken Specific Enemy Type
- Primary Terrain: Crush and Meadow

Stonehenge

LEGEND
C Crush
F Forest
L Labyrinth
M Meadow

After Seto Summons the Card Guardian, even he realizes that this demon is too evil to let live. Seto implores you, as the superior duelist, to defeat Manawyddan fab Llyr. Now the fate of England, and perhaps the world, rests in your hands.

Manawyddan sets up shop in Stonehenge, but he has changed the Normal arena into Crush squares.

Remember Pegasus? Well, Manawyddan fab Llyr is twice as bad, literally. His Deck Cost is a whopping 1,985! What takes up all that Deck Cost? Powerful Magic Cards.

As soon as you enter the duel, Manawyddan unleashes a barrage of attack spell cards, including Raigeki. He also plays Time Seal, which permanently spellbinds your strongest monster, and Just Desserts, which deals 300 damage for each monster and spell card you have on the Field, to a maximum of 3,000 LP damage! For monster destruction, Manawyddan also has the coveted instant-death Magic Cards, which destroy all creatures of that type on the Field. Last Day of Witch, for example, kills all Spellcasters, while Warrior Elimination kills all warrior monsters.

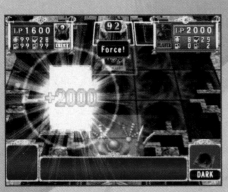

Manawyddan's Power-up Cards are also deadly, including Riryoku, which steals half your LP and adds that number to a monster's attack! Manawyddan also equips his weak monsters with Crush Card, which makes them turn terrain to Crush squares when they die, instantly killing all your monsters with ATK over 1,500.

His Trap Cards are also deadly. He plays Gorgon's Eye, which permanently spellbinds any monster that tries to move into the defense position, and Mirror Force, which kills every one of your monsters in the attack position when any of Manawyddan's monsters or Deck Leader is attacked. Both have unlimited range.

Clearly, if you don't have Magic Jammer, you won't survive. And bring as many healing cards as possible, and be patient about when you use them. Use them too early to boost your LP beyond 4,000 and you're just playing into Manawyddan's hands. Use Reverse Trap to make him pay, as this turns a power up into a reduction.

Don't be slow in attacking Manawyddan. With his Magic Cards, he benefits the longer the duel drags on. All he needs to do is throw out a Riryoku and a Just Desserts, and it's over. With Magic Jammer covering your beginning turns, play your most powerful monsters early, backed up with traps and power ups. Alter the Crush squares to your monsters' favorable terrain so they can move two squares and gain bonus points. Use Magic Cards of your own to directly damage Manawyddan's Deck Leader. If you load up your deck with three Tremendous Fires and three Ookazi, you can win with the right draw in a few rounds. Just hope Manawyddan

doesn't play his healing cards, which can restore him to 4,000 LP instantly. Don't let up with your monsters even as you use magic to attack and counterspell him.

Be prepared for many early exits against Manawyddan. But take heart. If you beat him, then the War of the Roses is over. Peace will be restored to England, and you can finally go home, with the thanks of King Yugi and a password to unlock one of the game's rarer cards. Congratulations! You proved yourself worthy of the name Rose Duelist.

Cards to Watch Out For
Mirror Force

Type: Trap
Usage: One-time
Deck Cost: 99
Effect: Disposable trap that triggers when an enemy initiates an attack against your Leader or other cards on the Field! Destroys every one of your opponent's attack-positioned cards on the Field!

Just Desserts

Type: Magic
Usage: One-time
Deck Cost: 80
Effect: Opponent's LP suffers damage equivalent to 300 points multiplied by the number of enemies on the Field!

Riryoku

Type: Power-up
Usage: One-time
Deck Cost: 99
Effect: Reduces opponent's LP by half and adds the reduced amount to the power of all monsters!

Creature Stats:
Manawyddan fab Llyr

- Main Race: Fiend
- Average Creature Attack: 1,661
- Average Creature Defense: 1,227

Sample Card List:
Manawyddan fab Llyr

NAME	ATK/DEF	TYPE
B. Dragon Jungle King	2,100/1,800	Dragon
Cosmo Queen's Prayer	—	Ritual
Crush Card	—	Power-up
Curse of Dragon	2,000/1,500	Dragon/Effect
Curse of Tri-Horned Dragon	—	Ritual
Dark Elf	2,000/800	Spellcaster/Effect
Dark-Piercing Light	—	Magic
Dian Keto the Cure Master	—	Magic
Feral Imp	1,300/1,400	Fiend
Gemini Elf	1,900/900	Spellcaster
Gorgon's Eye	—	Trap
Graverobber	—	Magic
Gravity Bind	—	Trap
Just Desserts	—	Magic
Kuriboh	300/200	Magic
Last Day of Witch	—	Magic
Mirror Force	—	Trap
Multiply	—	Power-up
Queen of Autumn Leaves	1,800/1,500	Plant
Princess of Tsurugi	900/700	Warrior
Raigeki	—	Magic
Riryoku	—	Power-up
Skull Knight	2,650/2,250	Spellcaster
Solomon's Lawbook	—	Magic
Time Seal	—	Magic
Tremendous Fire	—	Magic
Warrior Elimination	—	Magic

Tea
Vital Stats

- Name: Tea
- Location: Windsor
- Deck Cost: 933
- Deck Leader: Dancing Elf
- Deck Leader Rank: Second Lieutenant
- Leader Abilities: None
- Primary Terrain: Normal

Windsor

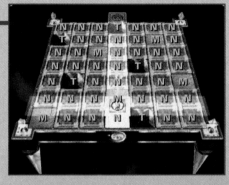

LEGEND	
M	Meadow
T	Mountain
N	Normal

Your first opponent in the Seto campaign is Tea, who is eager to punish you for betraying Yugi. She presents a modest challenge, but if you strike quickly and keep her off balance, you shouldn't have a problem defeating her.

Her deck consists of Fairy monsters, which for the most part are weak in ATK, but good in DEF. She only has two or three high ATK/DEF monsters, so her creatures shouldn't overwhelm you. Just don't get lured into attacking a Fairy on any of the Mountain squares on this map. And keep your Deck Leader away from the Mountains.

Go on the offensive against Tea, moving your Deck Leader closer to her and letting loose your strongest creatures. If you give her enough time, she can make her Fairy monsters very strong with her power ups and Effects Monsters. If she plays Gyakutenno Megami, you could be in trouble, as this monster adds +1,000 bonus points to all friendly monsters on the Field with 1,000 ATK or less. She also can play two Winged Trumpeters to further boost her Fairies another 600 points each.

 TIP

When Tea Summons the creature card, Tenderness, and uses its ability, all damage to Life Points is halved, including to your Deck Leader. This prolongs battles. But don't give Tea time to play many of her supporting creatures and power ups—destroy Tenderness quickly.

Two more supporting creature cards are Hoshiningen, which gives Fairy monsters another +300 bonus, and Mystical Elf, which gives all Light monsters +800 points. Add these together and a weak 700 ATK Fairy all of a sudden has 4,000 ATK! And her rare strong Fairy monsters, such as Airknight of Parshath, would be at 5,200 ATK! If Tea manages to pump up her monsters to this level, your only hope is to use lots of Trap Cards and Effects Monsters, backed up by direct damage spells.

Power increase!

Be wary of killing Hourglass of Life, which revives the four strongest monsters from either Graveyard under her control, or Hourglass of Courage, which when killed gives all her monsters bonus strength. However, these don't work if Tea is below 1,000 LP.

Tea does have good healing cards, including Soul of the Pure, which restores 2,000 LP. So strike hard and fast. If you use many Fiends in your deck, watch out, because Tea has Enchanted Javelin, which when equipped on a monster, lets it kill Fiends outright. She also has Binding Chain, which spellbinds all Fiends every turn when flipped face-up.

NOTE

Two good cards you can win from Tea are Gyakutenno Megami and the Trap Card, Tears of the Mermaid.

Cards to Watch Out For
Gyakutenno Megami

Type: Fairy
Attribute: Light
Attack: 1,800
Defense: 2,000
Effect: When this card is flipped face-up, all your own monsters with ATK of 1,000 or below are increased by 1,000 points!

Hourglass of Life

Type: Fairy
Attribute: Light
Attack: 700
Defense: 600
Effect: If LP is over 1,000 points when this card is destroyed in battle, the strength of your monsters are increased by 1,000 points, and your LP is reduced by 1,000!

Soul of the Pure

Type: Magic
Usage: One-time
Deck Cost: 30
Effect: 2000-point LP recovery for controlling player!

Creature Stats: Tea

- **Main Race:** Fairy
- **Average Creature Attack:** 1,000
- **Average Creature Defense:** 1,162

Sample Card List: Tea

NAME	ATK/DEF	TYPE
Airknight of Parshath	1,900/1,400	Fairy
Binding Chain	1,000/1,100	Fairy/Effect
Creature Swap	—	Magic
Dancing Elf	300/200	Fairy
Dark-Piercing Light	—	Magic
Doma the Angel of Silence	1,600/1,400	Fairy
Enchanted Javelin	—	Power-up
Goddess with the Third Eye	1,200/1,000	Fairy
Gyakutenno Megami	1,800/2,000	Fairy/Effect
Happy Lover	800/500	Fairy/Effect
Hoshiningen	500/700	Fairy/Effect
Hourglass of Courage	1,100/1,200	Fairy/Effect
Hourglass of Life	700/600	Fairy/Effect
Key Mace	400/300	Fairy/Effect
Mystical Elf	800/2,000	Spellcaster/Effect
Orion the Battle King	1,800/1,500	Fairy
Petit Angel	600/900	Fairy/Effect
Ray & Temperature	1,000/1,000	Fairy/Effect
Silver Bow and Arrow	—	Power-up
Soul of the Pure	—	Magic
Spirit of the Harp	800/2,000	Fairy
Tears of the Mermaid	—	Trap (Limited Range)
Tenderness	700/1,400	Fairy/Effect
Wing Egg Elf	500/1,300	Fairy
Winged Egg of New Life	1,400/1,700	Fairy
Winged Trumpeter	—	Magic

Prima's Official Strategy Guide

T. Tristan Grey
Vital Stats

- **Name:** T. Tristan Grey
- **Location:** London
- **Deck Cost:** 1,149
- **Deck Leader:** Karbonala Warrior
- **Deck Leader Rank:** Lieutenant Colonel
- **Leader Abilities:** None
- **Primary Terrain:** None

London

LEGEND

F	Forest
M	Meadow
N	Normal
S	Sea
W	Wasteland

T. Tristan Grey is a very straightforward guy. There aren't many tricks up his sleeve. Instead, he tries to overwhelm you with his great assortment of monsters.

Tristan's menagerie includes Warriors, Beasts, Fiends, Beast-warriors, and a few other monsters. His deck, with the exception of a small handful of cards, is made up entirely of monsters. You don't have to worry about traps or even power ups. With Tristan, what you see is what you get. So plow forward with abandon.

Only a few of Tristan's monsters really stand out, because most of them hover around the mid to high 1,000s in ATK/DEF. He can create several Chimera the Flying Mythical Beast Fusions, but if you have strong monsters with power ups, you are in no danger. Tristan tries to fight his battles over advantageous terrain, however, so that Chimera usually hovers around the Forest terrain.

Given the alternating lines of terrain, Tristan can move several monsters quickly across the map, because he has monster types that can take advantage of every terrain type on his level. But the monsters don't enjoy a clear terrain advantage across the entire map. Move your monsters so Tristan's monsters attack you on neutral terrain or terrain favorable to you.

The only two cards you should worry about are his Ritual Monster, Chakra, and his only Magic Card, Fairy Meteor Crash. Chakra is a very strong monster, but what's worse is that he resurrects himself if destroyed, so you have to beat him twice. Fairy Meteor Crash targets 10 spaces and destroys all cards in those spaces. Of course, because these cards are only two of 40, you're not likely to face them. But it helps to know about them.

Tristan should pose no problems if you play some strong monsters such as Great Mammoth of Goldfine, Kaiser Dragon, Rose Spectre of Dunn, or good Fusions, backed with power ups and traps.

Cards to Watch Out For
Chakra

Type: Fiend
Attribute: Dark
Attack: 2,450
Defense: 2,000
Effect: Revives in own Summoning Area other than current location when destroyed in battle!

Fairy Meteor Crash

Type: Magic
Usage: One-time
Deck Cost: 50
Effect: Randomly selects 10 spaces on the Field, and destroys any card in play on that space!

Chimera the Flying Mythical Beast

Type: Beast
Attribute: Wind
Attack: 2,100
Defense: 1,800
Effect: None

Creature Stats: T. Tristan Grey

- Main Race: Fiend, Beast, Warrior
- Average Creature Attack: 1,000
- Average Creature Defense: 1,162

Sample Card List: T. Tristan Grey

NAME	ATK/DEF	TYPE
Amazon of the Seas	1,300/1,400	Fish
Ansatsu	1,700/1,200	Warrior
Beautiful Beast Trainer	1,750/1,500	Warrior/Effect
Blocker	850/1,800	Machine/Effect
Chakra	2,450/2,000	Fiend/Effect
Chimera the Flying Mythical Beast	2,100/1,800	Beast
Cyber Saurus	1,800/1,400	Machine/Fusion
Dark Prisoner	600/1,000	Fiend/Effect
Deepsea Shark	1,900/1,600	Fish
Fairy Meteor Crash	—	Magic
Fire Kraken	1,600/1,500	Aqua
Garoozis	1,800/1,500	Beast-warrior
Gatekeeper	1,500/1,800	Machine
Giant Turtle Who Feeds on Flames	1,400/1,800	Aqua
Guardian of the Throne Room	1,650/1,600	Machine
Kanan the Swordmistress	1,400/1,400	Warrior
Leogun	1,750/1,550	Beast
Lord of the Lamp	1,400/1,200	Fiend
Mabarrel	1,700/1,400	Fiend
Madjinn Gunn	600/800	Fiend
Misairuzame	1,400/1,600	Fish/Effect
Monster Egg	600/900	Warrior/Effect
Mysterious Puppeteer	1,000/1,500	Warrior
Mystery Hand	500/500	Fiend/Effect
Neo the Magic Swordsman	1,700/1,000	Spellcaster
Pale Beast	1,500/1,200	Beast
Patrician of Darkness	2,000/1,400	Zombie
Resurrection of Chakra	—	Ritual
Rude Kaiser	1,800/1,600	Beast-warrior
Sleeping Lion	700/1,700	Beast
Sorcerer of the Doomed	1,450/1,200	Spellcaster
Spike Clubber	1,700/1,800	Machine
The Drdek	700/800	Fiend/Effect
The Illusory Gentleman	1,500/1,600	Spellcaster
Togek	1,600/1,800	Beast
Two-Mouth Darkruler	900/700	Dinosaur
Uraby	1,500/800	Dinosaur
Versago the Destroyer	1,100/900	Fiend
Warrior of Tradition	1,900/1,700	Warrior
Wicked Mirror	700/600	Fiend
Zanki	1,500/1,700	Warrior

Margaret Mai Beaufort
Vital Stats

- Name: Margaret Mai Beaufort
- Location: Canterbury
- Deck Cost: 1,003
- Deck Leader: Harpie Lady
- Deck Leader Rank: Colonel
- Leader Abilities: Increased Movement
- Primary Terrain: Mountain

Canterbury

LEGEND
T   Mountain
W   Wasteland

Compared to the previous duelist, Mai is an immense challenge. She is burning with your betrayal and can't wait to pay you back, so she is quick to roll out the heavy guns in her deck against you.

She employs mostly Winged Beasts in her deck, along with some female monsters. They are all very strong, with all above 1,000 ATK. Moreover, because almost the entire map is Mountain terrain, her average monster strength is more than 2,000. Like Tea, Mai uses lots of power ups and supporting Effects Monsters. In fact, less than half of her deck consists of monsters. The rest are power ups and a few traps and Magic Cards.

Expect many of her creatures to be in the high-2,000 range. Her most dangerous monster combinations are Harpie Lady Sisters and Harpie's Pet Dragon. Mai can play up to three Harpie Lady Sisters and two Harpie's Pet Dragons. When the Sisters are flipped face-up, they each give a 900-point bonus to their Pet Dragons. So potentially, you could have two behemoth monsters with ATK/DEF of 4,700/5,200! And that is before any power ups.

Mai's monsters are very aggressive and with the open Mountain terrain, all of them can move two spaces a turn. That means her monsters could be on your Deck Leader by turn two!

Changing the terrain helps, and so do traps. But Mai also has two Harpie's Feather Dusters, which sweep away all traps on the Field. This is the one instance where you want to add two Fake Trap cards to your deck. Other spell cards that Mai has that make her tough are Monster Reborn and Shadow of Eyes.

If you can erase Mai's terrain advantage and match her power ups, you should be in good shape. If her Pet Dragons come out to play though, use your Trap Cards and Effects Monsters. Because most of her monsters are Wind creatures, bring in Earth monsters to spellbind them.

For those using a Fairy deck, which has predominantly female monsters, Mai is a good duelist to keep playing because she offers Electro-Whip and Cyber Shield power ups in her Graveyard Slot Machine.

Cards to Watch Out For
Harpie's Pet Dragon

Type: Dragon
Attribute: Wind
Attack: 2,000
Defense: 2,500
Effect: None

Harpie's Feather Duster

Type: Magic
Usage: One-time
Range: Limited
Deck Cost: 70
Effect: Destroys all spells located in the vertical and horizontal lines from the activated space!

Monster Reborn

Type: Magic
Deck Cost: 50
Effect: Select, revive, and control 1 monster card from either Graveyard!

Creature Stats:
Margaret Mai Beaufort

- **Main Race:** Winged Beast
- **Average Creature Attack:** 1,697
- **Average Creature Defense:** 1,684

Sample Card List:
Margaret Mai Beaufort

Name	ATK/DEF	Type
Acid Trap Hole	—	Trap
Birdface	1,600/1,600	Winged Beast/Effect
Blue-Winged Crown	1,600/1,200	Winged Beast
Cursebreaker	—	Power-up
Cyber Shield	—	Power-up
Darkfire Dragon	1,500/1,250	Dragon
Electro-Whip	—	Power-up
Elegant Egotist	—	Power-up
Empress Judge	2,100/1,700	Warrior
Follow Wind	—	Power-up
Gust Fan	—	Power-up
Harpie Lady	1,300/1,400	Winged Beast/Effect
Harpie Lady Sisters	1,950/2,100	Winged Beast/Effect
Harpie's Feather Duster	—	Magic
Harpie's Pet Dragon	2,000/2,500	Dragon
Invisible Wire	—	Trap (Limited Range)
Kanan the Swordmistress	1,400/1,400	Warrior
Mesmeric Control	—	Trap (Limited Range)
Monster Reborn	—	Magic
Monstrous Bird	2,000/1,900	Winged Beast
Mountain	—	Magic
Peacock	1,700/1,500	Winged Beast
Punished Eagle	2,100/1,800	Winged Beast
Revived Serpent Night Dragon	—	Ritual
Shadow of Eyes	—	Trap (Full Range)
Tyhone	1,200/1,400	Winged Beast
Wing Eagle	1,800/1,500	Winged Beast

Mako
Vital Stats

- **Name:** Mako
- **Location:** Straits of Dover
- **Deck Cost:** 1,001
- **Deck Leader:** Kairyu-Shin
- **Deck Leader Rank:** Rear Admiral
- **Leader Abilities:** Movement Bonus for Same Type Friendlies
- **Primary Terrain:** Sea

Straits of Dover

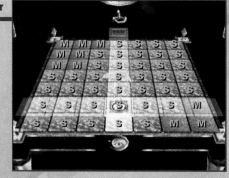

LEGEND
M   Meadow
S   Sea

After you beat Mai, your path to France lies open before you. Catch a ship to Amiens on the French coast. Along the way, the ship's captain, Mako, hijacks you and challenges you to a duel. You must defeat his Sea Serpent deck to make it to shore.

If you played the Yugi campaign already, you'll remember that Ishtar also used a deck full of Sea-friendly monsters. The difference here, though, is that Mako uses much more powerful creatures and spells, resulting in a more challenging duel. He is not a pushover.

Mako uses the best Aqua and Sea Serpent monsters. Many of his creatures are in the high 1,000s to low 2,000s, not counting bonuses. This means you'll battle monsters in the mid to high 2,000s. And while you can change the terrain to negate some of those bonuses, Mako can change it back with his creatures. Some, such as Kairyu-Shin and Violent Rain, revert the terrain around them to Sea whenever they are flipped face-up. And others, such as Aqua Dragon and Roaring Ocean Snake, turn every square in which they fight into Sea (guaranteeing them unbreakable terrain bonuses to strength). He has over a half-dozen monsters with

this ability, so in the long-run, any terrain altering you do will not stick—Mako will turn it all back to Sea.

With that in mind, build a deck that is also Sea friendly, using Aqua, Fish, Sea Serpent, and Thunder monsters. Mako also adds many power ups to his monsters, so you must match him there as well. Use your strong DEF cards and wait for Mako's monsters. They are aggressive and will charge you, so prepare a strong defense of monsters and traps.

Use cards such as Acid Trap Hole, which can kill his heavy monsters, or traps such as Mesmeric Control, which reduces a monster's strength 800 points. Gain both cards by replaying the previous duelists.

One powerful card Mako holds in reserve is Heavy Storm, which destroys all spell cards on the Field. Don't hold too many spell cards around your Deck Leader. Use them when you play them onto the Field, or you'll lose them. One curious fact is that Mako uses no traps.

Cards to Watch Out For
Aqua Dragon

Type: Sea Serpent
Attribute: Water
Attack: 2,250
Defense: 1,900
Effect: Space occupied in transformed to Sea terrain when engaged in battle!

Roaring Ocean Snake

Type: Aqua
Attribute: Water
Attack: 2,100
Defense: 1,800
Effect: When engaged in battle, transforms the space it occupies into Sea terrain! When this card is flipped face-up transforms all adjacent spaces into Sea terrain!

Heavy Storm

Type: Magic
Deck Cost: 50
Effect: Destroys all spell cards on the Field!

Creature Stats: Mako

- Main Race: Aqua, Fish, Sea Serpent
- Average Creature Attack: 1,375
- Average Creature Defense: 1,234

Sample Card List: Mako

NAME	ATK/DEF	TYPE
Akihiron	1,700/1,400	Aqua
Amazon of the Seas	1,300/1,400	Fish
Aqua Chorus	—	Magic
Aqua Dragon	2,250/1,900	Sea Serpent/Effect
Aqua Snake	1,050/900	Aqua/Effect
Bottom Dweller	1,650/1,700	Fish
Change Slime	400/300	Aqua/Effect
Crazy Fish	1,600/1,200	Fish
Enchanting Mermaid	1,200/900	Fish
Fiend Kraken	1,200/1,400	Aqua
Fortress Whale's Oath	—	Ritual
Heavy Storm	—	Magic
High Tide Gyojin	1,650/1,300	Aqua
Hightide	—	Power-up
Jellyfish	1,200/1,500	Aqua/Effect
Kairyu-Shin	1,800/1,500	Sea Serpent/Effect
Kanikabuto	650/900	Aqua
Maiden of the Aqua	700/2,000	Aqua/Effect
Man-eating Black Shark	2,100/1,300	Fish
Mech Bass	1,800/1,500	Machine
Octoberser	1,600/1,400	Aqua
Ooguchi	300/250	Aqua/Effect
Power of Kaishin	—	Power-up
Red Archery Girl	1,400/1,500	Aqua
Roaring Ocean Snake	2,100/1,800	Aqua/Effect
Root Water	900/800	Fish/Effect
Sea King Dragon	2,000/1,700	Sea Serpent
Spike Seadra	1,600/1,300	Sea Serpent/Effect
Spring of Rebirth	—	Power-up
Takriminos	1,500/1,200	Sea Serpent
The Furious Sea King	800/700	Aqua/Effect
Tongyo	1,350/800	Fish/Effect
Turu-Purun	450/500	Aqua/Effect
Umi	—	Magic
Violent Rain	1,550/800	Aqua/Effect
Zone Eater	250/200	Aqua/Effect

Joey
Vital Stats

- Name: Joey
- Location: Amiens
- Deck Cost: 970
- Deck Leader: Flame Swordsman
- Deck Leader Rank: Admiral
- Leader Abilities: Extended Support Range
- Primary Terrain: None

Amiens

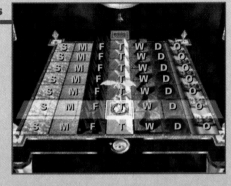

LEGEND	
D	Dark
F	Forest
M	Meadow
O	Toon
S	Sea
T	Mountain
W	Wasteland

Joey, like T. Tristan Grey, fights on a map of alternating terrain. The difference, though, is that he isn't as one-dimensional in his deck strategies. He employs several monsters, such as Warriors and Dragons. But he also has some spell cards up his sleeve, such as Ookazi. It makes him much more challenging than a straight creature deck duelist.

He can also take advantage of all his terrain with a variety of monsters. Joey's monsters are in the high 1,000s range, but he also has some stronger monsters in his deck, such as Thousand Dragon and Ryu-Ran. Watch out for his Dragons. He doesn't have anything like Seto's Blue-Eyes, but with his Time Wizard, he can turn all of them into an army of Thousand Dragons.

Joey, though, doesn't fight too fair. He sets up traps around his Deck Leader or his monsters to weaken your own monsters. His worst are Tears of the Mermaid and Acid Trap Hole. And he is fond of pumping up his monsters with power ups. He will probably play a strong creature such as Panther Warrior (2,000/1,900) and add two Kunai with Chains to make it a 3,000/2,900 monster. Make him pay by using Reverse Trap, which turns that bonus into a penalty.

Also beware of Shield & Sword and Copycat. Copycat essentially lets him use any of your spells, while Shield & Sword swaps ATK/DEF values of all monsters on the Field, which could be bad for you if you use monsters with high ATK but low DEF, such as Dinosaurs. Joey can also copy any spell you have, or play an extra Ookazi by using Copycat.

Joey is a very balanced duelist, with good magic and some very powerful monsters. Stick to traps and your own powered-up monsters to duel him.

Dragon deck holders should duel Joey several times to get Time Wizard from him, which is a great help for weak dragons. Shield & Sword is also a good Magic Card to have if you use a deck with high DEF creatures such as Fairies.

Cards to Watch Out For

Thousand Dragon

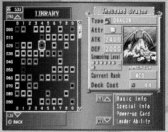

Type: Dragon
Attribute: Wind
Attack: 2,400
Defense: 2,000
Effect: None

Shield & Sword

Type: Magic
Deck Cost: 30
Effect: Swaps the respective ATK and DEF values of each monster on the Field!

Copycat

Type: Magic
Deck Cost: 50
Effect: Select, revive, and control 1 spell Card from an opponent's Graveyard!

Creature Stats: Joey

- **Main Race:** Beast-warrior, Dragon, Warrior
- **Average Creature Attack:** 1,592
- **Average Creature Defense:** 1,415

Sample Card List: Joey

NAME	ATK/DEF	TYPE
Acid Trap Hole	—	Trap (Limited Range)
Baby Dragon	1,200/700	Dragon
Battle Steer	1,800/1,300	Beast-warrior
Copycat	—	Magic
Crawling Dragon	1,600/1,400	Dragon
Dryad	1,200/1,400	Spellcaster/Effect
Flame Swordsman	1,800/1,600	Warrior/Effect
Garoozis	1,800/1,500	Beast-warrior
Judge Man	2,200/1,500	Warrior
Kojikocy	1,500/1,200	Warrior
Kunai with Chain	—	Power-up
Megasonic Eye	1,500/1,800	Machine
Metal Dragon	1,850/1,700	Machine
Metalmorph	—	Power-up
Mountain Warrior	600/1,000	Beast-warrior/Effect
Nails of Bane	—	Power-up
Ookazi	—	Magic
Panther Warrior	2,000/1,600	Beast-warrior
Rock Spirit	1,650/1,900	Spellcaster
Ryu-Ran	2,200/2,600	Dragon/Effect
Salamandra	—	Power-up
Shield & Sword	—	Magic
Tears of the Mermaid	—	Trap (Limited Range)
Thousand Dragon	2,400/2,000	Dragon
Tiger Axe	1,300/1,100	Beast-warrior
Time Wizard	500/400	Spellcaster/Effect
Twin-Headed Behemoth	1,500/1,200	Dragon
Wolf Axwielder	1,650/1,000	Beast-warrior

J. Shadi Morton
Vital Stats

- Name: J. Shadi Morton
- Location: Paris
- Deck Cost: 982
- Deck Leader: Millennium Golem
- Deck Leader Rank: Rear Admiral
- Leader Abilities: Extended Support Range, Increased Strength for Same Type Friendlies, Improved Resistance for Same Type Friendlies, Destroy Specific Enemy Type
- Primary Terrain: None

Paris

LEGEND

C	Crush
D	Dark
F	Forest
S	Sea
W	Wasteland

When J. Shadi Morton sets eyes on you, he is full of disdain and contempt. Teach him to show his betters proper respect.

This duelist uses a deck composed of Fiend, Rock, and Thunder monsters. More importantly, he has quite a few with a low ATK. But that is because of the makeup of the map. A cross of Crush squares divides this map into four sections, so moving between sections is lethal for any monsters with ATK of 1,500 or more. So it's natural for Morton to use low ATK monsters. You must change the terrain so you can get to him. But once you do that, Morton's strong monsters can get to you. So don't change it until you have the right monsters to beat his.

Morton's four quarters are Dark, Wasteland, Forest, and Sea, so he has some tough Fiend, Machine, Dinosaur, and Pyro monsters. He has at least one 2,000+ ATK monster of each of those types, and power ups to make them even stronger. His strongest monsters are Zoa, Bracchio-raidus, and Soul Hunter. But his scariest is Blast Juggler, which destroys all cards in a 3x3 area when it is killed. Proceed with caution when you see it.

If you don't have terrain cards, use low ATK/high DEF monsters such as Mystical Elf or Blocker, which have defenses of 2,000. Set them to defense on the Crush terrain in front of you and they'll handily deal with any monsters Morton sends directly down to you. If you want to attack, have your Deck Leader sit on a Crush square and Summon your monster onto the non-Crush terrain.

You can play offense or defense against Morton. If you leave your Deck Leader exposed to Morton's monsters, just one space away from the Crush squares, you can lure his monster toward you. As they pass the Crush squares they end their turn in the attack position. You know the monster is below 1,500 ATK, so Summon one of your stronger monsters next to it and attack to do good damage to Morton's Deck Leader. Don't Summon your creature until after the monster has passed into your section or you'll scare off Morton.

NOTE

A good card to get from J. Shadi Morton's Graveyard is Maha Vailo, a spellcaster monster that boosts all Power-up Cards by 200 points.

Cards to Watch Out For
Zoa

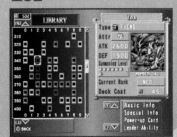

Type: Fiend
Attribute: Dark
Attack: 2,600
Defense: 1,900
Effect: None

Bracchio-raidus

Type: Dinosaur
Attribute: Water
Attack: 2,200
Defense: 2,000
Effect: None

Blast Juggler

Type: Machine
Attribute: Fire
Attack: 800
Defense: 900
Effect: All cards located in the surrounding 3x3 area are automatically destroyed when this card is destroyed in battle!

Creature Stats: J. Shadi Morton

- Main Race: Fiend, Rock, Thunder, Pyro
- Average Creature Attack: 1,492
- Average Creature Defense: 1,430

Sample Card List: J. Shadi Morton

NAME	ATK/DEF	TYPE
Berfomet	1,400/1,800	Fiend/Effect
Blast Juggler	800/900	Machine/Effect
Bracchio-raidus	2,200/2,000	Dinosaur
Burning Spear	—	Power-up
Dark-Piercing Light	—	Magic
Dimensionhole	—	Magic
Electric Lizard	850/800	Thunder/Effect
Electric Snake	800/900	Thunder/Effect
Final Flame	—	Magic
Fireyarou	1,300/1,000	Pyro
Flame Cerberus	2,100/1,800	Pyro
Giant Soldier of Stone	1,300/2,000	Rock
Hannibal Necromancer	1,400/1,800	Spellcaster/Effect
Hibikime	1,450/1,000	Warrior/Effect
Invader from Another Dimension	950/1,400	Fiend
Invigoration	—	Power-up
Kaminari Attack	1,900/1,400	Thunder
Maha Vailo	1,550/1,400	Spellcaster/Effect
Malevolent Nuzzler	—	Power-up
Mega Thunderball	750/600	Thunder/Effect
Molten Behemoth	1,000/2,200	Rock/Effect
Mystical Sand	2,100/1,700	Rock
Prisman	800/1,000	Rock/Effect
Saber Slasher	1,450/1,500	Machine
Salamandra	—	Power-up
Serpentine Princess	1,400/2,000	Reptile/Effect
Soul Hunter	2,200/1,800	Fiend
Spirit of the Books	1,400/1,200	Winged Beast/Effect
Spring of Rebirth	—	Power-up
Stone D.	2,000/2,300	Rock
Takuhee	1,450/1,000	Winged Beast
The Statue of Easter Island	1,100/1,400	Rock
Thunder Dragon	1,600/1,500	Thunder
Thunder Nyan Nyan	1,900/800	Thunder/Effect
Ushi Oni	2,150/1,950	Fiend
Vermillion Sparrow	1,900/1,500	Pyro
Wretched Ghost of the Attic	550/400	Fiend
Zoa	2,600/1,900	Fiend

Jasper Dice Tudor
Vital Stats

- **Name:** Jasper Dice Tudor
- **Location:** Le Mans
- **Deck Cost:** 1,078
- **Deck Leader:** Exodia the Forbidden One
- **Deck Leader Rank:** Secretary of Defense
- **Leader Abilities:** Extended Support Range, Increased Strength for Same Type Friendlies, Weaken Specific Enemy Type
- **Primary Terrain:** Dark, Meadow

Le Mans

LEGEND
D	Dark
L	Labyrinth
M	Meadow
S	Sea
T	Mountain
W	Wasteland

Fans of *Yu-Gi-Oh!* will recognize Yugi's kind grandfather, but this duelist is anything but nice.

Your first clue that you'll be up against a challenging fight is Jasper's Deck Leader: Exodia the Forbidden One. Yep, that means you could lose the duel if he manages to set up the Right and Left Arms and Legs of the Forbidden One. If he does that, the duel is over and you just lost. Clearly, this is one match that can't drag on.

You have to go on the offensive, but this map is designed to make all movement really slow. Jasper's Deck Leader is hiding inside a Labyrinth chamber, and the only entrance is a one-square opening at the top of the map. You start at the bottom. Rush up along either side of the map to reach the top and then come down into the walled-in area.

Jasper's main advantage is that you have to move around the Labyrinth squares. Negate that by adding a few monsters that can move through Labyrinth terrain, such as Shadow Ghoul, Labyrinth Tank, or Dungeon Worm.

Meanwhile, he has plenty of awesome spell cards to play against you, including Tremendous Fire and Just Desserts. The latter card does up to 3,000 damage to you if you have five monsters and five spells out! So don't clog your Summoning Squares with cards—it could get you killed.

Bring some direct damage spells of your own to attack Jasper's Deck Leader. Dark Hole is also a good counter to Exodia. When you see him play one of his limbs, use Dark Hole to cast it into his Graveyard.

As you are moving up to Exodia, watch out for traps. Jasper has plenty of traps that spellbind, weaken, or kill your monsters. Conversely, traps don't really work that well against him because Jasper's monsters are not aggressive. They won't budge from their defense positions.

Jasper can play the Yellow Luster Shield Magic Card, which boosts his monsters' high DEF by 900 points. Even the strongest monsters will find this tough to overcome. Get those monsters back down to a manageable level with Cursebreaker power ups. Bring a Dragon Piper or other cards that can break spellbinding because Jasper has lots of monsters that can spellbind, which creates a traffic jam trying to get to Exodia. Note that the incredibly low average ATK/DEF values for Jasper's monsters are brought down by the Limbs of Exodia, which aren't for battle but still count as monsters. Otherwise, his spellcasters (who all get a strength boost from Jasper's Leader Ability) have good DEF ratings.

TIP

Although Jasper can win with Exodia and his Limbs, he doesn't need to. He has enough direct damage spell cards to kill you outright. So bring in two or three healing cards. You need at least 6,000 LP, maybe even more, to survive long enough to reach his Deck Leader. Also add several Magic Jammer cards to your deck.

Cards to Watch Out For
Just Desserts

Type: Magic
Deck Cost: 80
Effect: Opponent's LP suffers damage equivalent to 300 points multiplied by the number of enemies on the Field!

Yellow Luster Shield

Type: Magic
Deck Cost: 10
Effect: Boosts the DEF of all your own monsters on the Field by 900 points!

Illusionist Faceless Mage

Type: Spellcaster
Attribute: Dark
Attack: 1,200
Defense: 2,200
Effect: When this card is flipped face-up in battle, spellbinds opposing monster for 3 turns!

Creature Stats: Jasper Dice Tudor
- Main Race: Spellcaster
- Average Creature Attack: 1,492
- Average Creature Defense: 1,430

Sample Card List: Jasper Dice Tudor

NAME	ATK/DEF	TYPE
Acid Trap Hole	—	Trap
Black Pendant	—	Power-up
Book of Secret Arts	—	Power-up
Curtain of the Dark Ones	600/500	Spellcaster
Fake Trap	—	Trap
Final Flame	—	Magic
Gravity Bind	—	Trap
Illusionist Faceless Mage	1,200/2,200	Spellcaster
Infinite Dismissal	—	Trap
Injection Fairy Lily	400/1,500	Spellcaster
Just Desserts	—	Magic
Left Arm of the Forbidden One	200/300	Spellcaster
Left Leg of the Forbidden One	200/300	Spellcaster
Magic Jammer	—	Trap
Nemuriko	800/700	Spellcaster
Phantom Dewan	700/600	Spellcaster
Right Arm of the Forbidden One	200/300	Spellcaster
Right Leg of the Forbidden One	200/300	Spellcaster
Tao the Chanter	1,200/900	Spellcaster
The Bewitching Phantom Thief	700/700	Spellcaster
Tremendous Fire	—	Magic
Witch's Apprentice	550/500	Spellcaster
Yellow Luster Shield	—	Magic

Bakura
Vital Stats

- Name: Bakura
- Location: Rennes
- Deck Cost: 757
- Deck Leader: Dark Plant
- Deck Leader Rank: Secretary of Defense
- Leader Abilities: LP Recovery, Extended Support Range, Increased Strength for Same Type Friendlies, Spellbind Specific Enemy Type, Destroy Specific Enemy Type
- Primary Terrain: Forest, Crush

NOTE

Bakura's Leader abilities are deadly against Dragon and Rock monsters. He spellbinds all Dragons and destroys all Rock monsters that approach within a 5x5 square around him.

Rennes

LEGEND

C   Crush
F   Forest

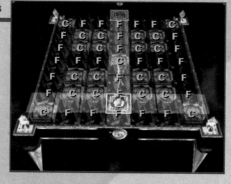

You are now only one step from Yugi. Bakura blocks your path, and he demands some stressful pre-dueling strategizing. His Deck Cost is an anemic 757, so you must clear out all your favorite cards just so you can play him.

Bakura's deck consists mostly of Plants, and his terrain is Forest. While the cards aren't very strong, Bakura has good power ups and the terrain is to his advantage. He also employs traps. Moreover, because Crush squares make up this level, you really can't move across the map with heavy monsters.

Ordinarily, you could defeat him handily, but with the Deck Cost limit, you will have to be creative. Go back to your Fusions. While the two component creatures might cost more in aggregate than the ultimate Fusion, they take up two spots in the deck, whereas a similarly priced single monster would still leave another space for you to fill.

You could, for example, bring a Dancing Elf (DC 5) and a Rainbow Flower (DC 9) and make a Queen of Autumn Leaves (ATK/DEF 1,800/ 1,500). Take along some power ups, and with a Vile Germs card, she could be a 2,800/2,500 monster on Forest terrain.

If you don't plan to fight his Plants with Plants, bring along a terrain-altering card to take away Bakura's terrain bonus and get rid of the Crush spaces. Preferably, the new terrain will be one that favors your monsters.

Because you can't bring lots of strong monsters, think about building a Fairy deck, and add Gyakutenno Megami as your lone high-cost monster. It adds +1,000 bonus points to all your monsters with ATK 1,000 or less. Go with a similar strategy if you don't want to go Fairies, such as Tactical Warrior for your warrior deck or Robotic Knight for your Machine deck. Bring in complementary Effects Monsters to make up for having only one high-level monster.

When you finally reach the duel, you'll find that Bakura uses power ups such as Rain of Mercy and Vile Germs to increase the strength of his Plants. Watch for specific monsters, such as Man Eater, which destroys all monsters on Forest terrain when flipped face-up, and Laughing Flower, which lets Bakura control your attacking monster.

Bakura's Deck Leader has five abilities! He gains 50 LP at the start of each turn. But despite his powers, Bakura isn't quite the opponent that J. Shadi Morton was, the other duelist who used Crush to divide his map.

If you can change the terrain and field some strong Fusions with power ups, you shouldn't have a problem defeating Bakura. Your real challenge lies next, with Yugi!

Cards to Watch Out For
Man Eater

Type: Plant
Attribute: Earth
Attack: 800
Defense: 600
Effect: When this card is flipped face-up, all card located on Forest terrain are destroyed!

Anti-Magic Fragrance

Type: Power-up
Deck Cost: 40
Effect: Plant monsters automatically destroy spell-caster monsters in battle! The opposing enemy's attack effects are rendered ineffective.

Dark Plant

Type: Plant
Attribute: Dark
Attack: 300
Defense: 400
Effect: When this card is destroyed in battle, all adjacent spaces are transformed into Crush terrain!

Creature Stats: Bakura

- Main Race: Plant, Beast
- Average Creature Attack: 873
- Average Creature Defense: 819

Sample Card List: Bakura

NAME	ATK/DEF	TYPE
Abyss Flower	750/400	Plant
Air Marmot of Nefariousness	400/600	Beast/Effect
Anti-Magic Fragrance	—	Power-up
Arlownay	800/1,000	Plant/Effect
Barrel Lily	1,100/600	Plant
Beast Fangs	—	Power-up
Dark Plant	300/400	Plant/Effect
Darkworld Thorns	1,200/900	Plant
Firegrass	700/600	Plant
Gate Deeg	700/800	Beast/Effect
Green Phantom King	500/1,600	Plant/Effect
Griggle	350/300	Plant
Laughing Flower	900/500	Plant/Effect
Leogun	1,750/1,550	Beast
Living Vase	900/1,100	Plant
Man Eater	800/600	Plant/Effect
Mushroom Man	800/600	Plant/Effect
Mystical Sheep #1	1,150/900	Beast
Nekogal #1	1,100/900	Beast
Queen of Autumn Leaves	1,800/1,500	Plant
Rain of Mercy	—	Magic
Rainbow Flower	400/500	Plant
Tentacle Plant	500/600	Plant
The Wicked Worm Beast	1,400/1,100	Beast
Vile Germs	—	Power-up
War-Lion Ritual	—	Ritual
Wilmee	1,000/1,200	Beast
Yashinoki	800/600	Plant/Effect

Yugi

Vital Stats

- Name: Yugi
- Location: Brest
- Deck Cost: 1,206
- Deck Leader: Dark Magician
- Deck Leader Rank: Secretary of Defense
- Leader Abilities: Extended Support Range, Increased Strength for Same Type Friendlies, Weaken Specific Enemy Type
- Primary Terrain: None

Brest

LEGEND	
C	Crush
D	Dark
F	Forest
L	Labyrinth
M	Meadow
N	Normal
O	Toon
S	Sea
T	Mountain
W	Wasteland

The final Red Rose Card is within your reach, held firmly in Yugi's hand. Now it's time for you to prove your mettle against the best Red Rose Duelist. He might not be as hard as Jasper Dice Tudor was, but Yugi presents a formidable challenge anyway.

His terrain is shockingly strange, a mishmash of all terrain types. Colorful Toon squares sit next to Normal terrain and Crush spaces. Mountains stand alongside Wastelands. Forget about terrain advantages and disadvantages. Just watch out for the Crush squares; they can get lost in the confusion.

> ### NOTE
>
> *Leader Abilities boost the strength of any of his spellcaster monsters within a 5x5 area surrounding him.*

Yugi has a strong all-around deck, but of course you can count on him using his Dark Magician. In fact, there are several Spellcasters in his deck. When he combines Dark Magician with Dark Magician Girl, along with his power ups, he can be a tough adversary to beat.

Among his other worthy monsters are Gaia the Fierce Knight, who can combine with Curse of Dragon to become Gaia the Dragon Champion. His Magician of Faith is very useful, as it can revive any spell. It provides the same ability as the 60 DC Graverobber card for 48 points less!

Yugi also has some incredibly strong spells, including Swords of Revealing Light and Raigeki. Even deadlier are his traps, which he is very fond of using. His best, and one of the game's best cards, is Mirror Force, which can decimate your monsters instantly and leave you open to attack. He also uses Spellbinding Circle,

Shadow Spell, and others. Unfortunately, Magic Jammer does nothing to traps, but if you can get Ancient Tree of Enlightenment, you should be in good shape. Although you also deprive yourself of being able to use traps, the trade-off is well worth it.

This just puts the onus on pumping up your monsters to a strong enough level to successfully battle Yugi's monsters. Power-up Cards and Effects Monsters are key here.

Like Seto and Manawyddan fab Llyr, Yugi also can attempt a Destiny Draw if he's desperate enough, and he could draw a powerful card, such as another Mirror Force or Raigeki.

Use all the strategies that worked so well for you on the rest of your campaign journey. Traps to weaken his monsters work well, followed by attack from your powered-up monsters. Change the terrain to your advantage, and use direct damage spells to soften up his Deck Leader.

Cards to Watch Out For
Mirror Force

Type: Trap (Full Range)

Deck Cost: 99

Effect: Disposable trap that triggers when an enemy initiates an attack against your Leader or other cards on the Field! Destroys every one of your opponent's attack-positioned cards on the Field!

Gaia the Dragon Champion

Type: Warrior

Attribute: Wind

Attack: 2,600

Defense: 2,100

Effect: None!

Swords of Revealing Light

Type: Magic

Deck Cost: 80

Effect: Flips all enemy cards on the Field face-up and spellbinds them for three turns!

Creature Stats: Yugi

- **Main Race:** Spellcaster, Warrior, Dragon
- **Average Creature Attack:** 1,668
- **Average Creature Defense:** 1,468

Sample Card List: Yugi

NAME	ATK/DEF	TYPE
Black Luster Ritual	—	Ritual
Black Pendant	—	Power-up
Blackland Fire Dragon	1,500/1,200	Dragon
Book of Secret Arts	—	Power-up
Celtic Guardian	1,400/1,200	Warrior/Effect
Curse of Dragon	2,000/1,500	Dragon
Cursebreaker	—	Power-up
Dark Energy	—	Power-up
Dark Magic Ritual	—	Ritual
Dark Magician Girl	2,000/1,700	Spellcaster/Effect
Dimensionhole	—	Magic
Feral Imp	1,300/1,400	Fiend
Gaia the Fierce Knight	2,300/2,100	Warrior
Gemini Elf	1,900/900	Spellcaster
Giant Soldier of Stone	1,300/2,000	Rock
Koumori Dragon	1,500/1,200	Dragon
Magician of Faith	300/400	Spellcaster/Effect
Meteor Dragon	1,800/2,000	Dragon
Monster Reborn	—	Magic
Mystical Elf	800/2,000	Spellcaster/Effect
Mystical Sand	2,100/1,700	Rock
Negate Attack	—	Trap (Full Range)
Paralyzing Potion	—	Power-up
Raigeki	—	Magic
Silver Fang	1,200/800	Beast
Spellbinding Circle	—	Trap (Limited Range)
Summoned Skull	2,500/1,200	Fiend
Winged Dragon Guardian of the Fortress #1	1,400/1,200	Dragon

Manawyddan fab Llyr (version two)
Vital Stats

- **Name:** Manawyddan fab Llyr (version two)
- **Location:** Stonehenge
- **Deck Cost:** 1,891
- **Deck Leader:** Chakra
- **Deck Leader Rank:** SD
- **Leader Abilities:** Extended Support Range, Increased Strength for Same Type Friendlies, Weaken Specific Enemy Type
- **Primary Terrain:** Dark and Meadow

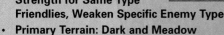

Stonehenge

LEGEND

D	**Dark**
F	**Forest**
L	**Labyrinth**
M	**Meadow**

After you defeat Yugi, things aren't over yet. Seto uses the Rose Cards to Summon what he believes will be a benevolent Card Guardian. But nothing could be further from the truth. Now, you must duel one last time to save yourself and the world.

As you enter the duel, you notice that the setup is similar to Seto's and the first Manawyddan's map. However, in the center of the arena is Dark terrain instead of Normal or Crush spaces.

Unlike his counterpart in the Yugi campaign, this Manawyddan concentrates on the best monsters in the game instead of the best spells. He still has a few nasty surprises, such as Riryoku, Dark Hole, and Magic Drain, but his strategy is to overwhelm you with behemoths such as Meteor B. Dragon, Blue-Eyes White Dragon, and Twin-Headed Thunder Dragon. And he can play them fast. He has Gate Deegs and Berfomets, monsters that give him maximum Summoning Points when flipped face-up.

NOTE

If you have a heavy Warrior deck, watch out for Manawyddan's Kinetic Soldier, which is ridiculously cheap (three Summoning Points) for its 2,350 ATK rating. Your main concern, though, is that it gets 2,000 bonus points against enemy warriors!

Manawyddan realizes that traps are a good way to beat him, so he usually plays his Royal Decree, which negates all enemy traps as long as it remains in play. Get rid of it quickly!

Manawyddan doesn't rely on the pure strength of his monsters. He loads them up with power ups as well, especially Riryoku. He has three of them! And if he uses them all in quick succession, that could mean a loss of 3,500 LP and a +2,000, +1,000, and +500 bonus to three already tough monsters!

Use Effects Monsters that kill the opposing monster when destroyed. Monsters such as Fiend's Hand and Blast Juggler work well. Second in effectiveness would be monsters that spellbind or weaken the enemy, such as Tongyo and Sectarian of Secrets. Use Cursebreaker to negate any power-up effects on Manawyddan's pumped-up monsters. Do anything you can to take away their strength or kill them outright.

Once you eliminate Royal Decree, things get more manageable. Traps, effects, and your own power ups added to your best monsters will save you. Use Magic Cards such as Tremendous Fire and Just Desserts. Good luck! If you defeat Manawyddan, then Seto will send you back home. While Yugi ultimately reclaims England, at least you have made an ally and a friend in Seto.

NOTE

Manawyddan weakens all enemy Spellcasters within two squares of him, lowering their attack and strength by 500 points. In contrast, all friendly Fiends have their attack and strength increased by 500. Seiyaryu is a good bet against them.

Cards to Watch Out For
Meteor B. Dragon

Type: Dragon
Attribute: Fire
Attack: 3,500
Defense: 2,000
Effect: None.

B. Skull Dragon

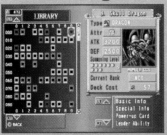

Type: Dragon
Attribute: Dark
Attack: 3,200
Defense: 2,500
Effect: None

Riryoku

Type: Power-up
Deck Cost: 99
Effect: Reduces opponent's LP by half and adds the reduced amount to the power of all monsters!

Creature Stats: Manawyddan fab Llyr

- Main Race: Dragon, Fiend
- Average Creature Attack: 2,270
- Average Creature Defense: 1,902

Sample Card List: Manawyddan fab Llyr

Name	ATK/DEF	Type
B. Skull Dragon	3,200/2,500	Dragon
Barrel Dragon	2,600/2,200	Machine/Effect
Berfomet	1,400/1,800	Fiend/Effect
Blue-Eyes White Dragon	3,000/2,500	Dragon
Dark Hole	—	Magic
Gaia the Fierce Knight	2,300/2,400	Warrior
Gate Deeg	700/800	Beast/Effect
Kazejin	2,400/2,200	Spellcaster/Effect
Kinetic Soldier	2,350/1,800	Machine/Effect
Labyrinth Tank	2,400/2,400	Machine/Effect
Magic Drain	—	Magic
Megamorph	—	Power-up
Meteor Dragon	1,800/2,000	Dragon
Red-Eyes B. Dragon	2,400/2,000	Dragon
Sanga of the Thunder	2,600/2,200	Thunder/Effect
Seiyaryu	2,500/2,300	Dragon/Effect
Skull Knight	2,650/2,250	Spellcaster
Suijin	2,500/2,400	Aqua/Effect
Summoned Skull	2,500/1,200	Fiend
Toon Summoned Skull	2,500/1,200	Fiend
Twin-Headed Thunder Dragon	2,800/2,100	Thunder

Complete Card List

30,000-YEAR WHITE TURTLE

Type: Aqua
Attr: Water
ATK: 1,250
DEF: 2,100
Level: 5
Deck Cost: 34
Number: 584
Effect: None

7 COLORED FISH

Type: Fish
Attr: Water
ATK: 1,800
DEF: 800
Level: 4
Deck Cost: 26
Number: 466
Effect: None

7 COMPLETED

Type: Power-up
Attr: —
ATK: —
DEF: —
Level: —
Deck Cost: 5
Number: 787
Effect: Increases the power of Slot Machine by 700 points

ABYSS FLOWER

Type: Plant
Attr: Earth
ATK: 750
DEF: 400
Level: 2
Deck Cost: 12
Number: 663
Effect: None

ACID CRAWLER

Type: Insect
Attr: Earth
ATK: 900
DEF: 700
Level: 3
Deck Cost: 16
Number: 426
Effect: Special Power-up: Transforms to Larva of Moth when strengthened with Cocoon of Evolution.

ACID TRAP HOLE

Type: Trap (Limited Range)
Attr: —
ATK: —
DEF: —
Level: —
Deck Cost: 30
Number: 811
Effect: Disposable trap that triggers against a monster with ATK of 4,000 or below and destroys it!

AIR EATER

Type: Fiend
Attr: Wind
ATK: 2,100
DEF: 1,600
Level: 6
Deck Cost: 38
Number: 367
Effect: None

AIR MARMOT OF NEFARIOUSNESS

Type: Beast
Attr: Earth
ATK: 400
DEF: 600
Level: 2
Deck Cost: 15
Number: 242
Effect: Able to move and attack without triggering an opponent's TRAP (LIMITED RANGE)!

AIRKNIGHT OF PARSHATH

Type: Fairy
Attr: Light
ATK: 1,900
DEF: 1,400
Level: 5
Deck Cost: 33
Number: 392
Effect: None

AKAKIEISU

Type: Spellcaster
Attr: Dark
ATK: 1,000
DEF: 800
Level: 3
Deck Cost: 18
Number: 68
Effect: None

AKIHIRON

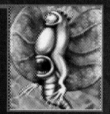

Type: Aqua
Attr: Water
ATK: 1,700
DEF: 1,400
Level: 5
Deck Cost: 31
Number: 555
Effect: None

ALINSECTION

Type: Insect
Attr: Earth
ATK: 950
DEF: 700
Level: 3
Deck Cost: 17
Number: 412
Effect: None

AMAZON OF THE SEAS

Type: Fish
Attr: Water
ATK: 1,300
DEF: 1,400
Level: 4
Deck Cost: 27
Number: 475
Effect: None

AMEBA

Type: Aqua
Attr: Water
ATK: 300
DEF: 350
Level: 1
Deck Cost: 12
Number: 589
Effect: Transforms all adjacent squares into Sea spaces when destroyed in battle!

AMPHIBIOUS BUGROTH

Type: Aqua
Attr: Water
ATK: 1,850
DEF: 1,300
Level: 5
Deck Cost: 32
Number: 607
Effect: None

ANCIENT BRAIN

Type: Fiend
Attr: Dark
ATK: 1,000
DEF: 700
Level: 3
Deck Cost: 17
Number: 318
Effect: None

ANCIENT ELF

Type: Spellcaster
Attr: Light
ATK: 1,450
DEF: 1,200
Level: 4
Deck Cost: 27
Number: 44
Effect: None

ANCIENT JAR

Type: Rock
Attr: Earth
ATK: 400
DEF: 200
Level: 1
Deck Cost: 11
Number: 627
Effect: The turn count for spellbound cards is not conducted while the card is in the face-up, defense position!

ANCIENT LIZARD WARRIOR

Type: Reptile
Attr: Earth
ATK: 1,400
DEF: 1,100
Level: 4
Deck Cost: 25
Number: 451
Effect: None

ANCIENT ONE OF THE DEEP FOREST

Type: Beast
Attr: Earth
ATK: 1,800
DEF: 1,900
Level: 6
Deck Cost: 37
Number: 258
Effect: None

ANCIENT SORCERER

Type: Spellcaster
Attr: Dark
ATK: 1,000
DEF: 1,300
Level: 4
Deck Cost: 23
Number: 71
Effect: None

ANCIENT TOOL

Type: Machine
Attr: Dark
ATK: 1,700
DEF: 1,400
Level: 5
Deck Cost: 31
Number: 482
Effect: None

ANCIENT TREE OF ENLIGHTENMENT

Type: Plant
Attr: Earth
ATK: 600
DEF: 1,500
Level: 3
Deck Cost: 26
Number: 655
Effect: While this card is face-up in the defense position, TRAP cards cannot be triggered!

ANSATSU

Type: Warrior
Attr: Earth
ATK: 1,700
DEF: 1,200
Level: 5
Deck Cost: 29
Number: 165
Effect: None

ANTHROSAURUS

Type: Dinosaur
Attr: Earth
ATK: 1,000
DEF: 850
Level: 3
Deck Cost: 19
Number: 442
Effect: None

ANTI RAIGEKI

Type: Trap
(Full Range)
Attr: —
ATK: —
DEF: —
Level: —
Deck Cost: 5
Number: 821
Effect: Permanent trap that triggers when Raigeki is activated, and nullifies the card's effect!

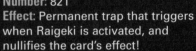

ANTI-MAGIC FRAGRANCE

Type: Power-up
Attr: —
ATK: —
DEF: —
Level: —
Deck Cost: 40
Number: 793
Effect:
PLANT monsters automatically destroy SPELLCASTER monsters in battle! The opposing enemy's attack effects are rendered ineffective.

Aqua Chorus

Type: Magic
Attr: —
ATK: —
DEF: —
Level: —
Deck Cost: 10
Number: 742
Effect: Boosts the ATK/DEF of all WATER monsters on the Field by 600 points!

Aqua Dragon

Type: Sea Serpent
Attr: Water
ATK: 2,250
DEF: 1,900
Level: 6
Deck Cost: 47
Number: 478
Effect: Space occupied is transformed to Sea terrain when engaged in battle!

Aqua Madoor

Type: Spellcaster
Attr: Water
ATK: 1,200
DEF: 2,000
Level: 4
Deck Cost: 32
Number: 100
Effect: None

Aqua Snake

Type: Aqua
Attr: Water
ATK: 1,050
DEF: 900
Level: 3
Deck Cost: 25
Number: 582
Effect: Spellbinds the opposing enemy for 1 turn when this card is flipped face-up in battle!

Arlwonay

Type: Plant
Attr: Earth
ATK: 800
DEF: 1,000
Level: 3
Deck Cost: 18
Number: 653
Effect: None

Arma Knight

Type: Aqua
Attr: Water
ATK: 1,000
DEF: 1,200
Level: 4
Deck Cost: 22
Number: 559
Effect: None

Armaill

Type: Warrior
Attr: Earth
ATK: 700
DEF: 1,300
Level: 3
Deck Cost: 20
Number: 174
Effect: None

Armed Ninja

Type: Warrior
Attr: Earth
ATK: 300
DEF: 300
Level: 1
Deck Cost: 11
Number: 193
Effect: Able to move or attack without triggering an opponent's TRAP (LIMITED RANGE)!

Armored Lizard

Type: Reptile
Attr: Earth
ATK: 1,500
DEF: 1,200
Level: 4
Deck Cost: 27
Number: 446
Effect: None

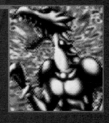

Armored Rat

Type: Beast
Attr: Earth
ATK: 950
DEF: 1,100
Level: 3
Deck Cost: 21
Number: 263
Effect: None

Armored Starfish

Type: Aqua
Attr: Water
ATK: 850
DEF: 1,400
Level: 4
Deck Cost: 23
Number: 603
Effect: None

Armored Zombie

Type: Zombie
Attr: Dark
ATK: 1,500
DEF: 0
Level: 3
Deck Cost: 15
Number: 105
Effect: None

Arsenal Bug

Type: Insect
Attr: Earth
ATK: 2,000
DEF: 2,000
Level: 3
Deck Cost: 50
Number: 429
Effect: ATTACK: All spaces within an area of 2 spaces are transformed into FOREST terrain!
FLIP: If an INSECT monster is Leader, this card's power is strengthened by 1,500 points when this card is flipped face-up!

AXE OF DESPAIR

Type: Power-up
Attr: —
ATK: —
DEF: —
Level: —
Deck Cost: 10
Number: 755
Effect: Increases the power of BEAST-WARRIOR and FIEND monsters by 500 points!

AXE RAIDER

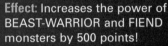

Type: Warrior
Attr: Earth
ATK: 1,700
DEF: 1,150
Level: 4
Deck Cost: 29
Number: 159
Effect: None

B. DRAGON JUNGLE KING

Type: Dragon
Attr: Earth
ATK: 2,100
DEF: 1,800
Level: 6
Deck Cost: 39
Number: 20
Effect: None

B. SKULL DRAGON

Type: Dragon
Attr: Dark
ATK: 3,200
DEF: 2,500
Level: 9
Deck Cost: 57
Number: 9
Effect: None

BABY DRAGON

Type: Dragon
Attr: Wind
ATK: 1,200
DEF: 700
Level: 3
Deck Cost: 19
Number: 21
Effect: None

BAD REACTION TO SIMOCHI

Type: Trap
(Full Range)
Attr: —
ATK: —
DEF: —
Level: —
Deck Cost: 25
Number: 815
Effect: Permanent trap that triggers against LP recovery and reduces an opponent's LP by the same amount!

BARON OF THE FIEND SWORD

Type: Fiend
Attr: Dark
ATK: 1,550
DEF: 800
Level: 4
Deck Cost: 24
Number: 360
Effect: None

BAROX

Type: Fiend
Attr: Dark
ATK: 1,380
DEF: 1,530
Level: 5
Deck Cost: 30
Number: 301
Effect: None

BARREL DRAGON

Type: Machine
Attr: Dark
ATK: 2,600
DEF: 2,200
Level: 7
Deck Cost: 53
Number: 502
Effect: When this card is flipped face-up, 1 card other than own is randomly selected for destruction!

BARREL LILY

Type: Plant
Attr: Earth
ATK: 1,100
DEF: 600
Level: 3
Deck Cost: 17
Number: 658
Effect: None

BARREL ROCK

Type: Rock
Attr: Earth
ATK: 1,000
DEF: 1,300
Level: 4
Deck Cost: 28
Number: 635
Effect: Can enter LABYRINTH squares, and transform the occupied space to NORMAL terrain!

BASIC INSECT

Type: Insect
Attr: Earth
ATK: 500
DEF: 700
Level: 2
Deck Cost: 12
Number: 397
Effect: None

BAT

Type: Machine
Attr: Wind
ATK: 300
DEF: 350
Level: 1
Deck Cost: 12
Number: 530
Effect: When this card is flipped face-up, if there's a Jigen Bakudan in any adjacent square, teleport 1 Jigen Bakudan to an opponent's Summoning Area.

BATTLE OX

Type: Beast-warrior
Attr: Earth
ATK: 1,700
DEF: 1,000
Level: 4
Deck Cost: 27
Number: 211
Effect: None

BATTLE STEER

Type: Beast-warrior
Attr: Earth
ATK: 1,800
DEF: 1,300
Level: 5
Deck Cost: 31
Number: 210
Effect: None

BATTLE WARRIOR

Type: Warrior
Attr: Earth
ATK: 700
DEF: 1,000
Level: 2
Deck Cost: 22
Number: 161
Effect: 500-point bonus when battling BEAST monsters!

BEAKED SNAKE

Type: Reptile
Attr: Earth
ATK: 800
DEF: 900
Level: 3
Deck Cost: 17
Number: 450
Effect: None

BEAN SOLDIER

Type: Plant
Attr: Earth
ATK: 1,400
DEF: 1,300
Level: 4
Deck Cost: 27
Number: 660
Effect: None

BEAR TRAP

Type: Trap
(Limited Range)
Attr: —
ATK: —
DEF: —
Level: —
Deck Cost: 10
Number: 809
Effect: Disposable trap that triggers against a monster with ATK of 2,000 or below, and destroys it.

BEAST FANGS

Type: Power-up
Attr: —
ATK: —
DEF: —
Level: —
Deck Cost: 10
Number: 759
Effect: Increases the power of BEAST monsters by 500 points!

BEASTKING OF THE SWAMP

Type: Aqua
Attr: Water
ATK: 1,000
DEF: 1,100
Level: 4
Deck Cost: 26
Number: 567
Effect: When destroyed, destroys the enemy engaged in battle with!

BEASTLY MIRROR RITUAL

Type: Ritual
Attr: —
ATK: —
DEF: —
Level: —
Deck Cost: 5
Number: 836
Effect: Sacrifice 1 FIEND monster with Wicked Mirror and Fiend Reflection #1 to summon Fiend's Mirror!

BEAUTIFUL BEAST TRAINER

Type: Warrior
Attr: Earth
ATK: 1,750
DEF: 1,500
Level: 5
Deck Cost: 38
Number: 192
Effect: When this card is flipped face-up, all BEAST monsters are increased 300 points!

BEAUTIFUL HEADHUNTRESS

Type: Warrior
Attr: Earth
ATK: 1,600
DEF: 800
Level: 4
Deck Cost: 24
Number: 180
Effect: None

BEAVER WARRIOR

Type: Beast-warrior
Attr: Earth
ATK: 1,200
DEF: 1,500
Level: 4
Deck Cost: 27
Number: 212
Effect: None

BEHEGON

Type: Aqua
Attr: Water
ATK: 1,350
DEF: 1,000
Level: 4
Deck Cost: 24
Number: 595
Effect: None

BERFOMET

Type: Fiend
Attr: Dark
ATK: 1,400
DEF: 1,800
Level: 5
Deck Cost: 37
Number: 364
Effect: Increases Summoning Power points to maximum level when this card is flipped face-up!

BICKURIBOX

Type: Fiend
Attr: Dark
ATK: 2,300
DEF: 2,000
Level: 7
Deck Cost: 43
Number: 341
Effect: Strong in TOON terrain!

BIG EYE

Type: Fiend
Attr: Dark
ATK: 1,200
DEF: 1,000
Level: 4
Deck Cost: 27
Number: 316
Effect: When destroyed in battle, the engaged enemy is spellbound for 1 turn!

BIG INSECT

Type: Insect
Attr: Earth
ATK: 1,200
DEF: 1,500
Level: 4
Deck Cost: 27
Number: 396
Effect: None

BINDING CHAIN

Type: Fairy
Attr: Light
ATK: 1,000
DEF: 1,100
Level: 3
Deck Cost: 26
Number: 386
Effect: While this card is face-up in the defense position, all WARRIOR monsters are spellbound!

BIO PLANT

Type: Fiend
Attr: Dark
ATK: 600
DEF: 1,300
Level: 3
Deck Cost: 19
Number: 336
Effect: None

BIRDFACE

Type: Winged Beast
Attr: Wind
ATK: 1,600
DEF: 1,600
Level: 5
Deck Cost: 37
Number: 291
Effect: While this card is face-up in the defense position, all WINGED BEAST monsters are awarded a power-up bonus of 300 points!

BLACK LUSTER RITUAL

Type: Ritual
Attr: —
ATK: —
DEF: —
Level: —
Deck Cost: 5
Number: 833
Effect: Sacrifice 2 monsters with ATKs of 1,500 or lower with Gaia the Fierce Knight to summon Black Luster Soldier

BLACK LUSTER SOLDIER

Type: Warrior/Ritual
Attr: Dark
ATK: 3,000
DEF: 2,500
Level: 8
Deck Cost: 60
Number: 143
Effect: 600-point bonus when battling DRAGON monsters!

BLACK PENDANT

Type: Power-up
Attr: —
ATK: —
DEF: —
Level: —
Deck Cost: 10
Number: 762
Effect: Increases the power of SPELLCASTER monsters of DARK by 500 points!

BLACKLAND FIRE DRAGON

Type: Dragon
Attr: Dark
ATK: 1,500
DEF: 1,200
Level: 4
Deck Cost: 23
Number: 4
Effect: None

BLADEFLY

Type: Insect
Attr: Wind
ATK: 600
DEF: 700
Level: 2
Deck Cost: 18
Number: 432
Effect: While this card is face-up in the defense position, all Wind monsters gain a 500-point power-up bonus.

BLAST JUGGLER

Type: Machine
Attr: Fire
ATK: 800
DEF: 900
Level: 3
Deck Cost: 22
Number: 509
Effect: All cards located in the surrounding 3x3 area are automatically destroyed when this card is destroyed in battle!

BLAST SPHERE

Type: Machine
Attr: Dark
ATK: 1,400
DEF: 1,400
Level: 4
Deck Cost: 33
Number: 506
Effect: All cards located in the surrounding 3x3 area are automatically destroyed when this card is destroyed in battle!

BLOCK ATTACK

Type: Trap
(Full Range)
Attr: —
ATK: —
DEF: —
Level: —
Deck Cost: 25
Number: 817
Effect: Disposable trap that triggers when an enemy card completes its move in the attack position. Cancels the card's action and ends further movement.

BLOCKER

Type: Machine
Attr: Dark
ATK: 850
DEF: 1,800
Level: 4
Deck Cost: 32
Number: 493
Effect: Whenever damage is inflicted to LP in battle, the damage amount is reduced to 0!

BLUE-EYED SILVER ZOMBIE

Type: Zombie
Attr: Dark
ATK: 900
DEF: 700
Level: 3
Deck Cost: 21
Number: 112
Effect: When this card is flipped face-up, all your monsters are transformed into ZOMBIE monsters!

BLUE-EYES ULTIMATE DRAGON

Type: Dragon/Ritual
Attr: Light
ATK: 4,500
DEF: 3,800
Level: 12
Deck Cost: 83
Number: 2
Effect: None

BLUE-EYES WHITE DRAGON

Type: Dragon
Attr: Light
ATK: 3,000
DEF: 2,500
Level: 8
Deck Cost: 55
Number: 0
Effect: None

BLUE-WINGED CROWN

Type: Winged Beast
Attr: Wind
ATK: 1,600
DEF: 1,200
Level: 4
Deck Cost: 28
Number: 290
Effect: None

BOLT ESCARGOT

Type: Thunder
Attr: Water
ATK: 1,400
DEF: 1,500
Level: 5
Deck Cost: 29
Number: 546
Effect: None

BOLT PENGUIN

Type: Thunder
Attr: Water
ATK: 1,100
DEF: 800
Level: 3
Deck Cost: 19
Number: 547
Effect: None

BONE MOUSE

Type: Zombie
Attr: Dark
ATK: 400
DEF: 300
Level: 1
Deck Cost: 12
Number: 127
Effect: Able to move and attack without triggering an opponent's TRAP (LIMITED RANGE)!

BOO KOO

Type: Spellcaster
Attr: Dark
ATK: 650
DEF: 500
Level: 2
Deck Cost: 17
Number: 74
Effect: When this card is flipped face-up, strengthens the Spirit of the Books by 700 points!

BOOK OF SECRET ARTS

Type: Power-up
Attr: —
ATK: —
DEF: —
Level: —
Deck Cost: 10
Number: 771
Effect: Increases the power of SPELLCASTER monsters other than DARK by 500 points!

BOTTOM DWELLER

Type: Fish
Attr: Water
ATK: 1,650
DEF: 1,700
Level: 5
Deck Cost: 34
Number: 465
Effect: None

BOULDER TORTOISE

Type: Aqua
Attr: Earth
ATK: 1,450
DEF: 2,200
Level: 6
Deck Cost: 37
Number: 549
Effect: None

BRACCHIO-RAIDUS

Type: Dinosaur
Attr: Aqua
ATK: 2,200
DEF: 2,000
Level: 6
Deck Cost: 42
Number: 445
Effect: None

BRAIN CONTROL

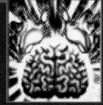

Type: Magic
Attr: —
ATK: —
DEF: —
Level: —
Deck Cost: 80
Number: 733
Effect: Take control of opponent's highest ATK monster for one turn!

BRAVE SCIZZAR

Type: Machine
Attr: Dark
ATK: 1,300
DEF: 1,000
Level: 4
Deck Cost: 23
Number: 499
Effect: None

BREATH OF LIGHT

Type: Magic
Attr: —
ATK: —
DEF: —
Level: —
Deck Cost: 50
Number: 724
Effect: Destroys all ROCK monsters on the Field

BRIGHT CASTLE

Type: Power-up
Attr: —
ATK: —
DEF: —
Level: —
Deck Cost: 10
Number: 781
Effect: Increases the power of LIGHT monsters by 500 points!

BURGLAR

Type: Beast
Attr: Earth
ATK: 850
DEF: 800
Level: 3
Deck Cost: 17
Number: 251
Effect: None

BURNING LAND

Type: Magic
Attr: —
ATK: —
DEF: —
Level: —
Deck Cost: 30
Number: 696
Effect: Transform a surrounding 2-space area into NORMAL terrain!

BURNING SPEAR

Type: Power-up
Attr: —
ATK: —
DEF: —
Level: —
Deck Cost: 10
Number: 786
Effect: Increases the power of PYRO monsters by 500 points!

CALL OF THE GRAVE

Type: Trap
(Full Range)
Attr: —
ATK: —
DEF: —
Level: —
Deck Cost: 5
Number: 822
Effect: Permanent trap that triggers when a card is resurrected from the Graveyard and cancels the card's effect!

CALL OF THE HAUNTED

Type: Magic
Attr: —
ATK: —
DEF: —
Level: —
Deck Cost: 1
Number: 745
Effect: All your monsters on the Field are transformed to ZOMBIE monsters!

CANDLE OF FATE

Type: Fiend
Attr: Dark
ATK: 600
DEF: 600
Level: 2
Deck Cost: 17
Number: 326
Effect: While this card is face-up in the defense position, all opponent monsters are reduced by 100 points each turn!

CANNON SOLDIER

Type: Machine
Attr: Dark
ATK: 1,400
DEF: 1,300
Level: 4
Deck Cost: 32
Number: 498
Effect: Can enter LABYRINTH squares, and transform the occupied space to a NORMAL terrain!

CARAT IDOL

Type: Immortal
Attr: Light
ATK: 2,600
DEF: 3,100
Level: 9
Deck Cost: 72
Number: 676
Effect: NATURE EFFECT: When this card enters a turn face-up and in the defense position, all cards are drawn 1 space toward CARAT IDOL! DESTRUCTION: Transforms adjacent spaces into CRUSH terrain when this card is destroyed in battle!

CASTLE OF DARK ILLUSIONS

Type: Fiend
Attr: Dark
ATK: 920
DEF: 1,930
Level: 4
Deck Cost: 34
Number: 298
Effect: While this card is face-up in the defense position, all FIEND monsters are awarded a power-up bonus of 500 points.

CATAPULT TURTLE

Type: Aqua
Attr: Water
ATK: 1,000
DEF: 2,000
Level: 5
Deck Cost: 35
Number: 552
Effect: Can enter LABYRINTH squares, and transform the occupied space to a NORMAL terrain!

CELTIC GUARDIAN

Type: Warrior
Attr: Earth
ATK: 1,400
DEF: 1,200
Level: 4
Deck Cost: 31
Number: 156
Effect: While this card is face-up in the defense position, all effects involving the taking of a card's control are rendered ineffective!

CHAKRA

Type: Fiend/Ritual
Attr: Dark
ATK: 2,450
DEF: 2,000
Level: 7
Deck Cost: 50
Number: 352
Effect: Revives in own Summoning Area, other than current location, when destroyed in battle!

CHANGE OF HEART

Type: Magic
Attr: —
ATK: —
DEF: —
Level: —
Deck Cost: 80
Number: 732
Effect: Select one of the opponent's cards on the Field and control it for 1 turn!

CHANGE SLIME

Type: Aqua
Attr: Water
ATK: 400
DEF: 300
Level: 1
Deck Cost: 12
Number: 570
Effect: Adopts opposing monster's ATK/DEF when this card is flipped face-up in battle!

CHARUBIN THE FIRE KNIGHT

Type: Pyro
Attr: Fire
ATK: 1,100
DEF: 800
Level: 3
Deck Cost: 19
Number: 615
Effect: None

CHIMERA THE FLYING MYTHICAL BEAST

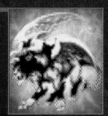

Type: Beast
Attr: Wind
ATK: 2,100
DEF: 1,800
Level: 6
Deck Cost: 39
Number: 267
Effect: None

CLAW REACHER

Type: Fiend
Attr: Dark
ATK: 1,000
DEF: 800
Level: 3
Deck Cost: 18
Number: 319
Effect: None

CLOWN ZOMBIE

Type: Zombie
Attr: Dark
ATK: 1,350
DEF: 0
Level: 2
Deck Cost: 14
Number: 107
Effect: None

COCKROACH KNIGHT

Type: Insect
Attr: Earth
ATK: 800
DEF: 900
Level: 3
Deck Cost: 17
Number: 413
Effect: None

COCOON OF EVOLUTION

Type: Power-up
Attr: —
ATK: —
DEF: —
Level: —
Deck Cost: 5
Number: 798
Effect: Changes Larvae Moth, Petit Moth, Kattapillar, Needle Worm, and Acid Crawler to Larva of Moth

COLD WAVE

Type: Magic
Attr: —
ATK: —
DEF: —
Level: —
Deck Cost: 50
Number: 730
Effect: Destroys all DINOSAUR monsters on the Field!

COMMENCEMENT DANCE

Type: Ritual
Attr: —
ATK: —
DEF: —
Level: —
Deck Cost: 5
Number: 838
Effect: Sacrifice 1 WINGED BEAST monster and 1 WARRIOR monster with Water Omotics to summon Performance of Sword!

CONSTRUCT OF MASK
Type: Ritual
Attr: —
ATK: —
DEF: —
Level: —
Deck Cost: 5
Number: 845
Effect: Sacrifice 2 SPELLCASTER monsters with Mask of Darkness to summon Mask of Shine & Dark!

COPYCAT

Type: Magic
Attr: —
ATK: —
DEF: —
Level: —
Deck Cost: 50
Number: 686
Effect: Select, revive, and control 1 SPELL Card from an opponent's Graveyard!

CORRODING SHARK
Type: Zombie
Attr: Dark
ATK: 1,100
DEF: 700
Level: 3
Deck Cost: 18
Number: 125
Effect: None

COSMO QUEEN
Type: Spellcaster/Ritual
Attr: Dark
ATK: 2,900
DEF: 2,450
Level: 8
Deck Cost: 59
Number: 76
Effect: When this card is flipped face-up, transforms the surrounding spaces within a range of two to DARK terrain!

COSMO QUEEN'S PRAYER
Type: Ritual
Attr: —
ATK: —
DEF: —
Level: —
Deck Cost: 5
Number: 850
Effect: Sacrifice Queen of Autumn Leaves, Princess of Tsurugi, and Dark Elf to summon Cosmo Queen!

CRAB TURTLE
Type: Aqua/Ritual
Attr: Water
ATK: 2,550
DEF: 2,500
Level: 8
Deck Cost: 51
Number: 596
Effect: None

CRASS CLOWN
Type: Fiend
Attr: Dark
ATK: 1,350
DEF: 1,400
Level: 4
Deck Cost: 28
Number: 304
Effect: None

CRAWLING DRAGON
Type: Dragon
Attr: Earth
ATK: 1,600
DEF: 1,400
Level: 5
Deck Cost: 30
Number: 18
Effect: None

CRAWLING DRAGON #2
Type: Dinosaur
Attr: Earth
ATK: 1,600
DEF: 1,200
Level: 4
Deck Cost: 28
Number: 438
Effect: None

CRAZY FISH

Type: Fish
Attr: Water
ATK: 1,600
DEF: 1,200
Level: 4
Deck Cost: 28
Number: 468
Effect: None

CREATURE SWAP

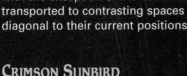

Type: Magic
Attr: —
ATK: —
DEF: —
Level: —
Deck Cost: 75
Number: 751
Effect: All cards in play on the Field with the exception of the Leaders are transported to contrasting spaces diagonal to their current positions!

CRIMSON SUNBIRD

Type: Winged Beast
Attr: Fire
ATK: 2,300
DEF: 1,800
Level: 6
Deck Cost: 41
Number: 269
Effect: None

CROW GOBLIN

Type: Winged Beast
Attr: Wind
ATK: 1,850
DEF: 1,600
Level: 5
Deck Cost: 35
Number: 287
Effect: None

CRUSH CARD

Type: Power-up
Attr: —
ATK: —
DEF: —
Level: —
Deck Cost: 80
Number: 794
Effect: Strengthens all monsters with ATK of 1,000 or below. When defeated in battle, the adjacent spaces are transformed into CRUSH terrain! The opposing enemy's destruction effects are rendered ineffective.

CURSE OF DRAGON

Type: Dragon
Attr: Dark
ATK: 2,000
DEF: 1,500
Level: 5
Deck Cost: 40
Number: 6
Effect: Transforms the occupied space to WASTELAND terrain when engaging in battle!

CURSE OF MILLENNIUM SHIELD

Type: Ritual
Attr: —
ATK: —
DEF: —
Level: —
Deck Cost: 5
Number: 830
Effect: Sacrifice 3 monsters with DEF factors of 2,000 or higher to summon Millennium Shield!

CURSE OF TRI-HORNED DRAGON

Type: Ritual
Attr: —
ATK: —
DEF: —
Level: —
Deck Cost: 5
Number: 842
Effect: Sacrifice Curse of Dragon, Feral Imp, and Koumori Dragon to summon Tri-Horned Dragon!

CURSEBREAKER

Type: Power-up
Attr: —
ATK: —
DEF: —
Level: —
Deck Cost: 1
Number: 796
Effect: Cancels all spellbind and power increase/decrease effects. Does not cancel any bonus effects involving terrain and leader abilities.

CURTAIN OF THE DARK ONES

Type: Spellcaster
Attr: Dark
ATK: 600
DEF: 500
Level: 2
Deck Cost: 16
Number: 62
Effect: When this card is flipped face-up in battle, the opposing enemy is spellbound for 1 turn!

CYBER COMMANDER

Type: Machine
Attr: Dark
ATK: 750
DEF: 700
Level: 2
Deck Cost: 20
Number: 496
Effect: While this card is face-up in the defense position, the strength of all your MACHINE monsters are increases by 300 bonus points!

CYBER SAURUS

Type: Machine
Attr: Earth
ATK: 1,800
DEF: 1,400
Level: 5
Deck Cost: 32
Number: 521
Effect: None

CYBER SHIELD

Type: Power-up
Attr: —
ATK: —
DEF: —
Level: —
Deck Cost: 10
Number: 768
Effect: Increases the power of female monsters by 500 points!

CYBER SOLDIER

Type: Machine
Attr: Dark
ATK: 1,500
DEF: 1,700
Level: 5
Deck Cost: 32
Number: 491
Effect: None

CYBER SOLDIER OF DARKWORLD

Type: Machine
Attr: Dark
ATK: 1,400
DEF: 1,200
Level: 4
Deck Cost: 26
Number: 484
Effect: None

CYBER-STEIN

Type: Machine
Attr: Dark
ATK: 700
DEF: 500
Level: 2
Deck Cost: 17
Number: 495
Effect: Transforms occupied space into WASTELAND when engaged in battle!

D. HUMAN

Type: Warrior
Attr: Earth
ATK: 1,300
DEF: 1,100
Level: 4
Deck Cost: 24
Number: 194
Effect: None

DANCING ELF

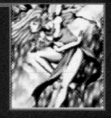

Type: Fairy
Attr: Wind
ATK: 300
DEF: 200
Level: 1
Deck Cost: 5
Number: 394
Effect: None

DARK ARTIST

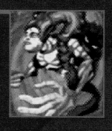

Type: Fiend
Attr: Dark
ATK: 600
DEF: 1,400
Level: 3
Deck Cost: 20
Number: 335
Effect: None

DARK ASSAILANT

Type: Zombie
Attr: Dark
ATK: 1,200
DEF: 1,200
Level: 4
Deck Cost: 24
Number: 120
Effect: None

DARK CHIMERA

Type: Fiend
Attr: Dark
ATK: 1,610
DEF: 1,460
Level: 5
Deck Cost: 31
Number: 302
Effect: None

DARK ELF

Type: Spellcaster
Attr: Dark
ATK: 2,000
DEF: 800
Level: 4
Deck Cost: 33
Number: 79
Effect: For every battle engaged with the enemy, the LP of the player controlling Dark Elf is reduced by 50 points!

DARK ENERGY

Type: Power-up
Attr: —
ATK: —
DEF: —
Level: —
Deck Cost: 10
Number: 754
Effect: Increases the power of DARK monsters by 300 points!

DARK GRAY

Type: Beast
Attr: Earth
ATK: 800
DEF: 900
Level: 3
Deck Cost: 17
Number: 234
Effect: None

DARK HOLE

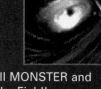

Type: Magic
Attr: —
ATK: —
DEF: —
Level: —
Deck Cost: 50
Number: 699
Effect: Destroys all MONSTER and SPELL Cards on the Field!

DARK KING OF THE ABYSS

Type: Fiend
Attr: Dark
ATK: 1,200
DEF: 800
Level: 3
Deck Cost: 20
Number: 315
Effect: None

DARK MAGIC RITUAL

Type: Ritual
Attr: —
ATK: —
DEF: —
Level: —
Deck Cost: 5
Number: 853
Effect: Sacrifice 2 monsters with ATKs of 1500 or less and Dark Magician to summon Magician of Black Chaos!

DARK MAGICIAN

Type: Spellcaster
Attr: Dark
ATK: 2,500
DEF: 2,100
Level: 7
Deck Cost: 46
Number: 60
Effect: None

Dark Magician Girl

Type: Spellcaster
Attr: Dark
ATK: 2,000
DEF: 1,700
Level: 6
Deck Cost: 42
Number: 87

Effect: When this card is flipped face-up, it is increased by 500 points for every Dark Magician and Dark Magician Girl found in all Graveyards!

Dark Plant

Type: Plant
Attr: Dark
ATK: 300
DEF: 400
Level: 1
Deck Cost: 12
Number: 647

Effect: When this card is destroyed in battle, all adjacent spaces are transformed into CRUSH terrain!

Dark Prisoner

Type: Fiend
Attr: Dark
ATK: 600
DEF: 1,000
Level: 3
Deck Cost: 21
Number: 317

Effect: Whenever damage is inflicted to LP in battle, the damage amount is reduced to 0!

Dark Rabbit

Type: Beast
Attr: Dark
ATK: 1,100
DEF: 1,500
Level: 4
Deck Cost: 26
Number: 225

Effect: Strong in TOON terrain!

Dark Shade

Type: Fiend
Attr: Wind
ATK: 1,000
DEF: 1,000
Level: 3
Deck Cost: 20
Number: 366
Effect: None

Dark Titan of Terror

Type: Fiend
Attr: Dark
ATK: 1,300
DEF: 1,100
Level: 4
Deck Cost: 25
Number: 324
Effect: None

Dark Witch

Type: Fairy
Attr: Light
ATK: 1,800
DEF: 1,700
Level: 5
Deck Cost: 35
Number: 385
Effect: None

Darkfire Dragon

Type: Dragon
Attr: Dark
ATK: 1,500
DEF: 1,250
Level: 4
Deck Cost: 28
Number: 8
Effect: None

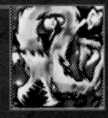

Darkness Approaches

Type: Magic
Attr: —
ATK: —
DEF: —
Level: —
Deck Cost: 20
Number: 717

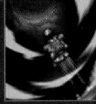

Effect: Flips all cards on the Field face-down!

Dark-Piercing Light

Type: Magic
Attr: —
ATK: —
DEF: —
Level: —
Deck Cost: 15
Number: 716

Effect: Flips all enemy cards on the Field face-up!

Darkworld Thorns

Type: Plant
Attr: Earth
ATK: 1,200
DEF: 900
Level: 3
Deck Cost: 21
Number: 662
Effect: None

Deepsea Shark

Type: Fish
Attr: Water
ATK: 1,900
DEF: 1,600
Level: 5
Deck Cost: 35
Number: 464
Effect: None

Destroyer Golem

Type: Rock
Attr: Earth
ATK: 1,500
DEF: 1,000
Level: 4
Deck Cost: 25
Number: 634
Effect: None

Prima's Official Strategy Guide

DHARMA CANNON

Type: Machine
Attr: Dark
ATK: 900
DEF: 500
Level: 2
Deck Cost: 19
Number: 500
Effect: Can enter LABYRINTH squares, and transform the occupied space to a NORMAL terrain!

DIAN KETO THE CURE MASTER

Type: Magic
Attr: —
ATK: —
DEF: —
Level: —
Deck Cost: 60
Number: 707
Effect: If LP is 4,000 or below, the number of points is increased to 4,000!

DICE ARMADILLO

Type: Machine
Attr: Earth
ATK: 1,650
DEF: 1,800
Level: 5
Deck Cost: 35
Number: 520
Effect: None

DIG BEAK

Type: Beast
Attr: Earth
ATK: 500
DEF: 800
Level: 2
Deck Cost: 13
Number: 237
Effect: None

DIMENSIONAL WARRIOR

Type: Warrior
Attr: Earth
ATK: 1,200
DEF: 1,000
Level: 4
Deck Cost: 27
Number: 183
Effect: Monsters destroyed in battles against Dimensional Warrior cannot be revived once they are sent to the Graveyard!

DIMENSIONHOLE

Type: Magic
Attr: —
ATK: —
DEF: —
Level: —
Deck Cost: 20
Number: 749
Effect: Transports your Leader to the space where this card is activated!

DISK MAGICIAN

Type: Machine
Attr: Dark
ATK: 1,350
DEF: 1,000
Level: 4
Deck Cost: 24
Number: 504
Effect: None

DISSOLVEROCK

Type: Rock
Attr: Earth
ATK: 900
DEF: 1,000
Level: 3
Deck Cost: 24
Number: 629
Effect: When this card is flipped face-up, all cards located in MOUNTAIN terrain are destroyed!

DJINN THE WATCHER OF THE WIND

Type: Spellcaster
Attr: Wind
ATK: 700
DEF: 900
Level: 3
Deck Cost: 16
Number: 97
Effect: None

DOKUROIZO THE GRIM REAPER

Type: Zombie
Attr: Dark
ATK: 900
DEF: 1,200
Level: 3
Deck Cost: 26
Number: 114
Effect: Able to move and attack without triggering an opponent's TRAP (LIMITED RANGE)!

DOKURORIDER

Type: Zombie/Ritual
Attr: Dark
ATK: 1,900
DEF: 1,850
Level: 6
Deck Cost: 43
Number: 128
Effect: During movement, transforms terrain of entered space into WASTELAND terrain!

DOMA THE ANGEL OF SILENCE

Type: Fairy
Attr: Dark
ATK: 1,600
DEF: 1,400
Level: 5
Deck Cost: 30
Number: 393
Effect: None

DORON

Type: Warrior
Attr: Earth
ATK: 900
DEF: 500
Level: 2
Deck Cost: 19
Number: 176
Effect: When this card is flipped face-up, adds another Doron face-up in own Summoning Area!

DOROVER

Type: Aqua
Attr: Water
ATK: 900
DEF: 800
Level: 3
Deck Cost: 22
Number: 561
Effect: When destroyed, spellbinds the enemy it engaged in battle for 1 turn!

DRAGON CAPTURE JAR

Type: Magic
Attr: —
ATK: —
DEF: —
Level: —
Deck Cost: 50
Number: 683
Effect: Permanently spellbinds all DRAGON monsters!

DRAGON PIPER

Type: Pyro
Attr: Fire
ATK: 200
DEF: 1,800
Level: 3
Deck Cost: 20
Number: 613
Effect: When this card is flipped face-up, all spellbound cards are freed and can move in the following turn!

DRAGON SEEKER

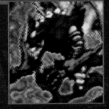

Type: Fiend
Attr: Dark
ATK: 2,000
DEF: 2,100
Level: 6
Deck Cost: 41
Number: 348
Effect: 500 bonus points added in battle against DRAGON monsters!

DRAGON STATUE

Type: Warrior
Attr: Earth
ATK: 1,100
DEF: 900
Level: 3
Deck Cost: 20
Number: 166
Effect: None

DRAGON TREASURE

Type: Power-up
Attr: —
ATK: —
DEF: —
Level: —
Deck Cost: 10
Number: 766
Effect: Increases the power of DRAGON and SEA SERPENT monsters by 500 points!

DRAGON ZOMBIE

Type: Zombie
Attr: Dark
ATK: 1,600
DEF: 0
Level: 3
Deck Cost: 16
Number: 106
Effect: None

DRAGONESS THE WICKED KNIGHT

Type: Warrior
Attr: Wind
ATK: 1,200
DEF: 900
Level: 3
Deck Cost: 21
Number: 205
Effect: None

DREAM CLOWN

Type: Warrior
Attr: Earth
ATK: 1,200
DEF: 900
Level: 3
Deck Cost: 26
Number: 164
Effect: When this card is flipped face-up in battle, the opponent is rendered eternally spellbound.

DROLL BIRD

Type: Winged Beast
Attr: Wind
ATK: 600
DEF: 500
Level: 2
Deck Cost: 16
Number: 276
Effect: When this card is flipped face-up, all monsters with an ATK of 500 or less are automatically flipped-up!

DROOLING LIZARD

Type: Reptile
Attr: Earth
ATK: 900
DEF: 800
Level: 3
Deck Cost: 17
Number: 449
Effect: None

DRYAD

Type: Spellcaster
Attr: Earth
ATK: 1,200
DEF: 1,400
Level: 4
Deck Cost: 31
Number: 89
Effect: When this card is flipped face-up in battle, the opposing monster is spellbound for 1 turn!

DUNGEON WORM

Type: Insect
Attr: Earth
ATK: 1,800
DEF: 1,500
Level: 5
Deck Cost: 33
Number: 409
Effect: Can enter LABYRINTH squares!

DUST TORNADO

Type: Magic
Attr: —
ATK: —
DEF: —
Level: —
Deck Cost: 50
Number: 729
Effect: Destroys all WINGED BEAST monsters on the Field!

EARTHSHAKER

Type: Magic
Attr: —
ATK: —
DEF: —
Level: —
Deck Cost: 70
Number: 750
Effect: Randomly shifts the position of cards and changes the terrain on the Field! In addition, all LABYRINTH squares are changed to NORMAL!

EATGABOON

Type: Trap (Limited Range)
Attr: —
ATK: —
DEF: —
Level: —
Deck Cost: 8
Number: 808
Effect: Disposable trap that triggers against a monster with ATK of 1,500 or below, and destroys it!

ELDEEN

Type: Spellcaster
Attr: Light
ATK: 950
DEF: 1,000
Level: 3
Deck Cost: 20
Number: 47
Effect: None

ELECTRIC LIZARD

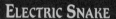

Type: Thunder
Attr: Earth
ATK: 850
DEF: 800
Level: 3
Deck Cost: 22
Number: 541
Effect: Spellbinds the opposing enemy for 1 turn when this card is flipped face-up in battle!

ELECTRIC SNAKE

Type: Thunder
Attr: Light
ATK: 800
DEF: 900
Level: 3
Deck Cost: 22
Number: 537
Effect: Increases 1,000 bonus points in battle against MACHINE monsters!

ELECTROMAGNETIC BAGWORM

Type: Immortal
Attr: Light
ATK: 200
DEF: 1,400
Level: 3
Deck Cost: 31
Number: 677
Effect: FLIP: When this card is flipped face-up, a player gains control of all opposing MACHINE monsters for the turn in play!
DESTRUCTION: Transforms adjacent spaces into CRUSH terrain when this card is destroyed in battle!

ELECTRO-WHIP

Type: Power-up
Attr: —
ATK: —
DEF: —
Level: —
Deck Cost: 10
Number: 767
Effect: Increases the power of female monsters by 500 points!

ELEGANT EGOTIST

Type: Power-up
Attr: —
ATK: —
DEF: —
Level: —
Deck Cost: 5
Number: 797
Effect: Changes Harpie Lady to Harpie Lady Sisters!

ELF'S LIGHT

Type: Power-up
Attr: —
ATK: —
DEF: —
Level: —
Deck Cost: 10
Number: 758
Effect: Increases the power of any monster with 'Elf' in its name by 700 points!

EMBRYONIC BEAST

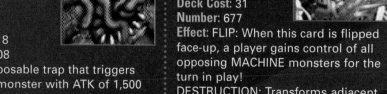

Type: Fiend
Attr: Dark
ATK: 500
DEF: 750
Level: 2
Deck Cost: 18
Number: 328
Effect: After being turned face-up, transforms into a Ryu-Kishin after surviving 3 turns in face-up defense position! However, the card must be turned up by the owning player.

EMPEROR OF THE LAND AND SEA

Type: Reptile
Attr: Water
ATK: 1,800
DEF: 1,500
Level: 5
Deck Cost: 33
Number: 455
Effect: None

EMPRESS JUDGE

Type: Warrior
Attr: Earth
ATK: 2,100
DEF: 1,700
Level: 6
Deck Cost: 38
Number: 199
Effect: None

ENCHANTED JAVELIN

Type: Power-up
Attr: —
ATK: —
DEF: —
Level: —
Deck Cost: 40
Number: 792
Effect: FAIRY monsters automatically destroy FIEND monsters in battle! The opposing enemy's attack effects are rendered ineffective.

ENCHANTING MERMAID

Type: Fish
Attr: Water
ATK: 1,200
DEF: 900
Level: 3
Deck Cost: 21
Number: 462
Effect: None

ERADICATING AEROSOL

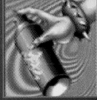

Type: Magic
Attr: —
ATK: —
DEF: —
Level: —
Deck Cost: 50
Number: 723
Effect: Destroys all INSECT monsters on the Field!

ETERNAL DRAUGHT

Type: Magic
Attr: —
ATK: —
DEF: —
Level: —
Deck Cost: 50
Number: 725
Effect: Destroys all FISH monsters on the Field!

ETERNAL REST

Type: Magic
Attr: —
ATK: —
DEF: —
Level: —
Deck Cost: 50
Number: 721
Effect: Destroys all ZOMBIE monsters on the Field!

EXILE OF THE WICKED

Type: Magic
Attr: —
ATK: —
DEF: —
Level: —
Deck Cost: 50
Number: 728
Effect: Destroys all FIEND monsters on the Field!

EXODIA THE FORBIDDEN ONE

Type: Spellcaster
Attr: Dark
ATK: 1,000
DEF: 1,000
Level: 3
Deck Cost: 30
Number: 58
Effect: As Leader, summon the four limbs from your own deck to adjacent Summon Areas, and enter your next turn face-up without being spellbound and victory is yours!

EYEARMOR

Type: Warrior
Attr: Earth
ATK: 600
DEF: 500
Level: 2
Deck Cost: 16
Number: 175
Effect: When this card is flipped face-up, adopt the ATK/DEF of the monster with the highest attack power on the Field!

FAIRY DRAGON

Type: Dragon
Attr: Wind
ATK: 1,100
DEF: 1,200
Level: 4
Deck Cost: 23
Number: 33
Effect: None

FAIRY KING TRUESDALE

Type: Plant
Attr: Aqua
ATK: 2,200
DEF: 1,500
Level: 6
Deck Cost: 42
Number: 670
Effect: While this card is face-up in the defense position, the power of all your PLANT monsters increases by 500 points.

FAIRY METEOR CRUSH

Type: Magic
Attr: —
ATK: —
DEF: —
Level: —
Deck Cost: 50
Number: 731
Effect: Randomly selects 10 spaces on the Field and destroys any card in-play on that space!

FAIRY OF THE FOUNTAIN

Type: Aqua
Attr: Water
ATK: 1,600
DEF: 1,100
Level: 4
Deck Cost: 27
Number: 605
Effect: None

FAIRY'S GIFT

Type: Spellcaster
Attr: Light
ATK: 1,400
DEF: 1,000
Level: 4
Deck Cost: 29
Number: 42
Effect: Gain 800 LP when this card is flipped face-up!

FAIRYWITCH

Type: Spellcaster
Attr: Dark
ATK: 800
DEF: 1,000
Level: 3
Deck Cost: 18
Number: 70
Effect: None

FAITH BIRD

Type: Winged Beast
Attr: Wind
ATK: 1,500
DEF: 1,100
Level: 4
Deck Cost: 26
Number: 275
Effect: None

FAKE TRAP

Type: Trap (Full Range)
Attr: —
ATK: —
DEF: —
Level: —
Deck Cost: 5
Number: 820
Effect: Disposable trap that triggers when Harpie's Feather Duster is activated and nullifies the card's effect!

FERAL IMP

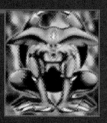

Type: Fiend
Attr: Dark
ATK: 1,300
DEF: 1,400
Level: 4
Deck Cost: 27
Number: 293
Effect: None

FIEND CASTLE

Type: Power-up
Attr: —
ATK: —
DEF: —
Level: —
Deck Cost: 10
Number: 782
Effect: Increases the power of FIEND monsters by 500 points!

FIEND KRAKEN

Type: Aqua
Attr: Water
ATK: 1,200
DEF: 1,400
Level: 4
Deck Cost: 26
Number: 550
Effect: None

FIEND REFLECTION #1

Type: Winged Beast
Attr: Wind
ATK: 1,300
DEF: 1,400
Level: 4
Deck Cost: 27
Number: 289
Effect: None

FIEND REFLECTION #2

Type: Winged Beast
Attr: Light
ATK: 1,100
DEF: 1,400
Level: 4
Deck Cost: 30
Number: 268
Effect: When this card is flipped face-up and a card has already been played from the hand, an additional card can be played from the hand!

FIEND SWORD

Type: Warrior
Attr: Dark
ATK: 1,400
DEF: 800
Level: 4
Deck Cost: 22
Number: 139
Effect: None

FIEND'S HAND

Type: Zombie
Attr: Dark
ATK: 600
DEF: 600
Level: 2
Deck Cost: 17
Number: 111
Effect: When destroyed in battle, it destroys the opposing monster as well!

FIEND'S MIRROR

Type: Fiend/Ritual
Attr: Dark
ATK: 2,100
DEF: 1,800
Level: 6
Deck Cost: 44
Number: 338
Effect: While this card is face-up in the defense position, reduce opponent's Summoning Power by 1 point.

FINAL FLAME

Type: Magic
Attr: —
ATK: —
DEF: —
Level: —
Deck Cost: 8
Number: 711
Effect: Inflicts 200 points of damage to opponent's LP!

FIRE EYE

Type: Pyro
Attr: Fire
ATK: 800
DEF: 600
Level: 2
Deck Cost: 19
Number: 616
Effect: Able to move and attack without triggering opponent's TRAP (LIMITED RANGE)!

FIRE KRAKEN

Type: Aqua
Attr: Fire
ATK: 1,600
DEF: 1,500
Level: 5
Deck Cost: 31
Number: 548
Effect: None

FIRE REAPER

Type: Zombie
Attr: Dark
ATK: 700
DEF: 500
Level: 2
Deck Cost: 17
Number: 115
Effect: When this card is flipped face-up, all cards located in Meadow terrain are destroyed!

FIREGRASS

Type: Plant
Attr: Earth
ATK: 700
DEF: 600
Level: 2
Deck Cost: 13
Number: 651
Effect: None

FIREWING PEGASUS

Type: Beast
Attr: Fire
ATK: 2,250
DEF: 1,800
Level: 6
Deck Cost: 41
Number: 226
Effect: None

FIREYAROU

Type: Pyro
Attr: Fire
ATK: 1,300
DEF: 1,000
Level: 4
Deck Cost: 23
Number: 618
Effect: None

FISSURE

Type: Magic
Attr: —
ATK: —
DEF: —
Level: —
Deck Cost: 50
Number: 726
Effect: Destroys the monster with the lowest ATK on the Field!

FLAME CEREBRUS

Type: Pyro
Attr: Fire
ATK: 2,100
DEF: 1,800
Level: 6
Deck Cost: 39
Number: 620
Effect: None

FLAME GHOST

Type: Zombie
Attr: Dark
ATK: 1,000
DEF: 800
Level: 3
Deck Cost: 23
Number: 118
Effect: When this card is flipped face-up, all cards located in Sea terrain are destroyed!

FLAME MANIPULATOR

Type: Spellcaster
Attr: Fire
ATK: 900
DEF: 1,000
Level: 3
Deck Cost: 19
Number: 88
Effect: None

FLAME SNAKE

Type: Pyro
Attr: Earth
ATK: 400
DEF: 450
Level: 2
Deck Cost: 9
Number: 623
Effect: None

FLAME SWORDSMAN

Type: Warrior
Attr: Fire
ATK: 1,800
DEF: 1,600
Level: 5
Deck Cost: 39
Number: 151
Effect: 300-point bonus when battling DINOSAUR monsters!

FLOWER WOLF

Type: Beast
Attr: Earth
ATK: 1,800
DEF: 1,400
Level: 5
Deck Cost: 32
Number: 253
Effect: None

FLYING PENGUIN

Type: Aqua
Attr: Water
ATK: 1,200
DEF: 1,000
Level: 4
Deck Cost: 22
Number: 572
Effect: None

FOLLOW WIND

Type: Power-up
Attr: —
ATK: —
DEF: —
Level: —
Deck Cost: 10
Number: 776
Effect: Increases the power of WINGED BEAST monsters by 500 points!

FOREST

Type: Magic
Attr: —
ATK: —
DEF: —
Level: —
Deck Cost: 30
Number: 689
Effect: Transforms a surrounding 2-space area into FOREST terrain!

FORTRESS WHALE

Type: Fish
Attr: Water
ATK: 2,350
DEF: 2,150
Level: 7
Deck Cost: 50
Number: 472
Effect: Automatically destroys WARRIOR monster in battle!

FORTRESS WHALE'S OATH

Type: Ritual
Attr: —
ATK: —
DEF: —
Level: —
Deck Cost: 5
Number: 852
Effect: Sacrifice 2 FISH monsters and Mech Bass to summon Fortress Whale!

FRENZIED PANDA

Type: Beast
Attr: Earth
ATK: 1,200
DEF: 1,000
Level: 4
Deck Cost: 22
Number: 241
Effect: None

FROG THE JAM

Type: Aqua
Attr: Water
ATK: 700
DEF: 500
Level: 2
Deck Cost: 17
Number: 594
Effect: While this card is face-up in the defense position, all LP recovery points are doubled!

FUNGI OF THE MUSK

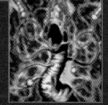

Type: Fiend
Attr: Dark
ATK: 400
DEF: 300
Level: 1
Deck Cost: 12
Number: 349
Effect: Reduces an enemy by 500 points when this card is flipped face-up in battle!

FUSIONIST

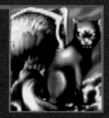

Type: Beast
Attr: Earth
ATK: 900
DEF: 700
Level: 3
Deck Cost: 16
Number: 240
Effect: None

GAIA THE DRAGON CHAMPION

Type: Dragon
Attr: Wind
ATK: 2,600
DEF: 2,100
Level: 7
Deck Cost: 47
Number: 23
Effect: None

GAIA THE FIERCE KNIGHT

Type: Warrior
Attr: Earth
ATK: 2,300
DEF: 2,100
Level: 7
Deck Cost: 44
Number: 155
Effect: None

GALE DOGRA

Type: Insect
Attr: Earth
ATK: 650
DEF: 600
Level: 2
Deck Cost: 18
Number: 418
Effect: While this card is face-up in the defense position, all enemy monsters are reduced 100 points each turn!

GANIGUMO

Type: Insect
Attr: Earth
ATK: 600
DEF: 800
Level: 2
Deck Cost: 19
Number: 411
Effect: Able to move and attack without triggering an opponent's TRAP (LIMITED RANGE)

GARMA SWORD

Type: Warrior/Ritual
Attr: Dark
ATK: 2,550
DEF: 2,150
Level: 7
Deck Cost: 47
Number: 148
Effect: 800-point bonus when battling SPELLCASTER monsters!

GARMA SWORD OATH

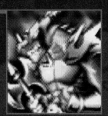

Type: Ritual
Attr: —
ATK: —
DEF: —
Level: —
Deck Cost: 5
Number: 849
Effect: Sacrifice 2 WARRIOR monsters and Swordstalker to summon Garma Sword

GAROOZIS

Type: Beast-warrior
Attr: Fire
ATK: 1,800
DEF: 1,500
Level: 5
Deck Cost: 33
Number: 208
Effect: None

GARVAS

Type: Beast
Attr: Earth
ATK: 2,000
DEF: 1,700
Level: 6
Deck Cost: 37
Number: 252
Effect: None

GATE DEEG

Type: Beast
Attr: Dark
ATK: 700
DEF: 800
Level: 3
Deck Cost: 20
Number: 224
Effect: When this card is flipped face-up, the owning player's Summoning Power points are increased to the maximum value!

GATE GUARDIAN

Type: Warrior/Ritual
Attr: Dark
ATK: 3,750
DEF: 3,400
Level: 11
Deck Cost: 77
Number: 145
Effect: Whenever damage is inflicted to LP in battle, the damage amount is reduced to 0!

GATE GUARDIAN RITUAL

Type: Ritual
Attr: —
ATK: —
DEF: —
Level: —
Deck Cost: 5
Number: 832
Effect: Sacrifice Kazejin, Suijin, and Sanga of the Thunder to summon Gate Guardian!

GATEKEEPER

Type: Machine
Attr: Dark
ATK: 1,500
DEF: 1,800
Level: 5
Deck Cost: 33
Number: 483
Effect: None

GAZELLE THE KING OF THE MYTHICAL BEASTS

Type: Beast
Attr: Earth
ATK: 1,500
DEF: 1,200
Level: 4
Deck Cost: 27
Number: 265
Effect: None

GEAR GOLEM THE MOVING FORTRESS

Type: Machine
Attr: Earth
ATK: 800
DEF: 2,200
Level: 5
Deck Cost: 30
Number: 527
Effect: None

GEMINI ELF

Type: Spellcaster
Attr: Earth
ATK: 1,900
DEF: 900
Level: 4
Deck Cost: 28
Number: 92
Effect: None

GENIN

Type: Spellcaster
Attr: Light
ATK: 600
DEF: 900
Level: 3
Deck Cost: 20
Number: 41
Effect: SPECIAL POWER-UP: Strong in TOON terrain!
FLIP: Spellbinds an opponent for 1 turn when this card is flipped face-up in battle!

GHOUL WITH AN APPETITE

Type: Zombie
Attr: Dark
ATK: 1,600
DEF: 1,200
Level: 4
Deck Cost: 28
Number: 131
Effect: None

GIANT FLEA

Type: Insect
Attr: Earth
ATK: 1,500
DEF: 1,200
Level: 4
Deck Cost: 27
Number: 400
Effect: None

GIANT MECH-SOLDIER

Type: Machine
Attr: Earth
ATK: 1,750
DEF: 1,900
Level: 6
Deck Cost: 37
Number: 515
Effect: None

GIANT RED SEASNAKE

Type: Aqua
Attr: Water
ATK: 1,800
DEF: 800
Level: 4
Deck Cost: 26
Number: 583
Effect: None

GIANT SCORPION OF THE TUNDRA

Type: Insect
Attr: Earth
ATK: 1,100
DEF: 1,000
Level: 3
Deck Cost: 21
Number: 424
Effect: None

GIANT SOLDIER OF STONE

Type: Rock
Attr: Earth
ATK: 1,300
DEF: 2,000
Level: 3
Deck Cost: 33
Number: 626
Effect: None

GIANT TURTLE WHO FEEDS ON FLAMES

Type: Aqua
Attr: Water
ATK: 1,400
DEF: 1,800
Level: 5
Deck Cost: 32
Number: 598
Effect: None

GIFT OF THE MYSTICAL ELF

Type: Magic
Attr: —
ATK: —
DEF: —
Level: —
Deck Cost: 25
Number: 708
Effect: Recover controlling player's LP by 1,500 points!

GIGA-TECH WOLF

Type: Machine
Attr: Earth
ATK: 1,200
DEF: 1,400
Level: 4
Deck Cost: 26
Number: 517
Effect: None

GILTIA THE D. KNIGHT

Type: Warrior
Attr: Light
ATK: 1,850
DEF: 1,500
Level: 5
Deck Cost: 34
Number: 134
Effect: None

GOBLIN FAN

Type: Trap
(Full Range)
Attr: —
ATK: —
DEF: —
Level: —
Deck Cost: 25
Number: 814
Effect: Permanent trap that triggers against an opponent's direct LP-attacking Riryoku and reverses the inflicted damage!

GOBLIN'S SECRET REMEDY

Type: Magic
Attr: —
ATK: —
DEF: —
Level: —
Deck Cost: 10
Number: 705
Effect: 1,000-point LP recovery for controlling player!

GODDESS OF WHIM

Type: Fairy
Attr: Light
ATK: 950
DEF: 700
Level: 3
Deck Cost: 22
Number: 382
Effect: Own ATK/DEF either increased or decreased by up to 1,500 points when entering battle!

GODDESS WITH THE THIRD EYE

Type: Fairy
Attr: Light
ATK: 1,200
DEF: 1,000
Level: 4
Deck Cost: 22
Number: 369
Effect: None

GOKIBORE

Type: Insect
Attr: Earth
ATK: 1200
DEF: 1400
Level: 4
Deck Cost: 26
Number: 399
Effect: None

GOLGOIL

Type: Machine
Attr: Earth
ATK: 900
DEF: 1,600
Level: 4
Deck Cost: 30
Number: 519
Effect: Revives in own Summoning Area, other than current location, when destroyed in battle

GORGON EGG

Type: Fiend
Attr: Dark
ATK: 300
DEF: 1,300
Level: 3
Deck Cost: 16
Number: 332
Effect: Transforms into a ZOMBIE/DARK monster when strengthened with Insect Imitation!

GORGON'S EYE

Type: Trap
(Full Range)
Attr: —
ATK: —
DEF: —
Level: —
Deck Cost: 50
Number: 819
Effect: Permanent Trap that triggers when an enemy card completes its move in the defense position! Automatically cancels the enemy card's move and eternally spellbinds it!

GRAPPLER

Type: Reptile
Attr: Water
ATK: 1,300
DEF: 1,200
Level: 4
Deck Cost: 25
Number: 453
Effect: None

GRAVEROBBER

Type: Magic
Attr: —
ATK: —
DEF: —
Level: —
Deck Cost: 60
Number: 688
Effect: Select, revive, and control 1 SPELL Card from either Graveyard!

GRAVEYARD AND THE HAND OF INVITATION

Type: Zombie
Attr: Dark
ATK: 700
DEF: 900
Level: 3
Deck Cost: 21
Number: 109
Effect: When this card is flipped face-up, all your monsters are transformed into ZOMBIE monsters!

GRAVITY BIND

Type: Trap
(Limited Range)
Attr: —
ATK: —
DEF: —
Level: —
Deck Cost: 60
Number: 806
Effect: Disposable trap that eternally spellbinds activated enemy card and reduces its strength by 1,500 points!

GREAT BILL

Type: Beast
Attr: Earth
ATK: 1,250
DEF: 1,300
Level: 4
Deck Cost: 26
Number: 262
Effect: None

GREAT MAMMOTH OF GOLDFINE

Type: Zombie
Attr: Dark
ATK: 2,200
DEF: 1,800
Level: 6
Deck Cost: 40
Number: 130
Effect: None

GREAT MOTH

Type: Insect
Attr: Earth
ATK: 2,600
DEF: 2,500
Level: 8
Deck Cost: 56
Number: 402
Effect: While this card is face-up in the defense position, all enemy monsters are reduced by 100 points each turn.

GREAT WHITE

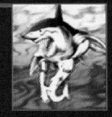

Type: Fish
Attr: Water
ATK: 1,600
DEF: 800
Level: 4
Deck Cost: 24
Number: 459
Effect: None

GREEN KAPPA

Type: Warrior
Attr: Dark
ATK: 650
DEF: 900
Level: 3
Deck Cost: 21
Number: 149
Effect: When this card is flipped face-up, adopts the ATK/DEF of the monster with the highest ATK power on the Field!

GREEN PHANTOM KING

Type: Plant
Attr: Earth
ATK: 500
DEF: 1,600
Level: 3
Deck Cost: 26
Number: 656
Effect: When this card is flipped face-up, all Queen of Autumn Leaves cards are strengthened by 500 points!

GRIFFORE

Type: Beast
Attr: Earth
ATK: 1,200
DEF: 1,500
Level: 4
Deck Cost: 27
Number: 229
Effect: None

GRIGGLE

Type: Plant
Attr: Earth
ATK: 350
DEF: 300
Level: 1
Deck Cost: 7
Number: 661
Effect: None

GROUND ATTACKER BUGROTH

Type: Machine
Attr: Earth
ATK: 1,500
DEF: 1,000
Level: 4
Deck Cost: 25
Number: 511
Effect: None

GRUESOME GOO

Type: Aqua
Attr: Water
ATK: 1,300
DEF: 700
Level: 3
Deck Cost: 20
Number: 608
Effect: None

GUARDIAN OF THE LABYRINTH

Type: Warrior
Attr: Earth
ATK: 1,000
DEF: 1,200
Level: 4
Deck Cost: 22
Number: 182
Effect: None

GUARDIAN OF THE SEA

Type: Aqua
Attr: Water
ATK: 1,300
DEF: 1,000
Level: 4
Deck Cost: 23
Number: 581
Effect: None

GUARDIAN OF THE THRONE ROOM

Type: Machine
Attr: Light
ATK: 1,650
DEF: 1,600
Level: 4
Deck Cost: 33
Number: 481
Effect: None

Complete Card List

GUST FAN

Type: Power-up
Attr: —
ATK: —
DEF: —
Level: —
Deck Cost: 10
Number: 785
Effect: Increases the power WIND monsters by 500 points!

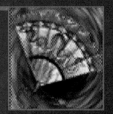

GYAKUTENNO MEGAMI

Type: Fairy
Attr: Light
ATK: 1,800
DEF: 2,000
Level: 6
Deck Cost: 43
Number: 368
Effect: When this card is flipped face-up, all your own monsters with ATK of 1,000 or below are increased by 1,000 points!

HAMBURGER RECIPE

Type: Ritual
Attr: —
ATK: —
DEF: —
Level: —
Deck Cost: 5
Number: 839
Effect: Sacrifice Battle Steer, Bio Plant, and Griggle to summon Hungry Burger!

HANE-HANE

Type: Beast
Attr: Earth
ATK: 450
DEF: 500
Level: 2
Deck Cost: 15
Number: 257
Effect: When this card is flipped face-up, return to own deck and re-shuffle the deck!

HANIWA

Type: Rock
Attr: Earth
ATK: 500
DEF: 500
Level: 2
Deck Cost: 10
Number: 628
Effect: None

HANNIBAL NECROMANCER

Type: Spellcaster
Attr: Dark
ATK: 1,400
DEF: 1,800
Level: 5
Deck Cost: 37
Number: 85
Effect: When this card is flipped face-up, all ZOMBIE monsters are increased by 300 points!

HAPPY LOVER

Type: Fairy
Attr: Light
ATK: 800
DEF: 500
Level: 2
Deck Cost: 18
Number: 375
Effect: Cancels all power increases or decreases of an enemy monster in battle! Does not cancel bonus effects such as terrain or Leader ability effects.

HARD ARMOR

Type: Warrior
Attr: Earth
ATK: 300
DEF: 1,200
Level: 3
Deck Cost: 15
Number: 169
Effect: None

HARPIE LADY

Type: Winged Beast
Attr: Wind
ATK: 1,300
DEF: 1,400
Level: 4
Deck Cost: 32
Number: 272
Effect: FLIP: When this card is flipped face-up, Harpie's Pet Dragon increases 300 points!
SPECIAL POWER-UP: When strengthened with Elgant Egotist, transforms into Harpie Lady Sisters!

HARPIE LADY SISTERS

Type: Winged Beast
Attr: Wind
ATK: 1,950
DEF: 2,100
Level: 6
Deck Cost: 46
Number: 273
Effect: When this card is flipped face-up, Harpie's Pet Dragon increases 900 points!

HARPIE'S FEATHER DUSTER

Type: Magic
Attr: —
ATK: —
DEF: —
Level: —
Deck Cost: 70
Number: 702
Effect: Destroys all spells located in the vertical and horizontal lines from the activated space!

HARPIE'S PET DRAGON

Type: Dragon
Attr: Wind
ATK: 2,000
DEF: 2,500
Level: 7
Deck Cost: 45
Number: 30
Effect: None

HEAVY STORM

Type: Magic
Attr: —
ATK: —
DEF: —
Level: —
Deck Cost: 50
Number: 701
Effect: Destroys all SPELL Cards on the Field!

HERCULES BEETLE

Type: Insect
Attr: Earth
ATK: 1,500
DEF: 2,000
Level: 5
Deck Cost: 35
Number: 398
Effect: None

HERO OF THE EAST

Type: Warrior
Attr: Earth
ATK: 1,100
DEF: 1,000
Level: 3
Deck Cost: 21
Number: 162
Effect: None

HIBIKIME

Type: Warrior
Attr: Earth
ATK: 1,450
DEF: 1,000
Level: 4
Deck Cost: 30
Number: 203
Effect: When this card is flipped face-up, all Sonic Maid cards are increased 500 points!

HIGH TIDE GYOJIN

Type: Aqua
Attr: Water
ATK: 1,650
DEF: 1,300
Level: 5
Deck Cost: 30
Number: 604
Effect: None

HIGHTIDE

Type: Power-up
Attr: —
ATK: —
DEF: —
Level: —
Deck Cost: 10
Number: 783
Effect: Increases the power of FISH and SEA SERPENT monsters by 500 points!

HINOTAMA

Type: Magic
Attr: —
ATK: —
DEF: —
Level: —
Deck Cost: 5
Number: 710
Effect: Inflicts 100 points of damage to opponent's LP!

HINOTAMA SOUL

Type: Pyro
Attr: Fire
ATK: 600
DEF: 500
Level: 2
Deck Cost: 16
Number: 617
Effect: When this card is destroyed in battle, all SPELL Cards positioned in adjacent spaces are destroyed!

HIRO'S SHADOW SCOUT

Type: Fiend
Attr: Dark
ATK: 650
DEF: 500
Level: 2
Deck Cost: 17
Number: 357
Effect: When this card is flipped face-up, identifies an opponent's face-down cards by type (MONSTER/MAGIC/POWER-UP/TRAP)!

HITODENCHAK

Type: Aqua
Attr: Water
ATK: 600
DEF: 700
Level: 2
Deck Cost: 18
Number: 564
Effect: None

HITOTSU-ME GIANT

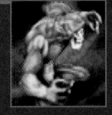

Type: Beast-warrior
Attr: Earth
ATK: 1,200
DEF: 1,000
Level: 4
Deck Cost: 22
Number: 209
Effect: None

HOLOGRAH

Type: Machine
Attr: Earth
ATK: 1,100
DEF: 700
Level: 3
Deck Cost: 18
Number: 512
Effect: None

HORN IMP

Type: Fiend
Attr: Dark
ATK: 1,300
DEF: 1,000
Level: 4
Deck Cost: 28
Number: 295
Effect: When this card is flipped face-up, if there's a Jigen Bakudan in any adjacent space, teleport 1 Jigen Bakudan to an opponent's Summoning Area.

HORN OF LIGHT

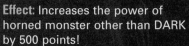

Type: Power-up
Attr: —
ATK: —
DEF: —
Level: —
Deck Cost: 10
Number: 764
Effect: Increases the power of horned monster other than DARK by 500 points!

HORN OF THE UNICORN

Type: Power-up
Attr: —
ATK: —
DEF: —
Level: —
Deck Cost: 10
Number: 765
Effect: Increases the power of horned monster of DARK by 500 points.

HOSHININGEN

Type: Fairy
Attr: Light
ATK: 500
DEF: 700
Level: 2
Deck Cost: 17
Number: 383
Effect: Own LIGHT monsters strengthened by 300 points when this card is flipped face-up!

HOURGLASS OF COURAGE

Type: Fairy
Attr: Light
ATK: 1,100
DEF: 1,200
Level: 4
Deck Cost: 28
Number: 390
Effect: If LP is over 1,000 points when this card is destroyed in battle, the strength of your monsters are increased by 1,000 points, and your LP is reduced by 1,000!

HOURGLASS OF LIFE

Type: Fairy
Attr: Light
ATK: 700
DEF: 600
Level: 2
Deck Cost: 18
Number: 377
Effect: If LP is higher than 1,000 at the moment this card is destroyed, a maximum of 4 monsters with the highest ATKs from own as well as opponent's Graveyard are revived under owning player's control. Following the revival, the owning player's LP is reduced by 1,000.

HOUSE OF ADHESIVE TAPE

Type: Trap (Limited Range)
Attr: —
ATK: —
DEF: —
Level: —
Deck Cost: 5
Number: 807
Effect: Disposable trap that triggers against a monster with ATK of 1,000 or below, and destroys it!

HUNGRY BURGER

Type: Warrior/Ritual
Attr: Dark
ATK: 2,000
DEF: 1,850
Level: 6
Deck Cost: 44
Number: 147
Effect: ATTACK: Allows the one-sided destruction of the opposition when battling BEAST monsters! SPECIAL POWER-UP: Strong in TOON terrain!

HUNTER SPIDER

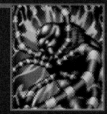

Type: Insect
Attr: Earth
ATK: 1,600
DEF: 1,400
Level: 5
Deck Cost: 30
Number: 425
Effect: None

HURRICAIL

Type: Spellcaster
Attr: Wind
ATK: 900
DEF: 200
Level: 2
Deck Cost: 16
Number: 98
Effect: When this card is flipped face-up, all spells within a range of a single space are destroyed!

HYO

Type: Warrior
Attr: Water
ATK: 800
DEF: 1,200
Level: 3
Deck Cost: 25
Number: 206
Effect: Spellbinds an opponent for 1 turn when destroyed in battle!

HYOSUBE

Type: Aqua
Attr: Water
ATK: 1,500
DEF: 900
Level: 4
Deck Cost: 24
Number: 609
Effect: None

ICE WATER

Type: Aqua
Attr: Water
ATK: 1,150
DEF: 900
Level: 3
Deck Cost: 21
Number: 577
Effect: None

ILL WITCH

Type: Spellcaster
Attr: Light
ATK: 1,600
DEF: 1,500
Level: 5
Deck Cost: 31
Number: 49
Effect: None

ILLUSIONIST FACELESS MAGE

Type: Spellcaster
Attr: Dark
ATK: 1,200
DEF: 2,200
Level: 5
Deck Cost: 39
Number: 61
Effect: When this card is flipped face-up in battle, spellbinds opposing monster for 3 turns!

INFINITE DISMISSAL

Type: Trap (Limited Range)
Attr: —
ATK: —
DEF: —
Level: —
Deck Cost: 20
Number: 805
Effect: Disposable trap that spellbinds activated enemy card for 3 turns!

INJECTION FAIRY LILY

Type: Spellcaster
Attr: Earth
ATK: 400
DEF: 1,500
Level: 3
Deck Cost: 24
Number: 95
Effect: While this card is in face-up in the defense position, LP increases 50 points at the start of each turn!

INSECT ARMOR WITH LASER CANNON

Type: Power-up
Attr: —
ATK: —
DEF: —
Level: —
Deck Cost: 10
Number: 757
Effect: Increases the power of INSECT monsters by 500 points!

INSECT IMITATION

Type: Power-up
Attr: —
ATK: —
DEF: —
Level: —
Deck Cost: 5
Number: 800
Effect: Randomly transforms any monster with 'Egg' in its name to another monster!

INSECT SOLDIERS OF THE SKY

Type: Insect
Attr: Wind
ATK: 1,000
DEF: 800
Level: 3
Deck Cost: 18
Number: 431
Effect: None

INVADER FROM ANOTHER DIMENSION

Type: Fiend
Attr: Dark
ATK: 950
DEF: 1,400
Level: 4
Deck Cost: 24
Number: 354
Effect: None

INVADER OF THE THRONE

Type: Warrior
Attr: Earth
ATK: 1,350
DEF: 1,700
Level: 5
Deck Cost: 31
Number: 202
Effect: None

INVIGORATION

Type: Power-up
Attr: —
ATK: —
DEF: —
Level: —
Deck Cost: 15
Number: 773
Effect: Increases the power of Earth monsters by 300 points

INVISIBLE WIRE

Type: Trap (Limited Range)
Attr: —
ATK: —
DEF: —
Level: —
Deck Cost: 20
Number: 810
Effect: Disposable trap that triggers against a monster with ATK of 3,000 or below, and destroys it!

INVITATION TO A DARK SLEEP

Type: Spellcaster
Attr: Dark
ATK: 1,500
DEF: 1,800
Level: 5
Deck Cost: 38
Number: 84
Effect: When this card is flipped face-up, all enemy cards are spellbound for 1 turn!

JAVELIN BEETLE

Type: Insect/Ritual
Attr: Earth
ATK: 2,450
DEF: 2,550
Level: 8
Deck Cost: 55
Number: 422
Effect: 600 bonus points added in battles against DRAGON monsters!

JAVELIN BEETLE PACT

Type: Ritual
Attr: —
ATK: —
DEF: —
Level: —
Deck Cost: 5
Number: 848
Effect: Sacrifice 2 INSECT monsters and Hercules Beetle to summon Javelin Beetle

JELLYFISH

Type: Aqua
Attr: Water
ATK: 1,200
DEF: 1,500
Level: 4
Deck Cost: 32
Number: 551
Effect: While this card is face-up in defense position, all THUNDER monsters are reduced by 500 points!

JIGEN BAKUDAN

Type: Pyro
Attr: Fire
ATK: 200
DEF: 1,000
Level: 2
Deck Cost: 17
Number: 621
Effect: When this card survives 2 turns face-up in the defense position, all cards located in surrounding 3x3 area are automatically destroyed! This only applies when the controlling player intentionally flips the card face-up.

JINZO #7

Type: Machine
Attr: Dark
ATK: 500
DEF: 400
Level: 2
Deck Cost: 9
Number: 497
Effect: None

JIRAI GUMO

Type: Insect
Attr: Earth
ATK: 2,200
DEF: 100
Level: 4
Deck Cost: 33
Number: 408
Effect: ATTACK: Cancels all power increases or decreases of an enemy monster in battle! Does not cancel bonus effects such as terrain or Leader ability effects.
MOVEMENT: Decreases LP by 100 points for each space moved!

JOB-CHANGE MIRROR

Type: Fiend
Attr: Dark
ATK: 800
DEF: 1,300
Level: 3
Deck Cost: 21
Number: 306
Effect: None

JOWLS OF DARK DEMISE

Type: Immortal
Attr: Water
ATK: 200
DEF: 100
Level: 2
Deck Cost: 18
Number: 672
Effect: FLIP: When this parasite card is flipped face-up in battle, it takes control of the oppposing card! When the controlled monster is destroyed in battle, this card is revived in controlling player's Summoning Area, other than its current location! The nature effect and destruction features of the monster that's taken over are rendered ineffective.
DESTRUCTION: Transforms all adjacent spaces into CRUSH terrain when this card is destroyed in battle!

JUDGE MAN

Type: Warrior
Attr: Earth
ATK: 2,200
DEF: 1,500
Level: 6
Deck Cost: 37
Number: 154
Effect: None

JUST DESSERTS

Type: Magic
Attr: —
ATK: —
DEF: —
Level: —
Deck Cost: 80
Number: 714
Effect: Opponent's LP suffers damage equivalent to 300 points multiplied by the number of enemies on the Field!

KAGEMUSHA OF THE BLUE FLAME

Type: Warrior
Attr: Earth
ATK: 800
DEF: 400
Level: 2
Deck Cost: 12
Number: 177
Effect: None

KAGENINGEN
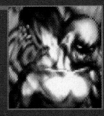
Type: Warrior
Attr: Dark
ATK: 800
DEF: 600
Level: 2
Deck Cost: 24
Number: 137
Effect: ATTACK: Whenever damage is inflicted to LP in battle, the damage amount is reduced to 0.
FLIP: When this card is flipped face-up, add one more Kageningen face-up in own Summoning Area.

KAIRYU-SHIN

Type: Sea Serpent
Attr: Water
ATK: 1,800
DEF: 1,500
Level: 5
Deck Cost: 38
Number: 476
Effect: All spaces within a range of 1 space are transformed to SEA terrain when this card is flipped face-up!

KAISER DRAGON

Type: Dragon
Attr: Light
ATK: 2,300
DEF: 2,000
Level: 7
Deck Cost: 43
Number: 3
Effect: None

KAMAKIRIMAN

Type: Insect
Attr: Earth
ATK: 1,150
DEF: 1,400
Level: 4
Deck Cost: 26
Number: 421
Effect: None

KAMINARI ATTACK

Type: Thunder
Attr: Wind
ATK: 1,900
DEF: 1,400
Level: 5
Deck Cost: 33
Number: 544
Effect: None

KAMINARIKOZOU

Type: Thunder
Attr: Wind
ATK: 700
DEF: 600
Level: 2
Deck Cost: 13
Number: 543
Effect: None

KAMIONWIZARD

Type: Spellcaster
Attr: Dark
ATK: 1,300
DEF: 1,100
Level: 4
Deck Cost: 24
Number: 63
Effect: None

KANAN THE SWORDMISTRESS

Type: Warrior
Attr: Earth
ATK: 1,400
DEF: 1,400
Level: 4
Deck Cost: 28
Number: 187
Effect: None

KANIKABUTO

Type: Aqua
Attr: Water
ATK: 650
DEF: 900
Level: 3
Deck Cost: 16
Number: 586
Effect: None

KAPPA AVENGER

Type: Aqua
Attr: Water
ATK: 1,200
DEF: 900
Level: 3
Deck Cost: 21
Number: 585
Effect: None

KARBONALA WARRIOR

Type: Warrior
Attr: Earth
ATK: 1,500
DEF: 1,200
Level: 4
Deck Cost: 27
Number: 157
Effect: None

KATTAPILLAR

Type: Insect
Attr: Earth
ATK: 250
DEF: 300
Level: 1
Deck Cost: 6
Number: 416
Effect: SPECIAL POWER-UP: Transforms to Larva of Moth when strengthened with Cocoon of Evolution!

KAZEJIN

Type: Spellcaster
Attr: Wind
ATK: 2,400
DEF: 2,200
Level: 7
Deck Cost: 51
Number: 99
Effect: Whenever damage is inflicted to LP in battle, the damage amount is reduced to 0!

KEY MACE

Type: Fairy
Attr: Light
ATK: 400
DEF: 300
Level: 1
Deck Cost: 17
Number: 374
Effect: When this card is flipped face-up, shifts all cards to defense position!

KEY MACE #2

Type: Fiend
Attr: Dark
ATK: 1,050
DEF: 1,200
Level: 4
Deck Cost: 23
Number: 356
Effect: None

KILLER NEEDLE

Type: Insect
Attr: Wind
ATK: 1,200
DEF: 1,000
Level: 4
Deck Cost: 22
Number: 430
Effect: None

KINETIC SOLDIER

Type: Machine
Attr: Earth
ATK: 2,350
DEF: 1,800
Level: 3
Deck Cost: 47
Number: 528
Effect: Increases 2,000 bonus points in battle against WARRIOR monsters!

KING FOG

Type: Fiend
Attr: Dark
ATK: 1,000
DEF: 900
Level: 3
Deck Cost: 19
Number: 333
Effect: None

KING OF YAMIMIKAI

Type: Fiend
Attr: Dark
ATK: 2,000
DEF: 1,530
Level: 5
Deck Cost: 36
Number: 300
Effect: None

KING TIGER WANGHU

Type: Beast
Attr: Earth
ATK: 1,700
DEF: 1,000
Level: 4
Deck Cost: 32
Number: 266
Effect: If face-up, can move 2 spaces at a time regardless of terrain!

KOJIKOCY

Type: Warrior
Attr: Earth
ATK: 1,500
DEF: 1,200
Level: 4
Deck Cost: 27
Number: 158
Effect: None

KOROGASHI

Type: Insect
Attr: Earth
ATK: 550
DEF: 400
Level: 2
Deck Cost: 15
Number: 415
Effect: Reduces all monsters located in vertical and horizontal spaces by 300 points when destroyed in battle!

KOUMORI DRAGON

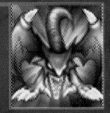

Type: Dragon/Fusion
Attr: Dark
ATK: 1,500
DEF: 1,200
Level: 4
Deck Cost: 27
Number: 5
Effect: None

KROKODILUS

Type: Reptile
Attr: Water
ATK: 1,100
DEF: 1,200
Level: 4
Deck Cost: 23
Number: 452
Effect: None

KRYUEL

Type: Fiend
Attr: Dark
ATK: 1,000
DEF: 1,700
Level: 4
Deck Cost: 32
Number: 365
Effect: While this card is face-up in the defense position, all damage to LP increased by 200 points!

KUMOOTOKO

Type: Insect
Attr: Earth
ATK: 700
DEF: 1,400
Level: 3
Deck Cost: 21
Number: 406
Effect: None

KUNAI WITH CHAIN

Type: Power-up
Attr: —
ATK: —
DEF: —
Level: —
Deck Cost: 15
Number: 778
Effect: Increases the power of WARRIOR and BEAST-WARRIOR monsters by 500 points!

KURAMA

Type: Winged Beast
Attr: Wind
ATK: 800
DEF: 800
Level: 3
Deck Cost: 16
Number: 278
Effect: None

KURIBOH

Type: Fiend
Attr: Dark
ATK: 300
DEF: 200
Level: 1
Deck Cost: 10
Number: 297
Effect: Whenever damage is inflicted to LP in battle, the damage amount is reduced to 0!

Kuwagata α

Type: Insect
Attr: Earth
ATK: 1,250
DEF: 1,000
Level: 4
Deck Cost: 23
Number: 414
Effect: None

Kwagar Hercules

Type: Insect
Attr: Earth
ATK: 1,900
DEF: 1,700
Level: 6
Deck Cost: 36
Number: 419
Effect: None

La Jinn the Mystical Genie of the Lamp

Type: Fiend
Attr: Dark
ATK: 1,800
DEF: 1,000
Level: 4
Deck Cost: 28
Number: 340
Effect: None

Labyrinth Tank

Type: Machine
Attr: Dark
ATK: 2,400
DEF: 2,400
Level: 7
Deck Cost: 53
Number: 486
Effect: Can enter LABYRINTH squares!

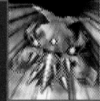

Labyrinth Wall

Type: Magic
Attr: —
ATK: —
DEF: —
Level: —
Deck Cost: 35
Number: 697
Effect: Transforms the occupied space into LABYRINTH terrain!

Lady of Faith

Type: Spellcaster
Attr: Light
ATK: 1,100
DEF: 800
Level: 3
Deck Cost: 19
Number: 48
Effect: None

Lala Li-oon

Type: Thunder
Attr: Wind
ATK: 600
DEF: 600
Level: 2
Deck Cost: 17
Number: 542
Effect: While this card is face-up in the defense position, all MACHINE monsters are reduced 500 points!

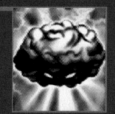

LaMoon

Type: Spellcaster
Attr: Light
ATK: 1,200
DEF: 1,700
Level: 5
Deck Cost: 29
Number: 39
Effect: None

Larva of Moth

Type: Insect
Attr: Earth
ATK: 0
DEF: 2,000
Level: 2
Deck Cost: 25
Number: 427
Effect: MOVEMENT: Cannot move!
NATURE EFFECT: Transforms into Pupa of Moth if the card survives 5 turns in face-up defense position after being flipped face-up by the controlling player. If destroyed prior to transformation, the card is revived as Larvae Moth in own Summoning Area other than the current location!

Larvae Moth

Type: Insect
Attr: Earth
ATK: 500
DEF: 400
Level: 2
Deck Cost: 9
Number: 401
Effect: SPECIAL POWER-UP: Transforms to Larva of Moth when strengthened with Cocoon of Evolution.

Larvas

Type: Beast
Attr: Earth
ATK: 800
DEF: 1,000
Level: 3
Deck Cost: 23
Number: 236
Effect: When this card is flipped face-up, all Mon Larvas cards are increased 500 points!

Laser Cannon Armor

Type: Power-up
Attr: —
ATK: —
DEF: —
Level: —
Deck Cost: 10
Number: 756
Effect: Increases the power of INSECT monsters by 500 points!

Last Day of Witch

Type: Magic
Attr: —
ATK: —
DEF: —
Level: —
Deck Cost: 50
Number: 727
Effect: Destroys all SPELLCASTER monsters on the Field!

LAUGHING FLOWER

Type: Plant
Attr: Earth
ATK: 900
DEF: 500
Level: 2
Deck Cost: 19
Number: 659
Effect: Control of opposing card is gained when this card is flipped face-up in battle!

LAUNCHER SPIDER

Type: Machine
Attr: Fire
ATK: 2,200
DEF: 2,500
Level: 7
Deck Cost: 47
Number: 508
Effect: None

LAVA BATTLEGUARD

Type: Warrior
Attr: Earth
ATK: 1,550
DEF: 1,800
Level: 5
Deck Cost: 39
Number: 197
Effect: When this card is flipped face-up, all Swamp Battleguards are increased 500 points!

LEFT ARM OF THE FORBIDDEN ONE

Type: Spellcaster
Attr: Dark
ATK: 200
DEF: 300
Level: 1
Deck Cost: 15
Number: 57
Effect: Left Arm of the Forbidden One. Awards victory to the one who brings together all four limbs and unleashes the monster!

LEFT LEG OF THE FORBIDDEN ONE

Type: Spellcaster
Attr: Dark
ATK: 200
DEF: 300
Level: 1
Deck Cost: 15
Number: 55
Effect: Left Leg of the Forbidden One. Awards victory to the one who brings together all four limbs and unleashes the monster!

LEGENDARY SWORD

Type: Power-up
Attr: —
ATK: —
DEF: —
Level: —
Deck Cost: 10
Number: 752
Effect: Increases the power of WARRIOR monsters of LIGHT and EARTH by 500 points!

LEGHUI

Type: Insect
Attr: Earth
ATK: 300
DEF: 350
Level: 1
Deck Cost: 12
Number: 410
Effect: Teleports to opponent's Summoning Area when this card is flipped face-up! When this card is flipped face-up in battle, the battle to be engaged is canceled!

LEO WIZARD

Type: Spellcaster
Attr: Earth
ATK: 1,350
DEF: 1,200
Level: 5
Deck Cost: 26
Number: 93
Effect: None

LEOGUN

Type: Beast
Attr: Earth
ATK: 1,750
DEF: 1,550
Level: 5
Deck Cost: 33
Number: 249
Effect: None

LESSER DRAGON

Type: Dragon
Attr: Wind
ATK: 1,200
DEF: 1,000
Level: 4
Deck Cost: 22
Number: 32
Effect: None

LIMITER REMOVAL

Type: Magic
Attr: —
ATK: —
DEF: —
Level: —
Deck Cost: 10
Number: 738
Effect: Boosts the ATK/DEF factors of all MACHINE monsters on the Field by 600 points

LIQUID BEAST

Type: Aqua
Attr: Water
ATK: 950
DEF: 800
Level: 3
Deck Cost: 18
Number: 601
Effect: None

LISARK

Type: Beast
Attr: Earth
ATK: 1,300
DEF: 1,300
Level: 4
Deck Cost: 26
Number: 238
Effect: None

LITTLE CHIMERA

Type: Beast
Attr: Fire
ATK: 600
DEF: 550
Level: 2
Deck Cost: 12
Number: 227
Effect: None

LITTLE D

Type: Dinosaur
Attr: Earth
ATK: 1,100
DEF: 700
Level: 3
Deck Cost: 18
Number: 444
Effect: None

LIVING VASE

Type: Plant
Attr: Earth
ATK: 900
DEF: 1,100
Level: 3
Deck Cost: 20
Number: 664
Effect: None

LORD OF D.

Type: Spellcaster
Attr: Dark
ATK: 1,200
DEF: 1,100
Level: 4
Deck Cost: 28
Number: 83
Effect: While this card is face-up in the defense position, all DRAGON monsters on the Field are immune to effects of an opponent's SPELL card!

LORD OF THE LAMP

Type: Fiend
Attr: Dark
ATK: 1,400
DEF: 1,200
Level: 4
Deck Cost: 26
Number: 312
Effect: None

LORD OF ZEMIA

Type: Fiend
Attr: Dark
ATK: 1,300
DEF: 1,000
Level: 4
Deck Cost: 23
Number: 314
Effect: None

LUCKY TRINKET

Type: Spellcaster
Attr: Light
ATK: 600
DEF: 800
Level: 2
Deck Cost: 19
Number: 40
Effect: All DARK monsters are reduced 100 points while this card is in the face-up, defense position!

LUMINOUS SOLDIER

Type: Warrior
Attr: Light
ATK: 1,600
DEF: 1,400
Level: 5
Deck Cost: 30
Number: 136
Effect: None

LUNAR QUEEN ELZAIM

Type: Fairy
Attr: Light
ATK: 750
DEF: 1,100
Level: 3
Deck Cost: 19
Number: 378
Effect: None

MABARREL

Type: Fiend
Attr: Dark
ATK: 1,700
DEF: 1,400
Level: 5
Deck Cost: 31
Number: 321
Effect: None

MACHINE ATTACKER

Type: Machine
Attr: Earth
ATK: 1,600
DEF: 1,300
Level: 5
Deck Cost: 29
Number: 525
Effect: None

MACHINE CONVERSION FACTORY

Type: Power-up
Attr: —
ATK: —
DEF: —
Level: —
Deck Cost: 10
Number: 774
Effect: Increases the power of MACHINE monsters by 500 points

MACHINE KING

Type: Machine
Attr: Earth
ATK: 2,200
DEF: 2,000
Level: 6
Deck Cost: 47
Number: 514
Effect: While this card is flipped face-up, this card is strengthened by 100 points for every MACHINE monster on the Field.

MADJINN GUNN

Type: Fiend
Attr: Dark
ATK: 600
DEF: 800
Level: 2
Deck Cost: 14
Number: 323
Effect: None

MAGIC DRAIN

Type: Magic
Attr: —
ATK: —
DEF: —
Level: —
Deck Cost: 60
Number: 748
Effect: Absorbs all of your opponent's Summoning Power!

MAGIC JAMMER

Type: Trap (Full Range)
Attr: —
ATK: —
DEF: —
Level: —
Deck Cost: 35
Number: 823
Effect: Disposable trap that triggers when an opponent's MAGIC or RITUAL card is activated, and cancels the cards effect

MAGICAL GHOST

Type: Zombie
Attr: Dark
ATK: 1,300
DEF: 1,400
Level: 4
Deck Cost: 27
Number: 124
Effect: None

MAGICAL LABYRINTH

Type: Magic
Attr: —
ATK: —
DEF: —
Level: —
Deck Cost: 10
Number: 698
Effect: Randomly selects 1 LABYRINTH terrain space, transforms it to NORMAL, and transforms the space where this card was triggered into LABYRINTH terrain! This card is effective only if there is at least one space containing LABYRINTH terrain on the Field.

MAGICAL NEUTRALIZING FORCE FIELD

Type: Magic
Attr: —
ATK: —
DEF: —
Level: —
Deck Cost: 10
Number: 734
Effect: Cancels all spellbind and power increase/decrease effects. In addition, destroys all face-up TRAP Cards! Does not cancel any bonus effects involving terrain and leader abilitites.

MAGICIAN OF BLACK CHAOS

Type: Spellcaster/Ritual
Attr: Dark
ATK: 2,800
DEF: 2,600
Level: 8
Deck Cost: 54
Number: 78
Effect: None

MAGICIAN OF FAITH

Type: Spellcaster
Attr: Light
ATK: 300
DEF: 400
Level: 1
Deck Cost: 12
Number: 43
Effect: When this card is flipped face-up, select 1 spell from all Graveyards and revive it in own Summoning Area! However, can only be activated in a turn when 'Magician of Faith' is being controlled.

MAHA VAILO

Type: Spellcaster
Attr: Light
ATK: 1,550
DEF: 1,400
Level: 5
Deck Cost: 35
Number: 45
Effect: When in the face-up defense position, the effect of all Power-up Cards are boosted an additional 200 points!

MAIDEN OF THE AQUA

Type: Aqua
Attr: Water
ATK: 700
DEF: 2,000
Level: 4
Deck Cost: 32
Number: 612
Effect: The power of all your AQUA monsters increases 500 points while this card is face-up in the defense position!

MAIDEN OF THE MOONLIGHT

Type: Spellcaster
Attr: Light
ATK: 1,500
DEF: 1,300
Level: 4
Deck Cost: 33
Number: 50
Effect: None

MALEVOLENT NUZZLER

Type: Power-up
Attr: —
ATK: —
DEF: —
Level: —
Deck Cost: 10
Number: 770
Effect: Increases the power of FIEND monsters by 500 points!

MAMMOTH GRAVEYARD

Type: Dinosaur
Attr: Earth
ATK: 1,200
DEF: 800
Level: 3
Deck Cost: 20
Number: 435
Effect: None

MAN EATER

Type: Plant
Attr: Earth
ATK: 800
DEF: 600
Level: 2
Deck Cost: 19
Number: 652
Effect: When this card is flipped face-up, all cards located on FOREST terrain are destroyed!

MAN-EATER BUG

Type: Insect
Attr: Earth
ATK: 450
DEF: 600
Level: 2
Deck Cost: 16
Number: 417
Effect: Destroys opposing enemy when this card is flipped face-up in battle.

MAN-EATING BLACK SHARK

Type: Fish
Attr: Water
ATK: 2,100
DEF: 1,300
Level: 5
Deck Cost: 34
Number: 473
Effect: None

MAN-EATING PLANT

Type: Plant
Attr: Earth
ATK: 800
DEF: 600
Level: 2
Deck Cost: 14
Number: 650
Effect: None

MAN-EATING TREASURE CHEST

Type: Fiend
Attr: Dark
ATK: 1,600
DEF: 1,000
Level: 4
Deck Cost: 26
Number: 359
Effect: None

MANGA RYU-RAN

Type: Dragon
Attr: Fire
ATK: 2,200
DEF: 2,600
Level: 7
Deck Cost: 48
Number: 17
Effect: SPECIAL POWER-UP: Strong in TOON terrain!
SPECIAL POWER-UP: Randomly transforms into a DRAGON/FIRE monster when powered up with Insect Imitation!

MARINE BEAST

Type: Fish
Attr: Water
ATK: 1,700
DEF: 1,600
Level: 5
Deck Cost: 33
Number: 474
Effect: None

MASAKI THE LEGENDARY SWORDSMAN

Type: Warrior
Attr: Earth
ATK: 1,100
DEF: 1,100
Level: 4
Deck Cost: 22
Number: 185
Effect: None

MASK OF DARKNESS

Type: Fiend
Attr: Dark
ATK: 900
DEF: 400
Level: 2
Deck Cost: 18
Number: 305
Effect: When this card is flipped face-up, revive 1 SPELL Card from the Graveyard and set it in own Summoning Area! This can only be done during the turn of a player controlling a Mask of Darkness card.

MASK OF SHINE AND DARK

Type: Spellcaster/ Ritual
Attr: Dark
ATK: 2,000
DEF: 1,800
Level: 6
Deck Cost: 43
Number: 77
Effect: 900-point bonus for battling against WARRIOR monsters!

MASKED CLOWN

Type: Warrior
Attr: Dark
ATK: 500
DEF: 700
Level: 2
Deck Cost: 12
Number: 138
Effect: None

MASKED SORCERER

Type: Spellcaster
Attr: Dark
ATK: 900
DEF: 1,400
Level: 4
Deck Cost: 23
Number: 69
Effect: None

MASTER & EXPERT

Type: Beast
Attr: Earth
ATK: 1,200
DEF: 1,000
Level: 4
Deck Cost: 22
Number: 244
Effect: None

MAVELUS

Type: Winged Beast
Attr: Wind
ATK: 1,300
DEF: 900
Level: 4
Deck Cost: 22
Number: 277
Effect: None

MECH BASS

Type: Machine
Attr: Water
ATK: 1,800
DEF: 1,500
Level: 5
Deck Cost: 33
Number: 532
Effect: None

MECH MOLE ZOMBIE

Type: Zombie
Attr: Dark
ATK: 500
DEF: 400
Level: 2
Deck Cost: 14
Number: 116
Effect: When turned face-up in battle, transforms an opponent into a ZOMBIE monster!

MECHALEON

Type: Reptile
Attr: Water
ATK: 800
DEF: 600
Level: 2
Deck Cost: 19
Number: 457
Effect: Flips all your SPELL cards face-down, when this card is flipped face-up!

MECHANICAL CHASER

Type: Machine
Attr: Dark
ATK: 1850
DEF: 800
Level: 4
Deck Cost: 27
Number: 492
Effect: None

MECHANICAL SNAIL

Type: Machine
Attr: Dark
ATK: 800
DEF: 1,000
Level: 3
Deck Cost: 18
Number: 503
Effect: None

MECHANICAL SPIDER

Type: Machine
Attr: Earth
ATK: 400
DEF: 500
Level: 2
Deck Cost: 9
Number: 516
Effect: None

MEDA BAT

Type: Fiend
Attr: Dark
ATK: 800
DEF: 400
Level: 2
Deck Cost: 12
Number: 327
Effect: None

MEGA THUNDERBALL

Type: Thunder
Attr: Wind
ATK: 750
DEF: 600
Level: 2
Deck Cost: 19
Number: 545
Effect: Gain control of an opposing monster if it is MACHINE for one turn when this card is flipped face-up in battle!

MEGAMORPH

Type: Power-up
Attr: —
ATK: —
DEF: —
Level: —
Deck Cost: 15
Number: 780
Effect: Increases the power of every monster by 300 points!

MEGASONIC EYE

Type: Machine
Attr: Dark
ATK: 1,500
DEF: 1,800
Level: 5
Deck Cost: 33
Number: 485
Effect: None

MEGAZOWLER

Type: Dinosaur
Attr: Earth
ATK: 1,800
DEF: 2,000
Level: 6
Deck Cost: 38
Number: 436
Effect: None

MEGIRUS LIGHT

Type: Fiend
Attr: Dark
ATK: 900
DEF: 600
Level: 3
Deck Cost: 15
Number: 331
Effect: None

MEOTOKO

Type: Beast
Attr: Earth
ATK: 700
DEF: 600
Level: 2
Deck Cost: 13
Number: 243
Effect: None

MESMERIC CONTROL

Type: Trap
(Limited Range)
Attr: —
ATK: —
DEF: —
Level: —
Deck Cost: 20
Number: 803
Effect: Disposable trap that spellbinds activated enemy card for 1 turn, and reduces its strength by 800 points!

METAL DRAGON

Type: Machine/ Fusion
Attr: Wind
ATK: 1,850
DEF: 1,700
Level: 6
Deck Cost: 36
Number: 529
Effect: None

METAL FISH

Type: Machine
Attr: Water
ATK: 1,600
DEF: 1,900
Level: 5
Deck Cost: 35
Number: 531
Effect: None

METAL GUARDIAN

Type: Fiend
Attr: Dark
ATK: 1,150
DEF: 2,150
Level: 5
Deck Cost: 33
Number: 303
Effect: None

METALMORPH

Type: Power-up
Attr: —
ATK: —
DEF: —
Level: —
Deck Cost: 5
Number: 799
Effect: Transforms Red-Eyes B. Dragon and Zoa to metal monsters!

METALZOA

Type: Machine
Attr: Dark
ATK: 3,000
DEF: 2,300
Level: 8
Deck Cost: 53
Number: 488
Effect: None

METEOR B. DRAGON

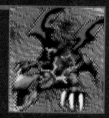

Type: Dragon
Attr: Fire
ATK: 3,500
DEF: 2,000
Level: 8
Deck Cost: 55
Number: 14
Effect: None

METEOR DRAGON

Type: Dragon
Attr: Earth
ATK: 1,800
DEF: 2,000
Level: 6
Deck Cost: 38
Number: 19
Effect: None

MIDNIGHT FIEND

Type: Fiend
Attr: Dark
ATK: 800
DEF: 600
Level: 2
Deck Cost: 19
Number: 322
Effect: While this card is face-up in the defense position, all damage to LP is increased by 100 points!

MIKAZUKINOYAIBA

Type: Dragon
Attr: Dark
ATK: 2,200
DEF: 2,350
Level: 7
Deck Cost: 46
Number: 12
Effect: None

MILLENNIUM GOLEM

Type: Rock
Attr: Earth
ATK: 2,000
DEF: 2,200
Level: 6
Deck Cost: 42
Number: 633
Effect: None

MILLENNIUM SHIELD

Type: Warrior/Ritual
Attr: Earth
ATK: 0
DEF: 3,000
Level: 5
Deck Cost: 35
Number: 189
Effect: While this card is face-up in the defense position, all your monsters receive 1,000 bonus points for their DEF!

MILUS RADIANT

Type: Beast
Attr: Earth
ATK: 300
DEF: 250
Level: 1
Deck Cost: 11
Number: 255
Effect: When this card is flipped face-up in battle, if the opposing card is a ZOMBIE monster, it is automatically destroyed!

MIMICAT

Type: Magic
Attr: —
ATK: —
DEF: —
Level: —
Deck Cost: 80
Number: 687
Effect: Select, revive, and control 1 card from either Graveyard!

MINAR

Type: Insect
Attr: Earth
ATK: 850
DEF: 750
Level: 3
Deck Cost: 17
Number: 420
Effect: None

MINOMUSHI WARRIOR

Type: Rock
Attr: Earth
ATK: 1,300
DEF: 1,200
Level: 4
Deck Cost: 25
Number: 636
Effect: None

MIRROR FORCE

Type: Trap
(Full Range)
Attr: —
ATK: —
DEF: —
Level: —
Deck Cost: 99
Number: 827
Effect: Disposable trap that triggers when an enemy inititiates an attack against your Leader or other cards on the Field! Destroys every one of your opponent's attack-positioned cards on the Field!

MIRROR WALL

Type: Trap
(Full Range)
Attr: —
ATK: —
DEF: —
Level: —
Deck Cost: 80
Number: 829
Effect: Permanent trap that triggers when an enemy initiates an attack against your Leader or other cards on the Field and reduces the ATK of the enemy by half!

MISAIRUZAME

Type: Fish
Attr: Water
ATK: 1,400
DEF: 1,600
Level: 5
Deck Cost: 35
Number: 469
Effect: Adds 500 bonus points for any battle against MACHINE monsters!

MOISTURE CREATURE

Type: Immortal
Attr: Light
ATK: 2,800
DEF: 2,900
Level: 9
Deck Cost: 72
Number: 682
Effect: NATURE EFFECT: While this card is face-up in the defense position, the opposing Leader's powers are rendered ineffective! DESTRUCTION: Transforms adjacent spaces into CRUSH terrain when this card is destroyed in battle!

MOLTEN BEHEMOTH

Type: Pyro
Attr: Fire
ATK: 1,000
DEF: 2,200
Level: 5
Deck Cost: 37
Number: 622
Effect: The power of all your PYRO monsters increases 500 points while this card is face-up in the defense position.

MON LARVAS

Type: Beast
Attr: Earth
ATK: 1,300
DEF: 1,400
Level: 4
Deck Cost: 27
Number: 259
Effect: None

MONSTER EGG

Type: Warrior
Attr: Earth
ATK: 600
DEF: 900
Level: 3
Deck Cost: 15
Number: 167
Effect: Randomly transforms into a BEAST-WARRIOR/EARTH monster when powered up with Insect Imitation!

MONSTER EYE

Type: Fiend
Attr: Dark
ATK: 250
DEF: 300
Level: 1
Deck Cost: 11
Number: 344
Effect: When turned face-up, flips the last card played by an opponent face-up!

MONSTER REBORN

Type: Magic
Attr: —
ATK: —
DEF: —
Level: —
Deck Cost: 50
Number: 685
Effect: Select, revive, and control 1 MONSTER card from either Graveyard!

Monster Recovery

Type: Magic
Attr: —
ATK: —
DEF: —
Level: —
Deck Cost: 5
Number: 744
Effect: All your monsters on the Field are returned to your Deck!

Monster Tamer

Type: Warrior
Attr: Earth
ATK: 1,800
DEF: 1,600
Level: 5
Deck Cost: 39
Number: 190
Effect: When this card is flipped face-up, all INSECT monsters are increased 300 points!

Monstrous Bird

Type: Winged Beast
Attr: Wind
ATK: 2,000
DEF: 1,900
Level: 6
Deck Cost: 39
Number: 285
Effect: None

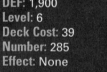

Monsturtle

Type: Aqua
Attr: Water
ATK: 800
DEF: 1,000
Level: 3
Deck Cost: 18
Number: 557
Effect: None

Moon Envoy

Type: Warrior
Attr: Light
ATK: 1,100
DEF: 1,000
Level: 4
Deck Cost: 21
Number: 133
Effect: None

Mooyan Curry

Type: Magic
Attr: —
ATK: —
DEF: —
Level: —
Deck Cost: 5
Number: 703
Effect: 200-point LP recovery for controlling player!

Morinphen

Type: Fiend
Attr: Dark
ATK: 1,550
DEF: 1,300
Level: 5
Deck Cost: 29
Number: 347
Effect: None

Morphing Jar

Type: Rock
Attr: Earth
ATK: 700
DEF: 600
Level: 2
Deck Cost: 13
Number: 643
Effect: None

Mountain

Type: Magic
Attr: —
ATK: —
DEF: —
Level: —
Deck Cost: 30
Number: 691
Effect: Transform a surrounding 2-space area into MOUNTAIN terrain

Mountain Warrior

Type: Beast-warrior
Attr: Earth
ATK: 600
DEF: 1,000
Level: 3
Deck Cost: 21
Number: 213
Effect: When this card is flipped face-up, all monsters in MOUNTAIN terrain are increased by 300 points!

Mucus Yolk

Type: Immortal
Attr: Dark
ATK: 0
DEF: 100
Level: 3
Deck Cost: 16
Number: 679
Effect: MOVEMENT: Each time Mucus Yolk moves, an opponent's LP is reduced by 50 points!
DESTRUCTION: Transforms adjacent spaces into CRUSH terrain when this card is destroyed in battle!

Muka Muka

Type: Rock
Attr: Earth
ATK: 600
DEF: 300
Level: 2
Deck Cost: 14
Number: 639
Effect: When this card is flipped face-up, the power of this card increases by 300 points for every monster in the controlling player's Graveyard!

Multiply

Type: Power-up
Attr: —
ATK: —
DEF: —
Level: —
Deck Cost: 10
Number: 790

Effect: Grants Kuriboh the power to resurrect on any Summoning Area space other than the one it's defeated in. Also, when the monster flips face-up, another Kuriboh is generated face-down in your own Summoning Area!

MUSE-A

Type: Fairy
Attr: Light
ATK: 850
DEF: 900
Level: 3
Deck Cost: 23
Number: 387
Effect: When this card is flipped face-up, all Musician King cards are strengthened 700 points!

MUSHROOM MAN

Type: Plant
Attr: Earth
ATK: 800
DEF: 600
Level: 2
Deck Cost: 18
Number: 649
Effect: When this card is flipped face-up, the power of all Mushroom Man #2 cards are increased by 500 points!

MUSHROOM MAN #2

Type: Warrior
Attr: Earth
ATK: 1,250
DEF: 800
Level: 3
Deck Cost: 21
Number: 196
Effect: None

MUSICIAN KING

Type: Spellcaster
Attr: Light
ATK: 1,750
DEF: 1,500
Level: 5
Deck Cost: 33
Number: 46
Effect: None

M-WARRIOR #1

Type: Warrior
Attr: Earth
ATK: 1,000
DEF: 500
Level: 3
Deck Cost: 20
Number: 170
Effect: When this card is flipped face-up, all M-Warrior #2s are increased 500 points!

M-WARRIOR #2

Type: Warrior
Attr: Earth
ATK: 500
DEF: 1,000
Level: 3
Deck Cost: 20
Number: 171
Effect: When this card is flipped face-up, all M-Warrior #1s are increased 500 points!

MYSTERIOUS PUPPETEER

Type: Warrior
Attr: Earth
ATK: 1,000
DEF: 1,500
Level: 4
Deck Cost: 25
Number: 173
Effect: None

MYSTERY HAND

Type: Fiend
Attr: Dark
ATK: 500
DEF: 500
Level: 2
Deck Cost: 15
Number: 310
Effect: When this card is flipped face-up, if there's a Jigen Bakudan in any adjacent space, teleport 1 Jigen Bakudan to an opponent's Summoning Area.

MYSTIC CLOWN

Type: Fiend
Attr: Dark
ATK: 1,500
DEF: 1,000
Level: 4
Deck Cost: 25
Number: 334
Effect: None

MYSTIC HORSEMAN

Type: Beast
Attr: Earth
ATK: 1,300
DEF: 1,550
Level: 4
Deck Cost: 29
Number: 233
Effect: None

MYSTIC LAMP

Type: Spellcaster
Attr: Dark
ATK: 400
DEF: 300
Level: 1
Deck Cost: 12
Number: 73
Effect: When this card is flipped face-up, strengthens the Lord of the Lamp by 700 points!

MYSTICAL CAPTURE CHAIR

Type: Fairy
Attr: Light
ATK: 700
DEF: 700
Level: 2
Deck Cost: 19
Number: 372
Effect: While this card is face-up, in defense position, spellbinds all FIEND monsters!

MYSTICAL ELF

Type: Spellcaster
Attr: Light
ATK: 800
DEF: 2,000
Level: 4
Deck Cost: 33
Number: 35
Effect: When this card is flipped face-up, powers up all of your own LIGHT monsters by 800 points!

MYSTICAL MOON

Type: Power-up
Attr: —
ATK: —
DEF: —
Level: —
Deck Cost: 10
Number: 769
Effect: Increases the power of BEAST and BEAST-WARRIOR monsters by 500 points!

MYSTICAL SAND

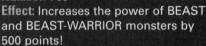

Type: Rock
Attr: Earth
ATK: 2,100
DEF: 1,700
Level: 6
Deck Cost: 38
Number: 641
Effect: None

MYSTICAL SHEEP #1

Type: Beast
Attr: Earth
ATK: 1,150
DEF: 900
Level: 3
Deck Cost: 21
Number: 264
Effect: None

MYSTICAL SHEEP #2

Type: Beast
Attr: Earth
ATK: 800
DEF: 1,000
Level: 3
Deck Cost: 23
Number: 247
Effect: When this card is flipped face-up in battle, the opposing monster is spellbound for 1 turn!

NAILS OF BANE

Type: Power-up
Attr: —
ATK: —
DEF: —
Level: —
Deck Cost: 10
Number: 788
Effect: Increases the power of DRAGON monsters of DARK by 700 points!

NECK HUNTER

Type: Fiend
Attr: Dark
ATK: 1,750
DEF: 1,900
Level: 6
Deck Cost: 37
Number: 351
Effect: None

NECROLANCER THE TIMELORD

Type: Spellcaster
Attr: Dark
ATK: 800
DEF: 900
Level: 3
Deck Cost: 17
Number: 65
Effect: None

NEEDLE BALL

Type: Fiend
Attr: Dark
ATK: 750
DEF: 700
Level: 2
Deck Cost: 20
Number: 346
Effect: Inflicts 500 points of damage against opponent's LP when destroyed in battle!

NEEDLE WORM

Type: Insect
Attr: Earth
ATK: 750
DEF: 600
Level: 2
Deck Cost: 14
Number: 423
Effect: SPECIAL POWER-UP: Transforms to Larva of Moth when strengthened with Cocoon of Evolution.

NEGATE ATTACK

Type: Trap
(Full Range)
Attr: —
ATK: —
DEF: —
Level: —
Deck Cost: 15
Number: 828
Effect: Disposable trap that triggers when an enemy initiates an attack against your leader or other cards on the Field and cancels the attack!

NEKOGAL #1

Type: Beast
Attr: Earth
ATK: 1,100
DEF: 900
Level: 3
Deck Cost: 20
Number: 245
Effect: None

NEKOGAL #2

Type: Beast-warrior
Attr: Earth
ATK: 1,900
DEF: 2,000
Level: 6
Deck Cost: 39
Number: 221
Effect: None

NEMURIKO

Type: Spellcaster
Attr: Dark
ATK: 800
DEF: 700
Level: 3
Deck Cost: 20
Number: 64
Effect: While this card is face-up in the defense position, spellbinds all enemy WARRIOR monsters.

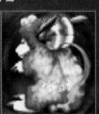

NEO THE MAGIC SWORDSMAN

Type: Spellcaster
Attr: Light
ATK: 1,700
DEF: 1,000
Level: 4
Deck Cost: 27
Number: 52
Effect: None

NIGHT LIZARD

Type: Aqua
Attr: Water
ATK: 1,150
DEF: 1,300
Level: 4
Deck Cost: 25
Number: 606
Effect: None

NIGHTMARE SCORPION

Type: Insect
Attr: Earth
ATK: 900
DEF: 800
Level: 3
Deck Cost: 22
Number: 404
Effect: Spellbinds opposing monster for 1 turn when this card is flipped face-up in battle!

NIWATORI

Type: Winged Beast
Attr: Earth
ATK: 900
DEF: 800
Level: 3
Deck Cost: 22
Number: 270
Effect: NATURE EFFECT: While this card is face-up in the defense position all recovery values to LP are doubled! SPECIAL POWER-UP: Strong in TOON terrain!

NOVOX'S PRAYER

Type: Ritual
Attr: —
ATK: —
DEF: —
Level: —
Deck Cost: 5
Number: 841
Effect: Sacrifice 2 WARRIOR monsters with Mystical Elf to summon Skull Guardian!

OBESE MARMOT OF NEFARIOUSNESS

Type: Beast
Attr: Earth
ATK: 750
DEF: 800
Level: 3
Deck Cost: 14
Number: 261
Effect: None

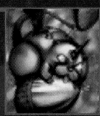

OCTOBERSER

Type: Aqua
Attr: Water
ATK: 1,600
DEF: 1,400
Level: 5
Deck Cost: 30
Number: 553
Effect: None

OCUBEAM

Type: Fairy
Attr: Light
ATK: 1,550
DEF: 1,650
Level: 5
Deck Cost: 32
Number: 381
Effect: None

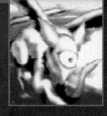

OGRE OF THE BLACK SHADOW

Type: Beast-warrior
Attr: Earth
ATK: 1,200
DEF: 1,400
Level: 4
Deck Cost: 26
Number: 218
Effect: None

ONE WHO HUNTS SOULS

Type: Beast-warrior
Attr: Earth
ATK: 1,100
DEF: 1,000
Level: 4
Deck Cost: 26
Number: 217
Effect: Monsters destroyed in battles against One Who Hunts Souls cannot be revived once they are sent to the Graveyard!

ONE-EYED SHIELD DRAGON

Type: Dragon
Attr: Wind
ATK: 700
DEF: 1,300
Level: 3
Deck Cost: 20
Number: 27
Effect: None

OOGUCHI

Type: Aqua
Attr: Water
ATK: 300
DEF: 250
Level: 1
Deck Cost: 11
Number: 575
Effect: Teleports to opponent's Summoning Area when this card is flipped face-up! When this card is flipped face-up in battle, that battle is cancelled.

OOKAZI

Type: Magic
Attr: —
ATK: —
DEF: —
Level: —
Deck Cost: 15
Number: 712
Effect: Inflicts 500 points of damage to opponent's LP!

111

ORION THE BATTLE KING

Type: Fairy
Attr: Light
ATK: 1,800
DEF: 1,500
Level: 5
Deck Cost: 33
Number: 370
Effect: None

OSCILLO HERO

Type: Warrior
Attr: Earth
ATK: 1,250
DEF: 700
Level: 3
Deck Cost: 20
Number: 198
Effect: None

OSCILLO HERO #2

Type: Thunder
Attr: Light
ATK: 1,000
DEF: 500
Level: 3
Deck Cost: 20
Number: 533
Effect: Increases 800 bonus points in battles against FISH monsters!

PALE BEAST

Type: Beast
Attr: Earth
ATK: 1,500
DEF: 1,200
Level: 4
Deck Cost: 27
Number: 260
Effect: None

PANTHER WARRIOR

Type: Beast-warrior
Attr: Earth
ATK: 2,000
DEF: 1,600
Level: 6
Deck Cost: 36
Number: 222
Effect: None

PARALYZING POTION

Type: Power-up
Attr: —
ATK: —
DEF: —
Level: —
Deck Cost: 15
Number: 795
Effect: Renders all monsters other than MACHINE eternally spellbound!

PARROT DRAGON

Type: Dragon
Attr: Wind
ATK: 2,000
DEF: 1,300
Level: 5
Deck Cost: 33
Number: 29
Effect: Strong in TOON terrain!

PATRICIAN OF DARKNESS

Type: Zombie
Attr: Dark
ATK: 2,000
DEF: 1,400
Level: 5
Deck Cost: 34
Number: 132
Effect: None

PATROL ROBO

Type: Machine
Attr: Earth
ATK: 1,100
DEF: 900
Level: 3
Deck Cost: 25
Number: 523
Effect: When this card is flipped face-up, flips all opponent SPELL Cards face-up!

PEACOCK

Type: Winged Beast
Attr: Wind
ATK: 1,700
DEF: 1,500
Level: 5
Deck Cost: 32
Number: 283
Effect: None

PENDULUM MACHINE

Type: Machine
Attr: Dark
ATK: 1,750
DEF: 2,000
Level: 6
Deck Cost: 38
Number: 487
Effect: None

PENGUIN KNIGHT

Type: Aqua
Attr: Water
ATK: 900
DEF: 800
Level: 3
Deck Cost: 22
Number: 560
Effect: All Penguin Soldiers increase 800 points when this card is flipped face-up!

PENGUIN SOLDIER

Type: Aqua
Attr: Water
ATK: 750
DEF: 500
Level: 2
Deck Cost: 18
Number: 600
Effect: When this card is flipped face-up, all Penguin Knights are strengthened by 800 points!

PERFECTLY ULTIMATE GREAT MOTH

Type: Insect
Attr: Earth
ATK: 3,500
DEF: 3,000
Level: 8
Deck Cost: 70
Number: 403
Effect: While this card is face-up in the defense position, all enemy monsters are reduced by 100 points each turn!

PERFORMANCE OF SWORDS

Type: Warrior/Ritual
Attr: Earth
ATK: 1,950
DEF: 1,850
Level: 6
Deck Cost: 43
Number: 195
Effect: 900-point bonus for battles with WARRIOR monsters!

PETIT ANGEL

Type: Fairy
Attr: Light
ATK: 600
DEF: 900
Level: 3
Deck Cost: 20
Number: 376
Effect: Revives in own Summoning Area, other than current location, when destroyed in battle!

PETIT DRAGON

Type: Dragon
Attr: Wind
ATK: 600
DEF: 700
Level: 2
Deck Cost: 13
Number: 26
Effect: None

PETIT MOTH

Type: Insect
Attr: Earth
ATK: 300
DEF: 200
Level: 1
Deck Cost: 5
Number: 407
Effect: SPECIAL POWER-UP: Transforms to Larva of Moth when strengthened with Cocoon of Evolution!

PHANTOM DEWAN

Type: Spellcaster
Attr: Dark
ATK: 700
DEF: 600
Level: 2
Deck Cost: 18
Number: 67
Effect: When this card is flipped face-up in battle, spellbinds opposing monster for 3 turns!

PHANTOM GHOST

Type: Zombie
Attr: Dark
ATK: 600
DEF: 800
Level: 2
Deck Cost: 14
Number: 117
Effect: None

POT THE TRICK

Type: Rock
Attr: Earth
ATK: 400
DEF: 400
Level: 2
Deck Cost: 13
Number: 642
Effect: When this card is flipped face-up, all your spellbound cards are freed and able to move at the start of your next turn!

POWER OF KAISHIN

Type: Power-up
Attr: —
ATK: —
DEF: —
Level: —
Deck Cost: 10
Number: 777
Effect: Increases the power of WATER monsters by 500 points!

PRACTICAL

Type: Dinosaur
Attr: Earth
ATK: 1,900
DEF: 1,500
Level: 5
Deck Cost: 34
Number: 441
Effect: None

PREVENT RAT

Type: Beast
Attr: Earth
ATK: 500
DEF: 2,000
Level: 4
Deck Cost: 25
Number: 246
Effect: None

PRINCESS OF TSURUGI

Type: Warrior
Attr: Wind
ATK: 900
DEF: 700
Level: 3
Deck Cost: 16
Number: 204
Effect: None

PRISMAN

Type: Rock
Attr: Light
ATK: 800
DEF: 1,000
Level: 3
Deck Cost: 23
Number: 624
Effect: When this card is flipped face-up, all your SPELL cards are flipped face-down!

PROTECTOR OF THE THRONE

Type: Warrior
Attr: Earth
ATK: 800
DEF: 1,500
Level: 4
Deck Cost: 23
Number: 184
Effect: None

PSYCHIC KAPPA

Type: Aqua
Attr: Water
ATK: 400
DEF: 1,000
Level: 2
Deck Cost: 19
Number: 571
Effect: Whenever damage is inflicted to LP in battle, the damage amount is reduced to 0!

PSYCHO-PUPPET

Type: Fiend/Ritual
Attr: Dark
ATK: 2,000
DEF: 2,350
Level: 7
Deck Cost: 49
Number: 353
Effect: If the Leader is a Mysterious Puppeteer, gains 1500 points when this card is flipped face-up!

PUMPKING THE KING OF GHOSTS

Type: Zombie
Attr: Dark
ATK: 1,800
DEF: 2,000
Level: 6
Deck Cost: 43
Number: 108
Effect: While this card is face-up in the defense position, all ZOMBIE monsters are increased 100 points at the start of each turn!

PUNISHED EAGLE

Type: Winged Beast
Attr: Wind
ATK: 2,100
DEF: 1,800
Level: 6
Deck Cost: 39
Number: 280
Effect: None

PUPA OF MOTH

Type: Insect
Attr: Earth
ATK: 0
DEF: 2,000
Level: 2
Deck Cost: 25
Number: 428
Effect: MOVEMENT: Cannot move. NATURE EFFECT: Transforms into Perfectly Ultimate Great Moth if the card survives 1 turn in face-up defense position after being flipped face-up by the controlling player. If destroyed prior to transformation in battle, the card is revived as Great Moth in own Summoning Area other than the current location!

PUPPET RITUAL

Type: Ritual
Attr: —
ATK: —
DEF: —
Level: —
Deck Cost: 5
Number: 847
Effect: Sacrifice 2 MACHINE monsters with Mysterious Puppeteer to summon Psycho-Puppet!

QUEEN BIRD

Type: Winged Beast
Attr: Wind
ATK: 1,200
DEF: 2,000
Level: 5
Deck Cost: 32
Number: 282
Effect: None

QUEEN OF AUTUMN LEAVES

Type: Plant
Attr: Earth
ATK: 1,800
DEF: 1,500
Level: 5
Deck Cost: 33
Number: 667
Effect: None

QUEEN'S DOUBLE

Type: Warrior
Attr: Earth
ATK: 350
DEF: 300
Level: 1
Deck Cost: 12
Number: 201
Effect: When this card is flipped face-up, all Princess of Tsurugi cards are increased 700 points!

RABID HORSEMAN

Type: Beast-warrior
Attr: Earth
ATK: 2,000
DEF: 1,700
Level: 6
Deck Cost: 37
Number: 215
Effect: None

Complete Card List

RAIGEKI

Type: Magic
Attr: —
ATK: —
DEF: —
Level: —
Deck Cost: 80
Number: 700
Effect: Destroys all monsters located in vertical and horizontal lines from the activated space!

RAIN OF MERCY

Type: Magic
Attr: —
ATK: —
DEF: —
Level: —
Deck Cost: 10
Number: 739
Effect: Boosts the ATK/DEF factors of all PLANT monsters on the Field by 600 points!

RAINBOW FLOWER

Type: Plant
Attr: Earth
ATK: 400
DEF: 500
Level: 2
Deck Cost: 9
Number: 657
Effect: None

RAINBOW MARINE MERMAID

Type: Fish
Attr: Water
ATK: 1,550
DEF: 1,750
Level: 5
Deck Cost: 33
Number: 467
Effect: None

RAISE BODY HEAT

Type: Power-up
Attr: —
ATK: —
DEF: —
Level: —
Deck Cost: 10
Number: 775
Effect: Increases the power of DINOSAUR and REPTILE monsters by 500 points!

RARE FISH

Type: Fish
Attr: Water
ATK: 1,500
DEF: 1,200
Level: 4
Deck Cost: 27
Number: 460
Effect: None

RAY & TEMPERATURE

Type: Fairy
Attr: Light
ATK: 1,000
DEF: 1,000
Level: 25
Deck Cost: 3
Number: 380
Effect: Cancels all power increases or decreases of an enemy monster in battle! Does not cancel bonus effects such as terrain or Leader ability effects!

REAPER OF THE CARDS

Type: Fiend
Attr: Dark
ATK: 1,380
DEF: 1,930
Level: 5
Deck Cost: 39
Number: 299
Effect: Able to move and attack without triggering an opponent's TRAP (LIMITED RANGE)!

RED ARCHERY GIRL

Type: Aqua
Attr: Water
ATK: 1,400
DEF: 1,500
Level: 4
Deck Cost: 29
Number: 610
Effect: None

RED MEDICINE

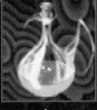

Type: Magic
Attr: —
ATK: —
DEF: —
Level: —
Deck Cost: 6
Number: 704
Effect: 500-point LP recovery for controlling player.

RED-EYES B. DRAGON

Type: Dragon
Attr: Dark
ATK: 2,400
DEF: 2,000
Level: 7
Deck Cost: 44
Number: 7
Effect: Transforms into Red-Eyes Black Metal Dragon when powered up with Metalmorph!

RED-EYES BLACK METAL DRAGON

Type: Machine
Attr: Dark
ATK: 2,800
DEF: 2,400
Level: 8
Deck Cost: 52
Number: 501
Effect: None

115

RESURRECTION OF CHAKRA

Type: Ritual
Attr: —
ATK: —
DEF: —
Level: —
Deck Cost: 5
Number: 846
Effect: Sacrifice 2 monsters with ATKs of 1,000 or less and Versago the Destroyer to summon Chakra!

REVERSE TRAP

Type: Trap (Full Range)
Attr: —
ATK: —
DEF: —
Level: —
Deck Cost: 25
Number: 816
Effect: Permanent trap that triggers against power-ups involving increases in ATK and DEF, reversing the positive effect to a negative amount.

REVIVAL OF DOKURORIDER

Type: Ritual
Attr: —
ATK: —
DEF: —
Level: —
Deck Cost: 5
Number: 851
Effect: Sacrifice 1 ZOMBIE monster, 1 MACHINE monster, and 1 INSECT monster to summon Dokurorider!

REVIVAL OF SENMIN GENJIN

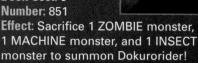

Type: Ritual
Attr: —
ATK: —
DEF: —
Level: —
Deck Cost: 5
Number: 840
Effect: Sacrifice 2 BEAST-WARRIOR monsters and Millenium Golem to summon Sengenjin!

REVIVED SERPENT NIGHT DRAGON

Type: Ritual
Attr: —
ATK: —
DEF: —
Level: —
Deck Cost: 5
Number: 843
Effect: Sacrifice 1 WARRIOR monster, 1 WINGED BEAST monster, and Darkfire Dragon to summon Serpent Night Dragon!

RHUIMUNDOS OF THE RED SWORD

Type: Warrior
Attr: Earth
ATK: 1,200
DEF: 1,300
Level: 4
Deck Cost: 25
Number: 168
Effect: None

RIGHT ARM OF THE FORBIDDEN ONE

Type: Spellcaster
Attr: Dark
ATK: 200
DEF: 300
Level: 1
Deck Cost: 15
Number: 56
Effect: Right Arm of the Forbidden One. Awards victory to the one who brings together all four limbs and unleashes the monster!

RIGHT LEG OF THE FORBIDDEN ONE

Type: Spellcaster
Attr: Dark
ATK: 200
DEF: 300
Level: 1
Deck Cost: 15
Number: 54
Effect: Right Leg of the Forbidden One. Awards victory to the one who brings together all four limbs and unleashes the monster!

RIGRAS LEEVER

Type: Immortal
Attr: Fire
ATK: 1,600
DEF: 100
Level: 3
Deck Cost: 32
Number: 681
Effect: FLIP: When this card is flipped face-up, all players must discard their current hand to their respective Graveyards!
DESTRUCTION: Transforms adjacent spaces into CRUSH terrain when this card is destroyed in battle!

RIRYOKU

Type: Power-up
Attr: —
ATK: —
DEF: —
Level: —
Deck Cost: 99
Number: 789
Effect: Reduces opponent's LP by half and adds the reduced amount to the power of all monsters!

ROARING OCEAN SNAKE

Type: Aqua
Attr: Water
ATK: 2,100
DEF: 1,800
Level: 6
Deck Cost: 49
Number: 563
Effect: ATTACK: When engaged in battle, transforms the space it occupies into Sea terrain!
FLIP: When this card is flipped face-up transforms all adjacent spaces into Sea terrain!

ROBOTIC KNIGHT

Type: Machine
Attr: Fire
ATK: 1,600
DEF: 1,800
Level: 5
Deck Cost: 39
Number: 510
Effect: While this card is face-up in the defense position, the power of all your MACHINE monsters are increased by 300 bonus points!

ROCK OGRE GROTTO #2

Type: Rock
Attr: Earth
ATK: 700
DEF: 1,400
Level: 3
Deck Cost: 21
Number: 631
Effect: None

ROCK OGRE GROTTO #1

Type: Rock
Attr: Earth
ATK: 800
DEF: 1,200
Level: 3
Deck Cost: 20
Number: 625
Effect: None

ROCK SPIRIT

Type: Spellcaster
Attr: Earth
ATK: 1,650
DEF: 1,900
Level: 5
Deck Cost: 36
Number: 94
Effect: None

ROGUE DOLL

Type: Spellcaster
Attr: Light
ATK: 1,600
DEF: 1,000
Level: 4
Deck Cost: 31
Number: 37
Effect: Allows the one-sided destruction of the opposition when battling ZOMBIE monsters!

ROOT WATER

Type: Fish
Attr: Water
ATK: 900
DEF: 800
Level: 3
Deck Cost: 22
Number: 461
Effect: All spaces within a range of 1 space are transformed to Sea terrain when this card is flipped face-up!

ROSE SPECTRE OF DUNN

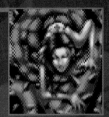

Type: Plant/Fusion
Attr: Dark
ATK: 2,000
DEF: 1,800
Level: 6
Deck Cost: 38
Number: 648
Effect: None

ROYAL DECREE

Type: Trap
(Full Range)
Attr: —
ATK: —
DEF: —
Level: —
Deck Cost: 80
Number: 825
Effect: Permanent trap that triggers against any activated TRAP Card and nullifies the card!

ROYAL GUARD

Type: Machine
Attr: Earth
ATK: 1,900
DEF: 2,200
Level: 6
Deck Cost: 41
Number: 524
Effect: None

RUDE KAISER

Type: Beast-warrior
Attr: Earth
ATK: 1,800
DEF: 1,600
Level: 5
Deck Cost: 34
Number: 219
Effect: None

RYU-KISHIN

Type: Fiend
Attr: Dark
ATK: 1,000
DEF: 500
Level: 3
Deck Cost: 15
Number: 292
Effect: None

RYU-KISHIN POWERED

Type: Fiend
Attr: Dark
ATK: 1,600
DEF: 1,200
Level: 4
Deck Cost: 28
Number: 339
Effect: None

RYU-RAN

Type: Dragon
Attr: Wind
ATK: 2,200
DEF: 2,600
Level: 7
Deck Cost: 48
Number: 16
Effect: Randomly transforms into a DRAGON/FIRE monster when powered up with Insect Imitation!

SABER SLASHER

Type: Machine
Attr: Dark
ATK: 1,450
DEF: 1,500
Level: 5
Deck Cost: 30
Number: 489
Effect: None

SAGGI THE DARK CLOWN

Type: Spellcaster
Attr: Dark
ATK: 600
DEF: 1,500
Level: 3
Deck Cost: 21
Number: 59
Effect: Strong in TOON terrain!

SALAMANDRA

Type: Power-up
Attr: —
ATK: —
DEF: —
Level: —
Deck Cost: 10
Number: 779
Effect: Increases the power of FIRE monsters by 500 points!

SAND STONE

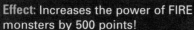

Type: Rock
Attr: Earth
ATK: 1,300
DEF: 1,600
Level: 5
Deck Cost: 29
Number: 640
Effect: None

SANGA OF THE THUNDER

Type: Thunder
Attr: Light
ATK: 2,600
DEF: 2,200
Level: 7
Deck Cost: 53
Number: 534
Effect: Whenever damage is inflicted to LP in battle, the damage amount is reduced to 0!

SANGAN

Type: Fiend
Attr: Dark
ATK: 1,000
DEF: 600
Level: 3
Deck Cost: 16
Number: 296
Effect: None

SEA KAMEN

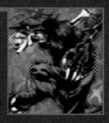

Type: Aqua
Attr: Water
ATK: 1,100
DEF: 1,300
Level: 4
Deck Cost: 24
Number: 588
Effect: None

SEA KING DRAGON

Type: Sea Serpent
Attr: Water
ATK: 2,000
DEF: 1,700
Level: 6
Deck Cost: 37
Number: 479
Effect: None

SEAL OF THE ANCIENTS

Type: Trap
(Full Range)
Attr: —
ATK: —
DEF: —
Level: —
Deck Cost: 5
Number: 826
Effect: Permanent trap that triggers against any activated RITUAL Card and nullifies the card!

SEBEK'S BLESSING

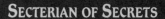

Type: Magic
Attr: —
ATK: —
DEF: —
Level: —
Deck Cost: 10
Number: 741
Effect: Boosts the ATK/DEF factors of all REPTILES monsters on the field by 600 points!

SECTERIAN OF SECRETS

Type: Spellcaster
Attr: Dark
ATK: 700
DEF: 500
Level: 2
Deck Cost: 17
Number: 72
Effect: Weakens an opposing enemy by 300 points when destroyed in battle!

SEIYARYU

Type: Dragon
Attr: Light
ATK: 2,500
DEF: 2,300
Level: 7
Deck Cost: 53
Number: 1
Effect: 300-point bonus for battles against FIEND monsters!

SENGENJIN

Type: Beast-warrior/
Ritual
Attr: Earth
ATK: 2,750
DEF: 2,500
Level: 8
Deck Cost: 58
Number: 220
Effect: 900-point bonus for battles against ROCK monsters!

SERPENT MARAUDER

Type: Reptile
Attr: Earth
ATK: 700
DEF: 600
Level: 2
Deck Cost: 18
Number: 447
Effect: While this card is face-up in the defense position, cancels any increased movement effects for all cards!

SERPENT NIGHT DRAGON

Type: Dragon/Ritual
Attr: Dark
ATK: 2,350
DEF: 2,400
Level: 7
Deck Cost: 53
Number: 11
Effect: 900-point bonus for battles against SPELLCASTER monsters!

SERPENTINE PRINCESS

Type: Reptile
Attr: Water
ATK: 1,400
DEF: 2,000
Level: 5
Deck Cost: 39
Number: 458
Effect: Own REPTILE monsters strengthened by 900 points when this card is flipped face-up!

SERVANT OF CATABOLISM

Type: Immortal
Attr: Light
ATK: 700
DEF: 500
Level: 3
Deck Cost: 27
Number: 680
Effect: NATURE EFFECT: While this card is face-up in the defense position, an additional point is added each turn during the recovery of the player's Summoning Power points!
DESTRUCTION: Transforms adjacent spaces into CRUSH terrain when this card is destroyed in battle!

SHADOW GHOUL

Type: Zombie
Attr: Dark
ATK: 1,600
DEF: 1,300
Level: 5
Deck Cost: 34
Number: 123
Effect: Can move into LABYRINTH terrain, and transforms into Wall Shadow!

SHADOW OF EYES

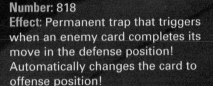

Type: Trap
(Full Range)
Attr: —
ATK: —
DEF: —
Level: —
Deck Cost: 20
Number: 818
Effect: Permanent trap that triggers when an enemy card completes its move in the defense position! Automatically changes the card to offense position!

SHADOW SPECTER

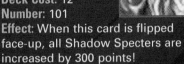

Type: Zombie
Attr: Dark
ATK: 500
DEF: 200
Level: 1
Deck Cost: 12
Number: 101
Effect: When this card is flipped face-up, all Shadow Specters are increased by 300 points!

SHADOW SPELL

Type: Trap
(Limited Range)
Attr: —
ATK: —
DEF: —
Level: —
Deck Cost: 40
Number: 802
Effect: Disposable trap that spellbinds activated enemy card for 3 turns, and reduces its strength by 1,000 points!

SHAPESNATCH

Type: Immortal
Attr: Dark
ATK: 1,200
DEF: 1,700
Level: 5
Deck Cost: 44
Number: 675
Effect: NATURE EFFECT: Shape Snatcher's ATK and DEF copies the enemy Leader's ATK for attacks and your own Leader's DEF when defending!
DESTRUCTION: Transforms adjacent spaces into CRUSH terrain when this card is destroyed in battle!

SHIELD & SWORD

Type: Magic
Attr: —
ATK: —
DEF: —
Level: —
Deck Cost: 30
Number: 736
Effect: Swaps the respective ATK and DEF values of each monster on the Field!

SHIFT

Type: Magic
Attr: —
ATK: —
DEF: —
Level: —
Deck Cost: 50
Number: 746
Effect: Your monster with the highest ATK on the Field is transported to the space where this card is activated!

SHINING FRIENDSHIP

Type: Fairy
Attr: Light
ATK: 1,300
DEF: 1,100
Level: 4
Deck Cost: 24
Number: 389
Effect: Spellbinds enemy for 1 turn when this card is flipped face-up in battle.

SHOVEL CRUSHER

Type: Machine
Attr: Dark
ATK: 900
DEF: 1,200
Level: 3
Deck Cost: 21
Number: 518
Effect: None

SILVER BOW AND ARROW

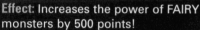

Type: Power-up
Attr: —
ATK: —
DEF: —
Level: —
Deck Cost: 10
Number: 763
Effect: Increases the power of FAIRY monsters by 500 points!

SILVER FANG

Type: Beast
Attr: Earth
ATK: 1,200
DEF: 800
Level: 3
Deck Cost: 20
Number: 232
Effect: None

SINISTER SERPENT

Type: Reptile
Attr: Water
ATK: 300
DEF: 250
Level: 1
Deck Cost: 11
Number: 456
Effect: Reduces opponent's Summoning Power to 0 when destroyed in battle!

SKELENGEL

Type: Fairy
Attr: Light
ATK: 900
DEF: 400
Level: 2
Deck Cost: 18
Number: 384
Effect: If a card has been played from the hand in the turn when this card is destroyed in battle, the owning player can play one more card from the hand!

SKELGON

Type: Zombie
Attr: Dark
ATK: 1,700
DEF: 1,900
Level: 6
Deck Cost: 36
Number: 126
Effect: None

SKULL GUARDIAN

Type: Warrior/Ritual
Attr: Light
ATK: 2,050
DEF: 2,500
Level: 7
Deck Cost: 56
Number: 135
Effect: ATTACK: 900-point bonus when battling FIEND monsters!
FLIP: When this card is flipped face-up, strengthen all LIGHT monsters by 300 points!

SKULL KNIGHT

Type: Spellcaster
Attr: Dark
ATK: 2,650
DEF: 2,250
Level: 7
Deck Cost: 49
Number: 75
Effect: None

SKULL RED BIRD

Type: Winged Beast
Attr: Wind
ATK: 1,550
DEF: 1,200
Level: 4
Deck Cost: 28
Number: 281
Effect: None

SKULL SERVANT

Type: Zombie
Attr: Dark
ATK: 300
DEF: 200
Level: 1
Deck Cost: 10
Number: 102
Effect: When this card is flipped face-up, all Skull Servants are increased by 300 points!

SKULL STALKER

Type: Warrior
Attr: Dark
ATK: 900
DEF: 800
Level: 3
Deck Cost: 22
Number: 140
Effect: Reduces opposing monster by 300 points when destroyed in battle!

SKULLBIRD

Type: Winged Beast
Attr: Wind
ATK: 1,900
DEF: 1,700
Level: 6
Deck Cost: 36
Number: 284
Effect: None

SKY DRAGON

Type: Dragon
Attr: Wind
ATK: 1,900
DEF: 1,800
Level: 6
Deck Cost: 37
Number: 31
Effect: None

SLATE WARRIOR

Type: Immortal
Attr: Wind
ATK: 1,900
DEF: 400
Level: 4
Deck Cost: 38
Number: 674
Effect: When this card is flipped face-up, all your IMMORTAL cards are strengthened by 500 points! Transforms adjacent spaces to CRUSH terrain when this card is destroyed in battle!

SLEEPING LION

Type: Beast
Attr: Earth
ATK: 700
DEF: 1,700
Level: 4
Deck Cost: 24
Number: 235
Effect: None

SLOT MACHINE

Type: Machine
Attr: Dark
ATK: 2,000
DEF: 2,300
Level: 7
Deck Cost: 43
Number: 505
Effect: None

SNAKEYASHI

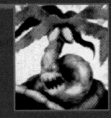

Type: Plant
Attr: Earth
ATK: 1,000
DEF: 1,200
Level: 4
Deck Cost: 22
Number: 665
Effect: None

SOGEN

Type: Magic
Attr: —
ATK: —
DEF: —
Level: —
Deck Cost: 30
Number: 692
Effect: Transforms a surrounding 2-space area into Meadow terrain!

SOLITUDE

Type: Beast-warrior
Attr: Earth
ATK: 1,050
DEF: 1,000
Level: 3
Deck Cost: 26
Number: 216
Effect: Spellbinds an opponent for 3 turns when destroyed in battle!

SOLOMON'S LAWBOOK

Type: Magic
Attr: —
ATK: —
DEF: —
Level: —
Deck Cost: 40
Number: 747
Effect: If a card has already been played from your hand, you can play another card!

SONIC MAID

Type: Warrior
Attr: Earth
ATK: 1,200
DEF: 900
Level: 3
Deck Cost: 26
Number: 186
Effect: When this card is flipped face-up, all Hibikime cards are increased 500 points!

SORCERER OF THE DOOMED

Type: Spellcaster
Attr: Dark
ATK: 1,450
DEF: 1,200
Level: 4
Deck Cost: 27
Number: 82
Effect: None

SOUL HUNTER

Type: Fiend
Attr: Dark
ATK: 2,200
DEF: 1,800
Level: 6
Deck Cost: 40
Number: 345
Effect: None

SOUL OF THE PURE

Type: Magic
Attr: —
ATK: —
DEF: —
Level: —
Deck Cost: 30
Number: 706
Effect: 2,000-point LP recovery for controlling player!

SOULEATER

Type: Immortal
Attr: Earth
ATK: 1,200
DEF: 0
Level: 4
Deck Cost: 27
Number: 673
Effect: NATURE EFFECT: When this card enters a turn face-up, and in the defense position, all MONSTER Cards are removed from the respective Graveyards, and the number of these removed cards are multiplied by 200 points. The result is added to the power of this card! DESTRUCTION: Transforms adjacent spaces into CRUSH terrain when this card is destroyed in battle!

SPACE MEGATRON

Type: Machine
Attr: Dark
ATK: 1,400
DEF: 2,000
Level: 4
Deck Cost: 34
Number: 507
Effect: None

SPARKS

Type: Magic
Attr: —
ATK: —
DEF: —
Level: —
Deck Cost: 2
Number: 709
Effect: Inflicts 50 points of damage to opponent's LP!

SPELLBINDING CIRCLE

Type: Trap
(Limited Range)
Attr: —
ATK: —
DEF: —
Level: —
Deck Cost: 30
Number: 801
Effect: Disposable trap that spellbinds activated enemy card for 3 turns, and reduces its strength by 600 points!

SPIKE CLUBBER

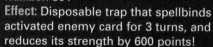

Type: Machine
Attr: Dark
ATK: 1,700
DEF: 1,800
Level: 5
Deck Cost: 35
Number: 494
Effect: None

SPIKE SEADRA

Type: Sea Serpent
Attr: Water
ATK: 1,600
DEF: 1,300
Level: 5
Deck Cost: 34
Number: 480
Effect: When this card is flipped face-up, this card is strengthened by 300 points for every THUNDER monster on the field!

SPIKED SNAIL

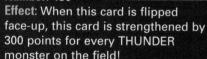

Type: Insect
Attr: Dark
ATK: 700
DEF: 1,300
Level: 3
Deck Cost: 25
Number: 395
Effect: Able to move 2 spaces regardless of terrain when this card is face-up!

SPIRIT OF THE BOOKS

Type: Winged Beast
Attr: Wind
ATK: 1,400
DEF: 1,200
Level: 4
Deck Cost: 31
Number: 274
Effect: When this card is flipped face-up, add a Boo Koo face-down to own Summoning Area!

SPIRIT OF THE HARP

Type: Fairy
Attr: Light
ATK: 800
DEF: 2,000
Level: 4
Deck Cost: 28
Number: 373
Effect: None

SPIRIT OF THE MOUNTAIN

Type: Spellcaster
Attr: Earth
ATK: 1,300
DEF: 1,800
Level: 5
Deck Cost: 31
Number: 91
Effect: None

SPIRIT OF THE WIND

Type: Spellcaster
Attr: Wind
ATK: 1,700
DEF: 1,400
Level: 5
Deck Cost: 31
Number: 96
Effect: None

SPRING OF REBIRTH

Type: Power-up
Attr: —
ATK: —
DEF: —
Level: —
Deck Cost: 10
Number: 784
Effect: Increases the power of THUNDER, AQUA, PYRO, and ROCK monsters by 500 points!

STAIN STORM

Type: Magic
Attr: —
ATK: —
DEF: —
Level: —
Deck Cost: 50
Number: 722
Effect: Destroys all MACHINE monsters on the Field!

STAR BOY

Type: Aqua
Attr: Water
ATK: 550
DEF: 500
Level: 2
Deck Cost: 16
Number: 593
Effect: When this card is flipped face-up, all of own AQUA monsters are strengthened by 300 points!

STEEL OGRE GROTTO #1

Type: Machine
Attr: Earth
ATK: 1,400
DEF: 1,800
Level: 5
Deck Cost: 32
Number: 522
Effect: None

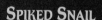

STEEL OGRE GROTTO #2

Type: Machine
Attr: Earth
ATK: 1,900
DEF: 2,200
Level: 6
Deck Cost: 41
Number: 526
Effect: None

STEEL SCORPION

Type: Machine
Attr: Earth
ATK: 250
DEF: 300
Level: 1
Deck Cost: 6
Number: 513
Effect: None

STEEL SHELL

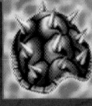

Type: Power-up
Attr: —
ATK: —
DEF: —
Level: —
Deck Cost: 10
Number: 760
Effect: Increases the power of any monsters with a shell by 500 points!

STONE ARMADILLER

Type: Rock
Attr: Earth
ATK: 800
DEF: 1,200
Level: 3
Deck Cost: 20
Number: 630
Effect: None

STONE D.

Type: Rock
Attr: Earth
ATK: 2,000
DEF: 2,300
Level: 7
Deck Cost: 43
Number: 632
Effect: None

STONE GHOST

Type: Rock
Attr: Earth
ATK: 1,200
DEF: 1,000
Level: 4
Deck Cost: 22
Number: 637
Effect: None

STONE OGRE GROTTO

Type: Rock
Attr: Earth
ATK: 1,600
DEF: 1,500
Level: 5
Deck Cost: 31
Number: 645
Effect: None

STONE STATUE OF THE AZTECS

Type: Rock
Attr: Earth
ATK: 300
DEF: 2,000
Level: 4
Deck Cost: 23
Number: 646
Effect: None

STOP DEFENSE

Type: Magic
Attr: —
ATK: —
DEF: —
Level: —
Deck Cost: 30
Number: 743
Effect: All of the enemy cards on the Field in defense position are shifted to attack position!

STUFFED ANIMAL

Type: Warrior
Attr: Earth
ATK: 1,200
DEF: 900
Level: 3
Deck Cost: 21
Number: 188
Effect: Strong in TOON terrain!

SUCCUBUS KNIGHT

Type: Warrior
Attr: Dark
ATK: 1,650
DEF: 1,300
Level: 5
Deck Cost: 30
Number: 150
Effect: None

SUIJIN

Type: Aqua
Attr: Water
ATK: 2,500
DEF: 2,400
Level: 7
Deck Cost: 54
Number: 573
Effect: Whenever damage is inflicted to LP in battle, the damage amount is reduced to 0!

SUMMONED SKULL

Type: Fiend
Attr: Dark
ATK: 2,500
DEF: 1,200
Level: 6
Deck Cost: 37
Number: 294
Effect: None

SUPER WAR-LION

Type: Beast/Ritual
Attr: Earth
ATK: 2,300
DEF: 2,100
Level: 7
Deck Cost: 49
Number: 248
Effect: If face-up, can move 2 spaces at a time regardless of terrain!

SUPPORTER IN THE SHADOWS

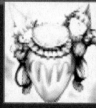

Type: Warrior
Attr: Earth
ATK: 1,000
DEF: 1,000
Level: 3
Deck Cost: 25
Number: 163
Effect: When this card is flipped face-up, all WARRIOR monsters are increased 300 points!

SWAMP BATTLEGUARD

Type: Warrior
Attr: Earth
ATK: 1,800
DEF: 1,500
Level: 5
Deck Cost: 38
Number: 153
Effect: When this card is flipped face-up, all Lava Battleguards are increased 500 points!

SWORD ARM OF DRAGON

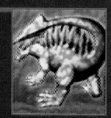

Type: Dinosaur
Attr: Earth
ATK: 1,750
DEF: 2,030
Level: 6
Deck Cost: 38
Number: 433
Effect: None

SWORD OF DARK DESTRUCTION

Type: Power-up
Attr: —
ATK: —
DEF: —
Level: —
Deck Cost: 10
Number: 753
Effect: Increases the power of WARRIOR monsters of DARK, FIRE, WATER, and WIND by 500 points!

SWORD OF DRAGON'S SOUL

Type: Power-up
Attr: —
ATK: —
DEF: —
Level: —
Deck Cost: 40
Number: 791
Effect: WARRIOR monsters automatically destroy DRAGON monsters in battle! The opposing enemy's attack effects are rendered ineffective.

SWORDS OF REVEALING LIGHT

Type: Magic
Attr: —
ATK: —
DEF: —
Level: —
Deck Cost: 80
Number: 715
Effect: Flips all enemy cards on the Field face-up and spellbinds them for 3 turns!

SWORDSMAN FROM A FOREIGN LAND

Type: Warrior
Attr: Earth
ATK: 250
DEF: 250
Level: 1
Deck Cost: 10
Number: 191
Effect: When destroyed in battle, it destroys the opposing monster as well!

SWORDSTALKER

Type: Warrior
Attr: Dark
ATK: 2,000
DEF: 1,600
Level: 6
Deck Cost: 41
Number: 146
Effect: When this card is flipped face-up, increased by 100 points for each monster in own Graveyard!

SYNCHAR

Type: Beast
Attr: Earth
ATK: 800
DEF: 900
Level: 3
Deck Cost: 17
Number: 239
Effect: None

TACTICAL WARRIOR

Type: Warrior
Attr: Fire
ATK: 1,200
DEF: 1,900
Level: 5
Deck Cost: 36
Number: 152
Effect: When this card is flipped face-up, all WARRIOR monsters are increased by 300 points!

TAINTED WISDOM

Type: Fiend
Attr: Dark
ATK: 1,250
DEF: 800
Level: 3
Deck Cost: 26
Number: 313
Effect: While this card is face-up in the defense position, a card's CLASS effects during battle can be identified even if the card is face-down!

TAKRIMINOS

Type: Sea Serpent
Attr: Water
ATK: 1,500
DEF: 1,200
Level: 4
Deck Cost: 27
Number: 477
Effect: None

TAKUHEE

Type: Winged Beast
Attr: Wind
ATK: 1,450
DEF: 1,000
Level: 4
Deck Cost: 25
Number: 288
Effect: None

TAO THE CHANTER

Type: Spellcaster
Attr: Earth
ATK: 1,200
DEF: 900
Level: 3
Deck Cost: 26
Number: 90
Effect: When this card is flipped face-up, all LIGHT monsters are transformed into DARK monsters!

TATSUNOOTOSHIGO

Type: Beast
Attr: Earth
ATK: 1,350
DEF: 1,600
Level: 5
Deck Cost: 30
Number: 250
Effect: None

TEARS OF THE MERMAID

Type: Trap
(Limited Range)
Attr: —
ATK: —
DEF: —
Level: —
Deck Cost: 15
Number: 804
Effect: Disposable trap that spellbinds activated enemy card for 1 turn, and reduces its strength by 600 points!

TEMPLE OF SKULLS

Type: Zombie
Attr: Dark
ATK: 900
DEF: 1,300
Level: 4
Deck Cost: 27
Number: 113
Effect: While this card is face-up in the defense position, all MAGIC and RITUAL Cards are rendered ineffective!

TENDERNESS

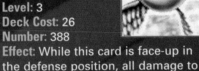

Type: Fairy
Attr: Light
ATK: 700
DEF: 1,400
Level: 3
Deck Cost: 26
Number: 388
Effect: While this card is face-up in the defense position, all damage to LP reduced by half!

TENTACLE PLANT

Type: Plant
Attr: Water
ATK: 500
DEF: 600
Level: 2
Deck Cost: 11
Number: 669
Effect: None

TERRA THE TERRIBLE

Type: Fiend
Attr: Dark
ATK: 1,200
DEF: 1,300
Level: 4
Deck Cost: 25
Number: 320
Effect: None

THAT WHICH FEEDS ON LIFE

Type: Fiend
Attr: Dark
ATK: 1,200
DEF: 1,000
Level: 4
Deck Cost: 22
Number: 307
Effect: None

THE 13TH GRAVE

Type: Zombie
Attr: Dark
ATK: 1,200
DEF: 900
Level: 3
Deck Cost: 21
Number: 110
Effect: None

THE BEWITCHING PHANTOM THIEF

Type: Spellcaster
Attr: Dark
ATK: 700
DEF: 700
Level: 2
Deck Cost: 19
Number: 66
Effect: Able to move and attack without triggering an opponent's TRAP (LIMITED RANGE)!

THE BISTRO BUTCHER

Type: Fiend
Attr: Dark
ATK: 1,800
DEF: 1,000
Level: 4
Deck Cost: 28
Number: 350
Effect: None

THE DRDEK

Type: Fiend
Attr: Dark
ATK: 700
DEF: 800
Level: 3
Deck Cost: 20
Number: 325
Effect: When this card is flipped face-up, all cards are shifted to attack position!

THE EYE OF TRUTH

Type: Magic
Attr: —
ATK: —
DEF: —
Level: —
Deck Cost: 25
Number: 718
Effect: Displays opponent's hand face-up for 5 seconds!

THE FURIOUS SEA KING

Type: Aqua
Attr: Water
ATK: 800
DEF: 700
Level: 3
Deck Cost: 20
Number: 568
Effect: All spaces within a range of 1 space are transformed to Sea terrain when this card is flipped face-up!

THE ILLUSORY GENTLEMAN

Type: Spellcaster
Attr: Dark
ATK: 1,500
DEF: 1,600
Level: 5
Deck Cost: 31
Number: 86
Effect: None

THE IMMORTAL OF THUNDER

Type: Thunder
Attr: Light
ATK: 1,500
DEF: 1,300
Level: 4
Deck Cost: 33
Number: 536
Effect: While this card is face-up in the defense position, all female monsters are reduced by 500 points!

THE INEXPERIENCED SPY

Type: Magic
Attr: —
ATK: —
DEF: —
Level: —
Deck Cost: 35
Number: 719
Effect: Regardless of facing, Type Icons of all opponent's card are displayed on the Field for 5 seconds!

THE JUDGEMENT HAND

Type: Warrior
Attr: Earth
ATK: 1,400
DEF: 700
Level: 3
Deck Cost: 21
Number: 172
Effect: None

THE LITTLE SWORDSMAN OF AILE

Type: Warrior
Attr: Water
ATK: 800
DEF: 1,300
Level: 3
Deck Cost: 21
Number: 207
Effect: None

THE MELTING RED SHADOW

Type: Aqua
Attr: Water
ATK: 500
DEF: 700
Level: 2
Deck Cost: 12
Number: 556
Effect: None

THE SHADOW WHO CONTROLS THE DARK

Type: Fiend
Attr: Dark
ATK: 800
DEF: 700
Level: 3
Deck Cost: 20
Number: 311
Effect: When this card is flipped face-up in battle, the engaged enemy is spellbound for 3 turns!

THE SNAKE HAIR

Type: Zombie
Attr: Dark
ATK: 1,500
DEF: 1,200
Level: 4
Deck Cost: 27
Number: 104
Effect: Eternally spellbinds an opponent when destroyed in battle!

THE STATUE OF EASTER ISLAND

Type: Rock
Attr: Earth
ATK: 1,100
DEF: 1,400
Level: 4
Deck Cost: 25
Number: 638
Effect: None

THE STERN MYSTIC

Type: Spellcaster
Attr: Light
ATK: 1,500
DEF: 1,200
Level: 4
Deck Cost: 32
Number: 51
Effect: When this card is flipped face-up, all face-down cards are automatically flipped face-up!

THE THING THAT HIDES IN THE MUD

Type: Rock
Attr: Earth
ATK: 1,200
DEF: 1,300
Level: 4
Deck Cost: 25
Number: 644
Effect: None

THE UNHAPPY MAIDEN

Type: Spellcaster
Attr: Light
ATK: 0
DEF: 100
Level: 1
Deck Cost: 6
Number: 53
Effect: Whenever damage is inflicted to LP in battle, the damage amount is reduced to 0!

THE WANDERING DOOMED

Type: Zombie
Attr: Dark
ATK: 800
DEF: 600
Level: 2
Deck Cost: 14
Number: 129
Effect: None

THE WICKED WORM BEAST

Type: Beast
Attr: Earth
ATK: 1,400
DEF: 700
Level: 3
Deck Cost: 26
Number: 228
Effect: When destroyed in battle, this card is returned to the deck, and the deck is re-shuffled!

THOUSAND DRAGON

Type: Dragon
Attr: Wind
ATK: 2,400
DEF: 2,000
Level: 7
Deck Cost: 44
Number: 24
Effect: None

THREE-HEADED GEEDO

Type: Fiend
Attr: Dark
ATK: 1,200
DEF: 1,400
Level: 4
Deck Cost: 26
Number: 363
Effect: None

THREE-LEGGED ZOMBIES

Type: Zombie
Attr: Dark
ATK: 1,100
DEF: 800
Level: 3
Deck Cost: 19
Number: 122
Effect: None

THUNDER DRAGON

Type: Thunder
Attr: Light
ATK: 1,600
DEF: 1,500
Level: 5
Deck Cost: 31
Number: 535
Effect: None

THUNDER NYAN NYAN

Type: Thunder
Attr: Light
ATK: 1,900
DEF: 800
Level: 4
Deck Cost: 32
Number: 539
Effect: While this card is face-up in the defense position, all face-up THUNDER monsters gain movement bonus!

TIGER AXE

Type: Beast-warrior
Attr: Earth
ATK: 1,300
DEF: 1,100
Level: 4
Deck Cost: 24
Number: 214
Effect: None

TIME SEAL

Type: Magic
Attr: —
ATK: —
DEF: —
Level: —
Deck Cost: 50
Number: 684
Effect: Permanently spellbinds the monster with the highest ATK on the Field!

TIME WIZARD

Type: Spellcaster
Attr: Light
ATK: 500
DEF: 400
Level: 2
Deck Cost: 14
Number: 36
Effect: When this card is flipped face-up, all DRAGON monsters with ATKs less than 2,400 are transformed into Thousand Dragons!

TIMEATER

Type: Immortal
Attr: Dark
ATK: 1,900
DEF: 1,700
Level: 6
Deck Cost: 51
Number: 678

Effect: NATURE EFFECT: While this card is face-up in the defense position, the countdown speed for spellbound cards are doubled should a Turn Count be involved.
DESTRUCTION: Transforms adjacent spaces into CRUSH terrain when this card is destroyed in battle!

TOAD MASTER

Type: Aqua
Attr: Water
ATK: 1,000
DEF: 1,000
Level: 3
Deck Cost: 25
Number: 554

Effect: Summons Frog The Jam face-up in own Summon Area when this card is flipped face-up!

TOGEX

Type: Beast
Attr: Earth
ATK: 1,600
DEF: 1,800
Level: 5
Deck Cost: 34
Number: 256

Effect: None

TOMOZAURUS

Type: Dinosaur
Attr: Earth
ATK: 500
DEF: 400
Level: 2
Deck Cost: 9
Number: 439

Effect: None

TONGYO

Type: Fish
Attr: Water
ATK: 1,350
DEF: 800
Level: 4
Deck Cost: 22
Number: 470

Effect: Decreases opposing enemy by 500 points when this card is flipped face-up in battle!

TOON ALLIGATOR

Type: Reptile
Attr: Water
ATK: 800
DEF: 1,600
Level: 4
Deck Cost: 24
Number: 454

Effect: Strong in TOON terrain!

TOON MERMAID

Type: Aqua
Attr: Water
ATK: 1,400
DEF: 1,500
Level: 4
Deck Cost: 29
Number: 611

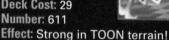

Effect: Strong in TOON terrain!

TOON SUMMONED SKULL

Type: Fiend
Attr: Dark
ATK: 2,500
DEF: 1,200
Level: 6
Deck Cost: 37
Number: 362

Effect: Strong in TOON terrain!

TOON WORLD

Type: Magic
Attr: —
ATK: —
DEF: —
Level: —
Deck Cost: 30
Number: 695

Effect: Transforms a surrounding 2-space area into TOON terrain!

TORIKE

Type: Beast
Attr: Earth
ATK: 1,200
DEF: 600
Level: 3
Deck Cost: 18
Number: 230

Effect: None

TRAKADON

Type: Dinosaur
Attr: Earth
ATK: 1,300
DEF: 800
Level: 3
Deck Cost: 21
Number: 443

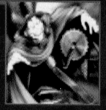

Effect: None

TRAP MASTER

Type: Warrior
Attr: Earth
ATK: 500
DEF: 1,100
Level: 3
Deck Cost: 21
Number: 178

Effect: Able to move and attack without triggering an opponent's TRAP (LIMITED RANGE)!

TREMENDOUS FIRE

Type: Magic
Attr: —
ATK: —
DEF: —
Level: —
Deck Cost: 40
Number: 713
Effect: Inflicts 1,000 points of damage to opponent's LP!

TRENT

Type: Plant
Attr: Earth
ATK: 1,500
DEF: 1,800
Level: 5
Deck Cost: 33
Number: 666
Effect: None

TRIAL OF NIGHTMARE

Type: Fiend
Attr: Dark
ATK: 1,300
DEF: 900
Level: 4
Deck Cost: 22
Number: 308
Effect: None

TRI-HORNED DRAGON

Type: Dragon/Ritual
Attr: Dark
ATK: 2,850
DEF: 2,350
Level: 8
Deck Cost: 52
Number: 10
Effect: None

TRIPWIRE BEAST

Type: Thunder
Attr: Earth
ATK: 1,200
DEF: 1,300
Level: 4
Deck Cost: 25
Number: 540
Effect: None

TURTLE BIRD

Type: Aqua
Attr: Water
ATK: 1,900
DEF: 1,700
Level: 6
Deck Cost: 36
Number: 592
Effect: None

TURTLE OATH

Type: Ritual
Attr: —
ATK: —
DEF: —
Level: —
Deck Cost: 5
Number: 844
Effect: Sacrifice 2 AQUA monsters and 30,000-Year White Turtle to summon Crab Turtle!

TURTLE RACCOON

Type: Aqua
Attr: Water
ATK: 700
DEF: 900
Level: 3
Deck Cost: 21
Number: 591
Effect: Teleports to own Summoning Area when this card is flipped face-up! When this card is flipped face-up in battle, that battle is cancelled!

TURTLE TIGER

Type: Aqua
Attr: Water
ATK: 1,000
DEF: 1,500
Level: 4
Deck Cost: 25
Number: 558
Effect: None

TURU-PURUN

Type: Aqua
Attr: Water
ATK: 450
DEF: 500
Level: 2
Deck Cost: 15
Number: 580
Effect: Gains 1,000 bonus points when fighting FISH monsters!

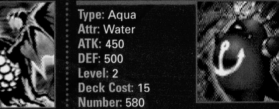

TWIN LONG RODS # 2

Type: Aqua
Attr: Water
ATK: 850
DEF: 700
Level: 3
Deck Cost: 16
Number: 602
Effect: None

TWIN LONG RODS #1

Type: Aqua
Attr: Water
ATK: 900
DEF: 700
Level: 3
Deck Cost: 14
Number: 562
Effect: None

TWIN-HEADED BEHEMOTH

Type: Dragon
Attr: Wind
ATK: 1,500
DEF: 1,200
Level: 4
Deck Cost: 27
Number: 34
Effect: None

TWIN-HEADED THUNDER DRAGON

Type: Thunder
Attr: Light
ATK: 2,800
DEF: 2,100
Level: 7
Deck Cost: 49
Number: 538
Effect: None

TWO-HEADED KING REX

Type: Dinosaur
Attr: Earth
ATK: 1,600
DEF: 1,200
Level: 4
Deck Cost: 28
Number: 434
Effect: None

TWO-MOUTH DARKRULER

Type: Dinosaur
Attr: Earth
ATK: 900
DEF: 700
Level: 3
Deck Cost: 16
Number: 440
Effect: None

TYHONE

Type: Winged Beast
Attr: Wind
ATK: 1,200
DEF: 1,400
Level: 4
Deck Cost: 26
Number: 271
Effect: None

TYHONE #2

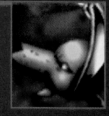

Type: Dragon
Attr: Fire
ATK: 1,700
DEF: 1,900
Level: 6
Deck Cost: 36
Number: 15
Effect: None

TYPE ZERO MAGIC CRUSHER

Type: Trap
(Limited Range)
Attr: —
ATK: —
DEF: —
Level: —
Deck Cost: 15
Number: 813
Effect: Disposable trap that triggers against an opponent's spell and destroys it!

ULTIMATE DRAGON

Type: Ritual
Attr: —
ATK: —
DEF: —
Level: —
Deck Cost: 5
Number: 837
Effect: Sacrifice 3 Blue-Eyes White Dragons to summon Blue-Eyes Ultimate Dragon!

UMI

Type: Magic
Attr: —
ATK: —
DEF: —
Level: —
Deck Cost: 30
Number: 693
Effect: Transforms a surrounding 2-space area into Sea terrain!

UNKNOWN WARRIOR OF FIEND

Type: Warrior
Attr: Dark
ATK: 1,000
DEF: 500
Level: 3
Deck Cost: 15
Number: 142
Effect: None

URABY

Type: Dinosaur
Attr: Earth
ATK: 1,500
DEF: 800
Level: 4
Deck Cost: 23
Number: 437
Effect: None

USHI ONI

Type: Fiend
Attr: Dark
ATK: 2,150
DEF: 1,950
Level: 6
Deck Cost: 41
Number: 343
Effect: None

VERMILLION SPARROW

Type: Pyro
Attr: Fire
ATK: 1,900
DEF: 1,500
Level: 5
Deck Cost: 34
Number: 619
Effect: None

VERSAGO THE DESTROYER

Type: Fiend
Attr: Dark
ATK: 1,100
DEF: 900
Level: 3
Deck Cost: 20
Number: 330
Effect: None

VILE GERMS

Type: Power-up
Attr: —
ATK: —
DEF: —
Level: —
Deck Cost: 10
Number: 761
Effect: Increases the power of PLANT monsters by 500 points!

VIOLENT RAIN

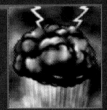

Type: Aqua
Attr: Water
ATK: 1,550
DEF: 800
Level: 4
Deck Cost: 29
Number: 599
Effect: When this card is flipped face-up, all adjacent spaces are transformed into Sea terrain!

VIOLET CRYSTAL

Type: Power-up
Attr: —
ATK: —
DEF: —
Level: —
Deck Cost: 10
Number: 772
Effect: Increases the power of ZOMBIE monsters by 500 points!

VISHWAR RANDI

Type: Warrior
Attr: Dark
ATK: 900
DEF: 700
Level: 3
Deck Cost: 21
Number: 141
Effect: When this card is flipped face-up, strengthen all Succubus Knights by 300 points!

WALL OF ILLUSION

Type: Fiend
Attr: Dark
ATK: 1,000
DEF: 1,850
Level: 4
Deck Cost: 34
Number: 361
Effect: Returns enemy monster to opponent's deck for re-shuffling when this card is flipped face-up in battle!

WALL SHADOW

Type: Warrior
Attr: Dark
ATK: 1,600
DEF: 3,000
Level: 7
Deck Cost: 51
Number: 144
Effect: Can move into LABYRINTH terrain!

WAR-LION RITUAL

Type: Ritual
Attr: —
ATK: —
DEF: —
Level: —
Deck Cost: 5
Number: 835
Effect: Sacrifice 2 BEAST monsters with Leogun to summon Super War-Lion!

WARRIOR ELIMINATION

Type: Magic
Attr: —
ATK: —
DEF: —
Level: —
Deck Cost: 50
Number: 720
Effect: Destroys all WARRIOR monsters on the Field!

WARRIOR OF TRADITION

Type: Warrior
Attr: Earth
ATK: 1,900
DEF: 1,700
Level: 6
Deck Cost: 36
Number: 200
Effect: None

WASTELAND

Type: Magic
Attr: —
ATK: —
DEF: —
Level: —
Deck Cost: 30
Number: 690
Effect: Transforms a surrounding 2-space area into WASTELAND terrain!

WATER ELEMENT

Type: Aqua
Attr: Water
ATK: 900
DEF: 700
Level: 3
Deck Cost: 21
Number: 565
Effect: When this card is flipped face-up, flips all of own SPELL cards face-down!

WATER GIRL

Type: Aqua
Attr: Water
ATK: 1,250
DEF: 1,000
Level: 4
Deck Cost: 23
Number: 579
Effect: None

WATER MAGICIAN

Type: Aqua
Attr: Water
ATK: 1,400
DEF: 1,000
Level: 4
Deck Cost: 24
Number: 576
Effect: None

WATER OMOTICS

Type: Aqua
Attr: Water
ATK: 1,400
DEF: 1,200
Level: 4
Deck Cost: 26
Number: 566
Effect: None

WATERDRAGON FAIRY

Type: Aqua
Attr: Water
ATK: 1,100
DEF: 700
Level: 3
Deck Cost: 18
Number: 578
Effect: None

WEATHER CONTROL

Type: Fairy
Attr: Light
ATK: 600
DEF: 400
Level: 2
Deck Cost: 15
Number: 371
Effect: When this card is flipped face-up, transforms all adjacent spaces to WASTELAND!

WEATHER REPORT

Type: Aqua
Attr: Water
ATK: 950
DEF: 1,500
Level: 4
Deck Cost: 25
Number: 597
Effect: None

WETHA

Type: Aqua
Attr: Water
ATK: 1,000
DEF: 900
Level: 3
Deck Cost: 19
Number: 569
Effect: None

WHIPTAIL CROW

Type: Fiend
Attr: Dark
ATK: 1,650
DEF: 1,600
Level: 5
Deck Cost: 33
Number: 358
Effect: None

WHITE DOLPHIN

Type: Fish
Attr: Water
ATK: 500
DEF: 400
Level: 2
Deck Cost: 9
Number: 463
Effect: None

WHITE HOLE

Type: Trap
(Full Range)
Attr: —
ATK: —
DEF: —
Level: —
Deck Cost: 10
Number: 824
Effect: Permanent trap that triggers when a Dark Hole is activated! Protects all your cards on the Field from destruction!

WHITE MAGICAL HAT

Type: Spellcaster
Attr: Light
ATK: 1,000
DEF: 700
Level: 3
Deck Cost: 22
Number: 38
Effect: Able to move and attack without triggering an opponent's TRAP (LIMITED RANGE)!

WICKED DRAGON WITH THE ERSATZ HEADS

Type: Dragon
Attr: Wind
ATK: 900
DEF: 900
Level: 3
Deck Cost: 18
Number: 28
Effect: None

WICKED MIRROR

Type: Fiend
Attr: Dark
ATK: 700
DEF: 600
Level: 2
Deck Cost: 13
Number: 329
Effect: None

WIDESPREAD RUIN

Type: Trap
(Limited Range)
Attr: —
ATK: —
DEF: —
Level: —
Deck Cost: 60
Number: 812
Effect: Disposable trap that triggers against any enemy card and destroys every card located within a 3x3-space area!

WILMEE

Type: Beast
Attr: Earth
ATK: 1,000
DEF: 1,200
Level: 4
Deck Cost: 22
Number: 254
Effect: None

WINDSTORM OF ETAQUA

Type: Magic
Attr: —
ATK: —
DEF: —
Level: —
Deck Cost: 10
Number: 740
Effect: Boosts the ATK/DEF factors of all WINGED BEAST monsters on the Field by 600 points!

WING EAGLE

Type: Winged Beast
Attr: Wind
ATK: 1,800
DEF: 1,500
Level: 5
Deck Cost: 33
Number: 279
Effect: None

WING EGG ELF

Type: Fairy
Attr: Light
ATK: 500
DEF: 1,300
Level: 3
Deck Cost: 18
Number: 379
Effect: None

WINGED CLEAVER

Type: Insect
Attr: Earth
ATK: 700
DEF: 700
Level: 2
Deck Cost: 14
Number: 405
Effect: None

WINGED DRAGON GUARDIAN OF THE FORTRESS #1

Type: Dragon
Attr: Wind
ATK: 1,400
DEF: 1,200
Level: 4
Deck Cost: 26
Number: 22
Effect: None

WINGED DRAGON GUARDIAN OF THE FORTRESS #2

Type: Winged Beast
Attr: Wind
ATK: 1,200
DEF: 1,000
Level: 4
Deck Cost: 22
Number: 286
Effect: None

WINGED EGG OF NEW LIFE

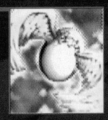

Type: Fairy
Attr: Light
ATK: 1,400
DEF: 1,700
Level: 5
Deck Cost: 31
Number: 391
Effect: None

WINGED TRUMPETER

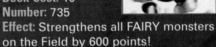

Type: Magic
Attr: —
ATK: —
DEF: —
Level: —
Deck Cost: 10
Number: 735
Effect: Strengthens all FAIRY monsters on the Field by 600 points!

WINGS OF WICKED FLAME

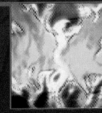

Type: Pyro
Attr: Fire
ATK: 700
DEF: 600
Level: 2
Deck Cost: 13
Number: 614
Effect: None

WITCH OF THE BLACK FOREST

Type: Spellcaster
Attr: Dark
ATK: 1,100
DEF: 1,200
Level: 4
Deck Cost: 28
Number: 80
Effect: While this card is face-up in the defense position, all LIGHT monsters are reduced 100 points.

WITCH'S APPRENTICE

Type: Spellcaster
Attr: Dark
ATK: 550
DEF: 500
Level: 2
Deck Cost: 11
Number: 81
Effect: None

WITTY PHANTOM

Type: Fiend
Attr: Dark
ATK: 1,400
DEF: 1,300
Level: 4
Deck Cost: 27
Number: 309
Effect: None

WODAN THE RESIDENT OF THE FOREST

Type: Warrior
Attr: Earth
ATK: 900
DEF: 1,200
Level: 3
Deck Cost: 26
Number: 181
Effect: When this card is flipped face-up, strengthens all PLANT monsters by 300 points!

WOLF

Type: Beast
Attr: Earth
ATK: 1,200
DEF: 800
Level: 3
Deck Cost: 20
Number: 231
Effect: None

WOLF AXWIELDER

Type: Beast-warrior
Attr: Earth
ATK: 1,650
DEF: 1,000
Level: 4
Deck Cost: 27
Number: 223
Effect: None

WOOD CLOWN

Type: Warrior
Attr: Earth
ATK: 800
DEF: 1,200
Level: 3
Deck Cost: 20
Number: 179
Effect: None

WOOD REMAINS

Type: Zombie
Attr: Dark
ATK: 1,000
DEF: 900
Level: 3
Deck Cost: 24
Number: 119
Effect: When this card is flipped face-up, all Wood Remains are increased 500 points!

WOODLAND SPRITE

Type: Plant
Attr: Earth
ATK: 2,100
DEF: 2,100
Level: 3
Deck Cost: 47
Number: 668
Effect: Power increases by 2,500 points in battle against FIEND monsters!

WOW WARRIOR

Type: Fish
Attr: Water
ATK: 1,250
DEF: 900
Level: 4
Deck Cost: 27
Number: 471
Effect: None

WRETCHED GHOST OF THE ATTIC

Type: Fiend
Attr: Dark
ATK: 550
DEF: 400
Level: 2
Deck Cost: 10
Number: 355
Effect: None

YADO KARU

Type: Aqua
Attr: Water
ATK: 900
DEF: 1,700
Level: 4
Deck Cost: 26
Number: 590
Effect: None

YAIBA ROBO

Type: Machine
Attr: Dark
ATK: 1,000
DEF: 1,300
Level: 4
Deck Cost: 28
Number: 490
Effect: Inflicts 300 points of damage to opponent's LP when destroyed in battle!

YAMADRON

Type: Dragon/Ritual
Attr: Fire
ATK: 1,600
DEF: 1,800
Level: 5
Deck Cost: 44
Number: 13
Effect: ATTACK: Transforms surrounding spaces into NORMAL terrain when engaged in battle! FLIP: Transforms surrounding spaces into NORMAL terrain when this card is flipped face-up!

YAMADRON RITUAL

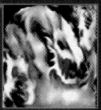

Type: Ritual
Attr: —
ATK: —
DEF: —
Level: —
Deck Cost: 5
Number: 831
Effect: Sacrifice 3 monsters respectively of BEAST-WARRIOR, DRAGON, and PYRO to summon Yamadron!

YAMATANO DRAGON SCROLL

Type: Dragon
Attr: Wind
ATK: 900
DEF: 300
Level: 2
Deck Cost: 17
Number: 25
Effect: Transforms into Yamadron after surviving 3 turns in a face-up defense position. However, the card must be voluntarily turned face-up.

YAMI

Type: Magic
Attr: —
ATK: —
DEF: —
Level: —
Deck Cost: 30
Number: 694
Effect: Transforms a surrounding 2-space area into DARK terrain!

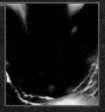

YARANZO

Type: Zombie
Attr: Dark
ATK: 1,300
DEF: 1,500
Level: 4
Deck Cost: 28
Number: 121
Effect: None

YASHINOKI

Type: Plant
Attr: Earth
ATK: 800
DEF: 600
Level: 2
Deck Cost: 19
Number: 654
Effect: When this card is flipped face-up, LP increases 500 points!

YELLOW LUSTER SHIELD

Type: Magic
Attr: —
ATK: —
DEF: —
Level: —
Deck Cost: 10
Number: 737
Effect: Boosts the DEF of all your own monsters on the Field by 900 points!

YORMUNGARDE

Type: Reptile
Attr: Earth
ATK: 1,200
DEF: 900
Level: 3
Deck Cost: 21
Number: 448
Effect: None

ZANKI

Type: Warrior
Attr: Earth
ATK: 1,500
DEF: 1,700
Level: 5
Deck Cost: 32
Number: 160
Effect: None

ZARIGUN

Type: Aqua
Attr: Water
ATK: 600
DEF: 700
Level: 2
Deck Cost: 13
Number: 587
Effect: None

ZERA RITUAL

Type: Ritual
Attr: —
ATK: —
DEF: —
Level: —
Deck Cost: 5
Number: 834
Effect: Sacrifice 2 FIEND monsters with King of Yamimikai to summon Zera the Mant!

ZERA THE MANT

Type: Fiend/Ritual
Attr: Dark
ATK: 2,800
DEF: 2,300
Level: 8
Deck Cost: 51
Number: 337
Effect: None

ZOA

Type: Fiend
Attr: Dark
ATK: 2,600
DEF: 1,900
Level: 7
Deck Cost: 45
Number: 342
Effect: None

ZOMBIE WARRIOR

Type: Zombie
Attr: Dark
ATK: 1,200
DEF: 900
Level: 3
Deck Cost: 21
Number: 103
Effect: None

ZONE EATER

Type: Aqua
Attr: Water
ATK: 250
DEF: 200
Level: 1
Deck Cost: 10
Number: 574
Effect: Transforms all horizontal spaces to Sea spaces when this card is flipped face-up!

Fusion

In *Yu-Gi-Oh!*, the winning duelist is usually the one with the strongest creatures. However, when you are just beginning with your initial deck, most of your creatures are low cost, and very weak. So how does a novice duelist compete against such juggernauts as Rex's Bracchio-raidus, Keith's Machine King, or, worst of all, Seto's Blue-Eyes White Dragon? Not with the low-level creatures in your default deck. Luckily, though, you can fuse two or more cards to create a stronger creature.

In the first few duels in the campaign, when you have mostly low-level creatures, Fusion is your only way of combating your opponents' strongest creatures.

Unlike in previous *Yu-Gi-Oh!* video games or the card game, you don't need to tribute monsters or use the Polymerization card to create a Fusion. This makes Fusions easy to create.

There are dozens of possible Fusion combinations, in fact, too many to list here. And half the fun is finding out the combinations on your own. Remember, though, that not every card can be part of a Fusion, and you'll find just as many unsuccessful combinations as you will successful ones. But we can give you a few tips and guidelines for exploiting this very useful ability.

 TIP

Use the computer to help learn new Fusion combinations. Play Custom Duels against the computer and let it use your deck. Then watch to see if it creates any Fusions during the duel. If it does, quickly view the Graveyard by pressing R1 and jot down the two or more creatures the computer Fused. You've just learned a new Fusion that you can try on your turn.

First, designate the creatures you will fuse by pushing up on your direction pad. The order in which you select these creatures usually isn't important, unless you are fusing more than two creatures together. In that case, be sure to fuse the first two creatures to create the first Fusion creature, which then fuses with your third selection, resulting in your ultimate Fusion creature goal.

The Correct Order for Multiple Fusions

Let's look at this example. To create the beast called Nekogal #2, we designate the Lisark, the Rainbow Flower, and the Goddess of Whim, in that order. The Lisark and Rainbow Flower form a Flower Wolf. The new Flower Wolf then combines with the Goddess of Whim to create a Nekogal #2. If the Goddess of Whim was designated first, then the Fusion would not work.

When you attempt a Fusion, you pay the Summoning Points only for the highest-level creature in the Summon. This lets you Summon higher-level monsters for fewer Summon Points. In the above example, the Nekogal #2 costs five Summon Points, but none of the three component creatures have a Summoning cost higher than three. That means you can attempt the Fusion when you only have three Summon Points available, allowing you to play a level-five monster in the very first turn of the game, something that is not ordinarily possible. Fusion lets you Summon more powerful creatures than you normally could, and it lets you creatively circumvent the limits of a low Summon Point.

If your attempted Fusion is successful, then the new creature is Summoned onto the Field, while the combining creatures go to your Graveyard.

When deciding what cards to fuse, first attempt to fuse creatures of different types, such as a Dragon and a Plant. Also try to use creatures with similar attributes, such as two Earth creatures or two Wind creatures. You can try to fuse creatures with different attributes, but stay away from combining cards with polar-opposite attributes, such as Fire and Water creatures.

Secondly, note that most fusions only operate with lower-cost cards, and that the ultimate card you Summon through the Fusion usually must be a higher level than the individual component cards.

Lastly, cards of the same type don't often combine to form a Fusion, so experiment with different type combinations, such as Dragon and Thunder, or Plant and Fiend.

Once you discover a Fusion combination, remember that it usually isn't the specific creatures that led to the Fusion, but the creature types and attributes. So, for example, a Dragon of Wind and a Thunder creature of Wind can fuse to create a Thunder Dragon. But it doesn't matter what Dragon of Wind you use. It could be a Baby Dragon, Petit Dragon, Fairy Dragon, or a Lesser Dragon. It's even easier for the Thunder component, which can have a Wind, Light, or Earth attribute. So your Thunder creature could be a Kaminarikozou, Electric Snake, Oscillo Hero #2, or a Thunder Lizard. Any combination of these Dragon and Thunder creatures will result in the Thunder Dragon. The only constant is each creature's Summoning level, which is three or less. If you try to create the Fusion with a Sky Dragon, which has a Summon level of five, the Fusion won't work.

Remember that in addition to creating stronger creatures, Fusions can be a very useful strategic tool in dueling. You can negate an enemy's spellbinding by creating a Fusion with the spellbound creature, or free up more spaces in your hand for additional cards in the draw phase by ridding your hand of multiple monsters, without wasting any, by creating a Fusion. And you can regain the element of surprise in a duel by fusing with a face-up monster on the Field, because the resulting Fusion comes into play face-down.

Fusion Samples

Here is a list of more than two dozen fusions. There are certainly more Fusions to discover in *The Duelists of the Roses*. Use these Fusions in your deck, or study them to figure out new combinations. The component creatures for each Fusion are listed, with each creature's type and attribute listed in parentheses after each creature.

Aqua Dragon
Component Creatures:
Roaring Ocean Snake
(Aqua/Water)
plus
Kairyu-Shin
(Sea Serpent/Water)

Bean Soldier
Component Creatures:
Guardian of the Labyrinth
(Warrior/Earth)
plus
Firegrass (Plant/Earth)

Other Successful Combinations:
Guardian of the Labyrinth (Warrior/Earth) plus
Arlownay (Plant/Earth)

Black Dragon Jungle King
Component Creatures:
Crawling Dragon
(Dragon/Earth)
plus
Arlownay (Plant/Earth)

Other Successful Combinations:
Crawling Dragon (Dragon/Earth) plus
Firegrass (Plant/Earth)

Blackland Fire Dragon

Component Creatures:
Mystical Elf (Spellcaster/Light)
plus
Winged Dragon Guardian of
the Fortress #1 (Dragon/Wind)

Other Successful Combinations:
Illusionist of the Faceless Mage (Spellcaster/Dark) plus
Winged Dragon Guardian of the Fortress #1 (Dragon/Wind)

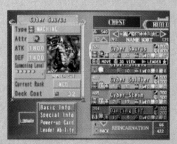

Cyber Saurus

Component Creatures:
Two Headed King Rex
(Dinosaur/Earth)
plus
Dice Armadillo
(Machine/Earth)

Cyber Soldier

Component Creatures:
Mechanical Snail
(Machine/Dark)
plus
Guardian of the Labyrinth
(Warrior/Earth)

Other Successful Combinations:
Mechanical Snail (Machine/Dark) plus
Unknown Warrior of Fiend (Warrior/Dark)

Steel Scorpion (Machine/Dark) plus
Guardian of the Labyrinth (Warrior/Earth)

Dark Witch

Component Creatures:
Lunar Queen of Elzaim
(Fairy/Light)
plus
Goddess with the Third Eye
(Fairy/Light)

Other Successful Combinations:
Goddess of Whim (Fairy/Light) plus
Spirit of the Winds (Spellcaster/Wind)

Goddess of Whim (Fairy/Light) plus
Beautiful Headhuntress (Warrior/Earth)

Special Note: At least one of the component creatures must be
a female or the Fusion will not work.

Dragon Zombie

Component Creatures:
Petit Dragon (Dragon/Wind)
plus
Flame Ghost (Zombie/Dark)

Other Successful Combinations:
Baby Dragon (Dragon/Wind) plus Flame Ghost (Zombie/Dark)

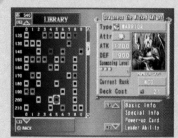

Dragoness the Wicked Knight

Component Creatures:
Fairy Dragon (Dragon/Wind)
plus
Guardian of the Labyrinth
(Warrior/Earth)

Flower Wolf

Component Creatures:
Lisark (Beast/Earth)
plus
Rainbow Flower (Plant/Earth)

Other Successful Combinations:
Fusionist (Beast/Earth) plus Firegrass (Plant/Earth)

Great Bill (Beast/Earth) plus Trent (Plant/Earth)

Gaia the Dragon Champion

Component Creatures:
Gaia the Fierce Knight
(Warrior/Earth)
plus
Curse of Dragon
(Dragon/Dark)

Garvas
Component Creatures:
Kurama (Winged Beast/Wind)
plus
Great Bill (Beast/Earth)

Other Successful Combinations:
Fiend Reflection #1 (Winged Beast/Wind) plus
Great Bill (Beast/Earth)

Crow Goblin (Winged Beast/Wind) plus Lisark (Beast/Earth)

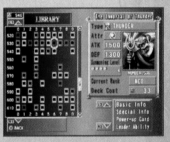

Immortal of Thunder
Component Creatures:
Secretarian of Secrets (Spellcaster/Dark)
plus
Kaminarikozou (Thunder/Wind)

Other Successful Combinations:
Necrolancer the Time Lord (Spellcaster/Dark) plus
Electric Snake (Thunder/Light)

Koumori Dragon
Component Creatures:
Fairy Dragon (Dragon/Wind)
plus
Ghost in the Attic (Fiend/Dark)

Other Successful Combinations:
Lesser Dragon (Dragon/Wind) plus
Ghost in the Attic (Fiend/Dark)

Petit Dragon (Dragon/Wind) plus
Ghost in the Attic (Fiend/Dark)

Baby Dragon (Dragon/Wind) plus
Ghost in the Attic (Fiend/Dark)

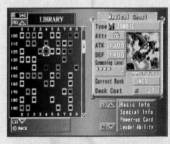

Magical Ghost
Component Creatures:
Dark Assailant (Zombie/Dark)
plus
Necrolancer the Time Lord (Spellcaster/Dark)

Metal Dragon
Component Creatures:
Mechanical Snail (Machine/Dark)
plus
Petit Dragon (Dragon/Wind)

Other Successful Combinations:
Guardian of the Throne (Machine/Light) plus
Lesser Dragon (Dragon/Wind)

Steel Scorpion (Machine/Dark) plus
Baby Dragon (Dragon/Wind)

Meteor Black Dragon
Component Creatures:
Meteor Dragon (Dragon/Earth)
plus
Red-Eyes Black Dragon (Dragon/Dark)

Mystical Elf
Component Creatures:
Dancing Elf (Fairy/Wind)
plus
Lunar Queen of Elzaim (Fairy/Light)

Mystical Sand
Component Creatures:
Stone Ghost (Rock/Earth)
plus
Beautiful Headhuntress (Warrior/Earth)

Other Successful Combinations:
Minomushi Warrior (Rock/Earth) plus
Red Archery Girl (Aqua/Water)

Special Note: At least one of the component creatures must be a female or the Fusion will not work.

Prima's Official Strategy Guide

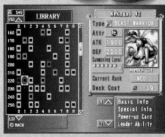

Nekogal #2
Component Creatures:
Flower Wolf (Beast/Earth)
plus
Goddess of Whim (Fairy/Light)

Other Successful Combinations:
Fusionist (Beast/Earth) plus
Beautiful Headhuntress (Warrior/Earth)

Fusionist (Beast/Earth) plus Goddess of Whim (Fairy/Light)

Rude Kaiser (Beast-warrior/Earth) plus
Queen of Autumn Leaves (Plant/Earth)

Arlownay (Plant/Earth) plus Firegrass (Plant/Earth) plus
Rude Kaiser (Beast-warrior/Earth)

Rude Kaiser (Beast-warrior/Earth) plus
Goddess with the Third Eye (Fairy/Light)

Special Note: At least one of the component creatures must be a female or the Fusion will not work.

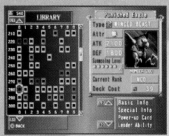

Punished Eagle
Component Creatures:
Skull Red Bird
(Winged Beast/Wind)
plus
Oscillo Hero (Warrior/Earth)

Other Successful Combinations:
Fiend Reflection #1 (Winged Beast/Wind) plus
Unknown Warrior of Fiend (Warrior/Dark)

Crow Goblin (Winged Beast/Wind) plus
Beautiful Headhuntress (Warrior/Earth)

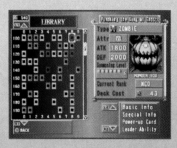

Pumpking the King of Ghosts
Component Creatures:
Arlownay (Plant/Earth)
plus
Ghoul with an Appetite
(Zombie/Dark)

Queen of Autumn Leaves
Component Creatures:
Arlownay (Plant/Earth)
plus
Firegrass (Plant/Earth)

Other Successful Combinations:
Arlownay (Plant/Earth) plus
Goddess with the Third Eye (Fairy/Light)

Trent (Plant/Earth) plus Spirit of the Winds (Spellcaster/Wind)

Firegrass (Plant/Earth) plus Lunar Queen of Elzaim (Fairy/Light)

Special Note: At least one of the component creatures must be a female or the Fusion will not work.

Red-Eyes Black Dragon
Component Creatures:
Koumori Dragon
(Dragon/Dark)
plus
Tyhone #2 (Dragon/Fire)

Other Successful Combinations:
Lesser Dragon (Dragon/Wind) plus
Ghost in the Attic (Fiend/Dark) plus Tyhone #2 (Dragon/Fire)

Rose Spectre of Dunn
Component Creatures:
Trent (Plant/Earth)
plus
King Fog (Fiend/Dark)

Other Successful Combinations:
Arlownay (Plant/Earth) plus Meda Bat (Fiend/Dark)

Skelgon
Component Creatures:
Fiend's Hand (Zombie/Dark)
plus
Dragon Zombie (Zombie/Dark)

Other Successful Combinations:
Petit Dragon (Dragon/Wind) plus Flame Ghost (Zombie/Dark)
plus Ghoul with an Appetite (Zombie/Dark)

Tatstunootoshigo
Component Creatures:
Great Bill (Beast/Earth)
plus
Wow Warrior (Fish/Water)

Winged Egg of New Life
Component Creatures:
Fiend Reflection #1
(Winged Beast/Wind)
plus
Goddess with the Third Eye
(Fairy/Light)

Thunder Dragon
Component Creatures:
Petit Dragon (Dragon/Wind)
plus
Kaminarikozou
(Thunder/Wind)

Zombie Warrior
Component Creatures:
Unknown Warrior of Fiend
(Warrior/Dark)
plus
Flame Ghost (Zombie/Dark)

Other Successful Combinations:
Baby Dragon (Dragon/Wind) plus
Electric Snake (Thunder/Light)

Lesser Dragon (Dragon/Wind) plus
Oscillo Hero #2 (Thunder/Light)

Strategies

Once you've beaten the campaigns of *Yu-Gi-Oh! The Duelists of the Roses*, the game doesn't end. You can play all the duelists in the game as many times as you want, gaining new cards and advancing your Deck Leader to new heights.

You can also play against other human players, engaging in friendly or not-so-friendly one-on-one duels. Here are a few tips and tactics to help you hone your game, whether you play against the computer or a friend.

Tips and Tactics
Know Your Foe

When playing against other humans, the benefits of surprise are huge. Of course, it's hard to guarantee that surprise when both players are playing on the same screen. Cards such as Dark-Piercing Light and Monster Eye allow you to see your opponent's hand. Knowing what cards your foe has lets you prepare better defenses, or attack without worrying about whether a trap lies in wait for you. Adding Dark-Piercing Light is thus key for any deck, and Fiend decks can afford to add Monster Eye for little cost.

Defending With Spell Cards

If your Deck Leader is being chased by a monster in its favorable terrain, remember that the monster can move two squares in a turn and thus quickly run down your Leader.

If you are in that situation, but you can't play a monster in defense position to guard your Deck Leader—either because of the Shadow of Eyes or Gorgon's Eye—then place a spell card between you and the incoming monster. The card stops the monster's movement, preventing it from moving two squares into you.

Pick Up Your Cards!

Don't leave power ups near your enemy's monsters. Any monster can benefit from a power up if it moves into its square, so by leaving a power up in an opponent's monster's path, you're giving it a free 500-point bonus.

Drawing Twice

If you've stacked your deck with some specific game-winning cards, such as Just Desserts or Blue-Eyes White Dragon, you need to get to those cards quickly. Solomon's Lawbook comes in handy just for that. Its primary use is to play two cards in one turn, but it also lets you draw a second time, getting that much closer to the card you want.

Maximum Summoning Points Instantly

Try to get Gate Deeg and Berfomet by dueling Manawyddan fab Llyr. With these two cards in your deck, you're in a better position to play your high-cost monsters, such as Summoned Skull or Dark Magician. Of these two, Gate Deeg is better simply because its Deck Cost is 17 points lower, so it won't eat up so much of your total Deck Cost. Of course, when dueling other human players, Deck Cost isn't a concern.

Cursebreaker

This card is perfect for erasing any damage done by traps. It negates any spellbinding and restores a monster to its original ATK/DEF ratings.

Bringing Powered-up Monsters Down to Size

Cursebreaker isn't just good for your units. It can also severely weaken powered-up enemy monsters. And it only costs 1 DC. It works beautifully to deflate a pumped-up creature, erasing power ups and effects. Having three in your deck is a cheap investment and, combined with your own Power-up cards, allows you to outmuscle your enemy. If you don't use it to help your own units, you can still use it to hinder your enemy.

Nastiest Combo!

Players don't think to use Reverse Trap as an offensive tool, but you can. While this card is in effect, all power ups drain their amount of strength points rather than adding it as a bonus. Therefore, place Power-up cards face-down in front of the enemy's monsters. When they run over it, they get a nasty surprise: a reduction in ATK strength. That will make your foe think twice before attacking.

Custom Game

Playing a game against the computer in Custom Game is great for a variety of reasons. Chief among those is that it lets you learn from the computer. It knows the Fusions, and when it performs them with your deck, you can look into the Graveyard to see what creatures were just fused. Then you can try it yourself. Custom Games also let you win multiple copies of your own cards. It's great for building up your deck.

Good Additions

Any of these following cards would be good fits for any deck. In most cases, the effects from these monsters only trigger when they are face-up and in the defense position. Refer to the cards themselves for details. The good thing about these cards is that they aren't rare. You can win them easily from dueling in the single-player campaign, and they are low in Deck Cost.

Hourglass of Courage: Gives all surviving monsters +1,000 bonus points, but deals you 1,000 LP damage. Not usable if LP is under 1,000.

Hourglass of Life: Resurrects up to four of the strongest monsters from both Graveyards when it dies, but deals you 1,000 LP damage. Not usable if LP is under 1,000.

Injection Fairy Lily: +50 LP every turn.

Maha Vailo: Increases the bonus from Power-up Cards 200 points.

Tenderness: Halves all LP damage.

Yashinoki: Gain 500 LP when flipped face-up.

Ask for Help

Finally, no good duelist ever became great by going it alone. Follow Yugi's example and learn from your friends. Two heads are better than one, so discuss strategies with your buddies and practice against them. You'll be better duelists for it.

Card Passwords

Finding passwords in *Yu-Gi-Oh! The Duelists of the Roses* is a little more difficult than it was in previous Yu-Gi-Oh! games. Konami has changed the password structure to include both letters and numbers now, and the passwords you find on the actual cards do not work in the game. To make things even tougher, the cards no longer show their passwords when you win them in duels. The *only* way to get a password is to beat the entire game. Once you beat the campaign, you are rewarded with a password. Unfortunately, you can't keep replaying the same end duel. Each time you defeat the final boss, you get the same password. So, you'll need to start an entirely new game under a new name if you want to acquire multiple passwords.

We do have a few passwords for you, though, and some of them are great cards. There are excellent Effects monsters, such as Ancient Tree of Enlightenment, which negates all Trap Cards, and Fairy's Gift, which gives you 800 LP when it's flipped face-up. There are other Effects monsters as well that give bonus points to others of their type, such as Birdface and Robotic Knight. Among the sample password list you will also find very strong monsters like Seiyaryu, Aqua Dragon, and Barrel Dragon. There are some incredibly powerful Spell Cards, as well, such as Dark Hole, Earthshaker, Harpie's Feather Duster, and Mimicat. All of these cards would make fine additions to your deck, and give you a competitive advantage over the duelists in the campaign.

Sample Password List

NAME	PASSWORD	TYPE	ATK/DEF	EFFECT
Ancient Tree of Enlightenment	EKJHQ109	Plant	600/1500	While this card is face-up in the defense position, TRAP cards cannot be triggered!
Aqua Dragon	JXCB6FU7	Sea Serpent	2250/1900	Space occupied in transformed to Sea terrain when engaged in battle!
Barrel Dragon	GTJXSBJ7	Machine	2600/2200	When this card is flipped face-up, 1 card other than own is randomly selected for destruction!
Beastking of the Swamps	QXNTQPAX	Aqua	1000/1100	When destroyed, destroys the enemy engaged in battle with!
Birdface	N54T4TY5	Winged-Beast	1600/1600	While this card is face up in the defense position, all WINGED-BEAST monsters are awarded a power-up bonus of 300 points!
Blast Sphere	CZN5GD2X	Machine	1400/1400	All cards located in the surrounding 3x3 area are automatically destroyed when this card is destroyed in battle!
Dark Hole	UMJ10MQB	Magic	—	Destroys all MONSTER and SPELL Cards on the Field!
Dragon Seeker	81EZCH8B	Fiend	2000/2100	Destroys all MONSTER and SPELL Cards on the Field!
Earthshaker	Y34PN1SV	Magic	—	Randomly shifts the position of cards and changes the terrain on the Field! In addition, all LABYRINTH squares are changed
Elf's Light	E5G3NRAD	Power Up	—	Increases the power of any monster with 'Elf' in its name by 700 points!
Fairy King Truesdale	YF07QVEZ	Plant	2200/1500	While this card is face-up in the defense position, the power of all your PLANT monsters increases by 500 points.
Fairy's Gift	NVE7A3EZ	Spellcaster	1400/1000	Gain 800 LP when this card is flipped face-up!
Greenkappa	YBJMCD6Z	Aqua	650/900	When this card is flipped face-up, adopts the ATK/DEF of the monster with the highest ATK power on the Field!
Harpie's Feather Duster	8HJHQPNP	Magic	—	Destroys all spells located in the vertical and horizontal lines from the activated space!
Horn of the Unicorn	S14FGKQ1	Power Up	—	Increases the power of horned monster of DARK by 500 points!
Left Arm of The Forbidden One	A5CF6HSH	Spellcaster	200/300	Left Arm of the Forbidden One. Awards victory to the one who brings together all four limbs and unleashes the monster!
Magician of Faith	GME1S3UM	Spellcaster	300/400	When this card is flipped face-up, select 1 spell from all Graveyards and revive it in own Summoning Area! However, can only be activated in a turn when 'Magician of Faith' is being controlled.
Mimicat	69YDQM85	Magic	—	Select, revive, and control 1 card from either Graveyard!
Mystical Capture Chain	N1NDJMQ3	Fairy	700/700	While this card is face-up, in defense position, spell binds all FIEND monsters!
Robotic Knight	S5S7NKNH	Machine	1600/1800	While this card is face-up in the defense position, the power of all your MACHINE monsters are increased by 300 bonus points
Seiyaryu	2H4D85J7	Dragon	2500/2300	300-point bonus for battles against FIEND monsters!
Serpentine Princess	UMQ3WZUZ	Reptile	1400/2000	Own REPTILE monsters strengthened by 900 points when this card is flipped face-up!
Swordsman from a Foreign Land	CZ81UVGR	Warrior	250/250	When destroyed in battle, it destroys the opposing monster as well!
Swordstalker	AH0PSHEB	Warrior	2000/1600	When this card is flipped face-up, increased by 100 points for each monster in own Graveyard!
Tactical Warrior	054TC727	Warrior	1200/1900	When this card is flipped face-up, all WARRIOR monsters are increased by 300 points!